Human Resource Management in the Hospitality Industry

A Practitioner's Perspective

D.V. Tesone

Rosen School of Hospitality Management
University of Central Florida
Orlando, Florida

PEARSON
Prentice
Hall

Upper Saddle River, New Jersey 07458

Library of Congress Cataloging-in-Publication Data
Human resource management in the hospitality industry :
a practitioner's perspective / Dana V. Tesone.
    p. cm.
Includes bibliographical references and index.
ISBN 0-13-110092-0
  1. Hospitality industry—Personnel management.   I. Title.
TX911.3.P4T47 2004
647.94'068'3--dc22

                                                        2004006733

Executive Editor: Vernon R. Anthony
Editorial Assistant: Beth Dyke
Director of Manufacturing and Production: Bruce Johnson
Managing Editor: Mary Carnis
Production Liaison: Adele M. Kupchik
Senior Marketing Manager: Ryan DeGrote
Senior Marketing Coordinator: Elizabeth Farrell
Marketing Assistant: Les Roberts
Production Management: Pine Tree Composition, Inc.
Production Editor: Jessica Balch, Pine Tree Composition, Inc.
Manufacturing Manager: Ilene Sanford
Manufacturing Buyer: Cathleen Petersen
Creative Director: Cheryl Asherman
Senior Design Coordinator: Miguel Ortiz
Cover Designer: Marianne Frasco
Cover Image: Comstock IMAGES
Printer/Binder: Von Hoffman
Cover Printer: Phoenix Color Corp.

Pearson Education LTD.
Pearson Education Australia PTY, Limited
Pearson Education Singapore, Pte. Ltd
Pearson Education North Asia Ltd
Pearson Education Canada, Ltd.
Pearson Educación de Mexico, S.A. de C.V.
Pearson Education—Japan
Pearson Education Malaysia, Pte. Ltd

10 9 8
ISBN 0-13-110092-0

To my partner, Dawn;
the Ts, the Bs,
and to the big G

Brief Contents

Contents

PART III HOW DO WE DO IT?

CHAPTER 15
Putting It All Together   199

Preface

Human Resource Management in the Hospitality Industry is designed to provide readers with the planning, organizing, influencing, and control functions associated with human resource management in hospitality and tourism organizations. It is presented from the standpoint of a practitioner, which means it is applicable to the actual tasks, duties and responsibilities that are performed by human resource generalists and specialists alike. The book may be used for educational programs as well as training programs in any service industry. The information that is presented includes all of the activities performed by human resource practitioners. So, what if the reader does not wish to become an HR practitioner?

This may be good news. If everyone were interested in human resource management, there would be no one left in the operating departments. However, the objective of the manager in the hospitality and tourism industries is to learn the practice of professional management. This practice includes having a solid foundation of human resource management knowledge and skills. The operating manager who is in possession of these skills will be less likely to incur organizational liability resulting from inappropriate management practices and would be free to manage a work unit with little reliance on the advice of human resource practitioners. This person will be a better manager for the organization.

This book is written in a straightforward and condensed manner designed to provide the reader with an inclusive yet precise presentation of the material. The intention is to place the reader in the imaginary workplace. At the beginning of each chapter, a vignette entitled In the Real World . . . sets the stage. The chapter concludes with the outcome of the applied role-play with the vignette called In the Real World . . . *(Continued)*, to provide reinforcement of the material absorbed through reading the chapter.

A section called *Discussion Questions* appears after each vignette to provide thoughtful consideration of the topics presented. Questions are arranged in formats ranging from open ended to true or false. *Key Terms* are then listed; these terms appear throughout each chapter to reinforce the marginal *definitions* placed in the margins.

The 15 chapters of this book are arranged in three parts. The chapters in Part I focus on the evolution of the practice of commerce to include the development of complex employer/employee relationships. The chapters present the case that historical practices have brought the practice of human resource management into its current status within organizations. Part II contains chapters that present the reader with a snapshot of duties and responsibilities associated with the practice of professional management. Part III demonstrates the practical (applied) skills required for effective human resource management.

It is recommended that readers reflect on actual scenarios in the workplace or classroom role-play while digesting the content of *Human Resource Management in the Hospitality Industry.* If the book is being used as part of a college course or workplace training program, the facilitator may encourage discussions of actual events to bring each topic to life. The reader is encouraged to convert the knowledge gained from this book into actual skills to be applied in the workplace. This may be accomplished through two activities. First, apply the knowledge immediately. Turning knowledge into skills requires practice. Practice the knowledge 24 to 48 hours after reading it. Second, teach these concepts to someone else. We learn through teaching. As one presents this new information to another person, the exchange process will reinforce the knowledge and "teacher" will be better prepared to use the knowledge in the workplace. This technique should be applied 24 to 48 hours after reading and discussing the information.

D. V. Tesone

CHAPTER ONE

Hospitality Human Resource Management: An Overview

OBJECTIVES

By the end of this chapter, the reader will be able to:

1. Understand the relationships of human resource practitioners with members of the stakeholder group.

2. Understand the evolution of human resource management.

3. Identify the legal and ethical practices of management as a function of human resource practice.

4. Recognize the tools used by human resource practitioners to meet their responsibilities.

In the Real World . . .

You have just completed your first day as an intern in the human resource office for a large cruise line. You normally work in the reservations department, but since you have expressed an interest in learning human resource management, the director has arranged for you to do a one-day internship per week. For you, this day has just flown by. The office is a madhouse, with the phones ringing off the hook all day long. Everyone works at a frenetic pace in an effort to handle employment inquiries, pre-employment screening interviews, employee complaints, and demands by the operations managers to fill vacant positions.

At the end of the day, you kick back with a friend to talk about your experience. You say, "I had no idea that so many things happen in that office. It's even busier than the rez department. I'm not so sure I want to work in this field—it's so negative." Your friend replies, "Give it a chance, it's just your first day. . ."

INTRODUCTION

HRM—Human resource management.
HR—Human resources.
HRD—Human resource development.

It is common knowledge that the practice of human resource management **(HRM)** is prevalent in organizations of all sizes. The current-day human resource **(HR)** manager has direct influence on the strategic direction and thinking of both private and public sector organizations. As a result of this influence, HRM and human resource development **(HRD)** officers command large salaries that are often in the six-figure range, with some senior practitioners reported to earn annual direct compensation in excess of $250,000.[1] The reason for this is a relatively current shift in organizational thinking. From the time of the Industrial Revolution through the middle of the 20th century, workers were considered to be nothing more than expenses for labor that created a financial burden on the profits of their companies. Since **employees** were considered to be expense items, managers believed they were as expendable as any material resource used to get the job done, such as a jackhammer or a shovel. When a worker became too tired or ill to do the job, he was replaced by a worker who was willing to take that job. For this reason, scientific managers (usually trained as engineers) espoused supervisory practices that completely overlooked the human factor in worker productivity enhancement.[2] During the early 1960s, a small group of progressive management practitioners changed their thinking about workers from that of expense item to one of **human capital**, which means that an employee is an **asset** to the organization and is thus worthy of investment and development. This chapter takes us on the journey from "then" to "now."

employees—A stakeholder group consisting of the workers for an organization.

human capital—The belief that the development of workers will add value to an organization.

asset—Something that adds value to an organization.

scientific management—An engineering approach to management aimed at finding the single most efficient means of performing work tasks.

A HISTORICAL PERSPECTIVE

Look back in history that occurred during the last few decades of the 19th century, just before the commencement of **scientific management**. An agrarian economy existed at that time in which wealthy landowners employed the services of ten or more workers who were labeled as slaves, serfs, sharecroppers, or indentured servants. Unfortunately, these landowners served as role models for the unenlightened managers who ran large factories during the Industrial Revolution.

During the early Industrial Revolution, top managers were usually wealthy factory owners; supervisors were individuals with the ability to coerce and intimidate the workers. History books are full of examples of factory owners abusing child labor, paying insufficient wages and utilizing the "my way or the highway" form of motivation. Human resource management had not even occurred to these early managers, much less been considered a viable practice. Employees were as disposable as tissues.

The fact is, the first corporate HR department is barely 100 years old. When compared with the disciplines of medicine, mathematics, and the fine arts, the practice of human resource management may be considered to be in its infancy. For this reason, some managers continue to challenge the viability of human capital investment and development practices that are championed by their HRM peers.

Some of corporate America's chief executive officers **(CEOs)** have been accused of providing mere lip service concerning HRM practices.[3] Most annual reports commence with a letter to the stockholders proclaiming that the workers are the firm's most valuable assets. Some individuals note that this is the only attention paid to the employees throughout a typical fiscal year.[4] While some executives continue to label human resource practices as necessary evils, more proactive managers embrace them as part of the mainstream of corporate strategic planning and direction. Interestingly, many of these firms are those held in good standing among **shareholders**, **customers** and the **community** at large. A proactive CEO will tell you that solid HR practices are just good business.

CEO—Chief executive officer, usually the top-level manager in an organization.

shareholders—A stakeholder group consisting of the investors or owners of a company.

customers—A stakeholder group consisting of those who purchase products and services.

OVERVIEW

Who are the stakeholders or constituents served by human resource management practitioners? In actuality, HR practitioners have the same responsibilities in the area of stakeholder service as any corporate manager. The **stakeholder group** consists of shareholders (stockholders in publicly traded firms), employees, customers, and the community. The trick here is balance.

community—Outside stakeholders who are not within other stakeholder groups.

stakeholder group—Groups of constituents for an organization.

HOSPITALITY NEWS *Want a Successful Career? Live by these rules.*

- Always think like your customer.
- Build on a sound foundation. Pay your dues through education or the school of hard knocks.
- Always deliver a positive experience to your customers.
- Join professional associations, and keep learning by attending seminars and trade shows.
- Make friends with your competitors and others in your community who can serve as mentors.

- Look to those who went before you, and then combine their old ways with some of your new ways.
- Never forget the power of advertising, promotion, surveying, and researching as you try to improve your business.

Source: Hospitality News, 2001, p. 4.

In a healthy organization, the needs of each stakeholder group will be satisfied more or less equally. On the other hand, dysfunctional companies will serve the needs of one stakeholder group (the shareholders, for instance) at the expense of another group (such as the employees). When this happens, the senior HR manager is at odds with the value system of the organization (or at least the CEO), and will attempt to stabilize the imbalance in the interests of both groups. This is discussed in detail in Chapter 2. Figure 1.1 provides a description of the stakeholders as the people who the HR practitioner and every other manager in the organization should serve in proportion.

In Chapter 3 we discuss the good and bad news associated with government regulation of employer/employee relationships. This regulation takes place through legislation aimed at protecting workers and applicants from unfair and unsafe treatment, as well as providing accommodations for those who have special needs in the workplace. Some consider the regulations to be bad news, as there are very high costs associated with legal compliance as determined by the courts. However, certain HR practitioners consider this good news, as the legal environment has created high-level positions in organizations to ensure the protection of a firm's assets through legal compliance strategies.

We discuss legal compliance strategies in Chapter 4, just after a description of the legal environment of employment law. It is important for HR practitioners to balance sound managerial practices with legal compliance issues. Some individuals incorrectly contend that all that is needed in this area is the services of a labor attorney. While this person may be well versed in the law, it is likely she will not be trained in the field of management. For instance, if you operate in a state in which the courts have established that employee handbooks are construed to be implied-in-fact contracts, an attorney will advise you to refrain from the distribution of the handbooks. Good legal advice, perhaps; but what about your duty as a manager to clearly and effectively articulate the expectations for performance in the organization, as well as identify all terms, conditions and privileges of employment? This scenario and others are discussed at length in the chapter. Some individuals tend to confuse the term *labor law* with another term, *labor relations*. These are two discrete concepts. Labor law deals with the state and federal legal regulation of employment relationships. Labor relations law, however, deals with the right of individuals to elect union representation within organizations.

Labor relations is the topic of Chapter 5, which is an aspect of the legal environment that is separate from the field of employment law. This chapter identifies the legal rights of workers and organizations. As in Chapter 4, strategies are presented to assist practitioners in dealing with union, as well

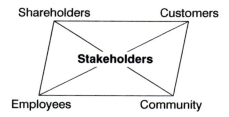

Figure 1.1. Stakeholder Groups.

as non-union workplace environments. Of course (as we will soon find out), all of the aspects of the employment legal environment arose from prior practices in organizations that were deemed by society to be detrimental to those engaged in employment relationships. This would lead us to believe that certain managers acted unethically in their dealings with employees in the past, which created the perceived need for society to protect employees through the actions of the legislature and the courts. Business ethics is the topic of discussion for Chapter 6, which leads to the role of human resource managers as protectors of employee rights, in Chapter 7. Figure 1.2 shows the relationship of these concepts as the "what" of human resource management.

At the conclusion of Chapter 7, we ask the question, "Now that we know how we got here and what we should do, how do we do it?" Part III is the crucial element in the book, as we proceed to engage in discussions about doing the job of an HR practitioner. This is the "how to" of the book.

Chapter 8 provides the steps necessary to develop and implement sound strategies for recruitment and selection practices. As we will find out, recruitment is the process of generating a qualified pool of applicants; selection is the process of choosing the best one for a position. How do we know which one is best? Chapter 9 gives us that answer. Now that we have the new or existing employee, how do we go about giving him the knowledge, skills and abilities to do the job? Or, how do we develop her for the next higher level position? These are the topics addressed in Chapter 9.

Once we train employees, we would like for them to remain with our organization for a reasonable period of time. HR practitioners call this function employee retention, as opposed to employee turnover. In Chapter 10, strategies are provided for the reader to develop skills in the area of retaining the best and brightest staff members. A big part of employee retention comes from clearly established expectations for performance and honest, objective feedback on how well one meets those expectations. These components and others are contained within a performance management system for an organization, a topic that we discuss thoroughly in Chapter 11. Figure 1.3 depicts the "how" of human resource management practice, the chapters we will discuss next.

Now, we don't want to say we saved the best for last, but we did. And we did this because, now that we know what we know, we are ready to engage in the three most important processes of management. The first process (and the topic of Chapter 12) is effective communications, which is perhaps the manager's most powerful tool. It is possible for a person to know all there is

Figure 1.2. Stakeholder Responsibilities.

HOSPITALITY NEWS *Beyond Yesterday's Basics*

Reading, writing and arithmetic used to be considered the basics of education. But the jobs of tomorrow, while still requiring these essential skills, will also require a new set of workplace skills, according to a study by the American Society for Training and Development, a professional organization of corporate trainers.

- Creative thinking: As work becomes more flexible, workers' solutions will need to become more creative.
- Goal setting/motivation: Workers will need to be able to set objectives and persist in achieving them.
- Interpersonal skills: Being able to get along with suppliers, co-workers and customers will be essential in future work.
- Leadership: Workers will be asked to assume more responsibility and direct their co-workers when needed.
- Learning to learn: Workers will need to learn new information and develop new skills, and to be able to apply the new information and skills to their jobs.
- Listening: Good listening skills will help workers understand the concerns of co-workers, suppliers and customers.

- Negotiation: Workers should be able to build agreement through give-and-take negotiating.
- Oral communications: Workers must be able to respond clearly to the concerns of co-workers, suppliers and customers.
- Organizational effectiveness: Employees will need to understand how the company's business goals are met and how their jobs contribute to fulfilling those goals.
- Personal/career development skills: The most valuable employees will be those who understand that they need to continually develop new skills on the job.
- Problem solving: In work organizations, workers will be asked to find answers, and solve problems.
- Self-esteem: Supervisors say they want (and will expect) workers who are proud of themselves and their abilities.
- Teamwork: Working cooperatively means workers must effectively and equitably divide work to achieve team goals.

Source: Hospitality News, August 2002, p. 33.

---

synthesis—The ability to apply abstract concepts in a realistic setting.

to know about management and yet be unable to perform as an effective manager, if he lacks the ability to communicate effectively with individuals and groups. Since it is our contention that an HR practitioner is a "manager's manager," that is a person who shows other managers how to manage, it is important for her to know about leadership skills, as discussed in Chapter 13. Finally, all of this information is merely academic if we are not able to apply it in a real world setting. We call this ability **synthesis**. Chapter 14 provides a real world experience with all of us as human resource practitioners. We are confident that you will join in our success at this point in the book. Figure 1.4 shows the whole picture after we put together the who, what, and how.

Notice that we begin the book with our constituent group, otherwise referred to as the stakeholder group, that consists of shareholders, customers, employees and the community. This is represented by the square in the center of the diagram, in which it is our contention that the interests of all parties should be kept in balance. The eclipse balances the "what" of our responsibilities to the stakeholder group. We possess the responsibility to do business in

a legal and ethical fashion. In so doing, the HR practitioner protects the long-term interests of the shareholders by protecting the assets of the organization from legal liability. She protects the employees by ensuring fair, uniform and consistent management practices, which trickles down to the customers, who deserve to be treated in the same manner. Finally, by being legally and ethically responsible, the organization is guaranteed to be a good neighbor to the community in which it does business, which includes vendors, other suppliers, the competition, the general industry, government officials, and neighbors in the vicinity surrounding the physical plant, as well as other members of society.

We conclude the book with chapters that present the skills that enable the HR practitioner to make these things happen. The human resource practi-

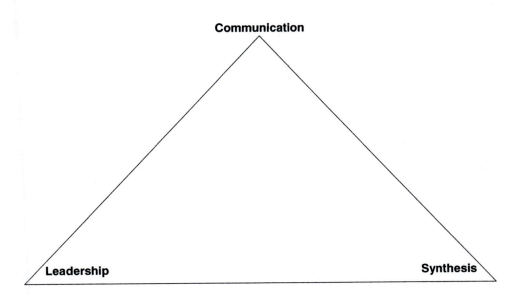

Figure 1.3. How to Practice Human Resource Management

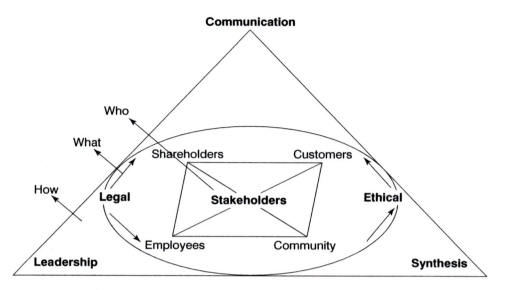

Figure 1.4. The Whole Picture.

tioner must be an effective communicator in order to ensure that the organization balances its responsibilities to each of the stakeholder groups. This effort requires leadership capability, which is particularly necessary if the HR practitioner intends to become a "manager's manager," as we recommended earlier. And, as noted in the song, "It don't mean a thing if you ain't got that swing,"[5] we must swing into action as practitioners by using the skills at each angle of the outer triangle in the figure, which are communication, leadership, and synthesis.

SUMMARY

In this chapter, we have provided an overview of management within organizations as related to the service of the stakeholder groups. After a brief review of historical events in management, we noted that the function of human resource management exists to protect the assets of the organization and to en-

---

In the Real World. . . (Continued)

A couple of months have passed since you started your internship in the HR office. You have worked alongside most of the managers and staff who perform various functions. You have gained a little experience in each area of the office. Now you know a little about recruitment and selection, compensation, training and orientation, employee counseling, performance management systems, and legal compliance.

One night, you are sitting with your friend, who says, "Hey, how's that internship going? I haven't heard you complain about it since your first day. What did you do, give it up?"

"No," you reply, "I'm still doing it and I really like it. I think I want to learn some more human resources from a management perspective."

sure the development of human capital. We have discussed the upcoming chapters of the book to describe briefly the journey to discover the "who, what, and how" of human resource management. Finally, we have described how we would practice newly formed knowledge and skills in the practice of human resource management when we reach the end of the book.

DISCUSSION QUESTIONS

1. Do you know anyone who works in human resource management? Have they ever talked about their jobs? Is it a "love/hate" relationship in their view? If so, why?

2. What type of people do you think are attracted to becoming HR practitioners? Why do you think certain types are more prone to do human resource management than others?

3. The In the Real World vignette portrayed a hectic environment in the HR office. Is this accurate? Does it have to be this way?

4. Is there any area in the overview of HR management that you find interesting? Why do you like that area—or why don't you like any of the areas?

KEY TERMS

asset	employees	human capital	stakeholder group
CEO	HR	scientific	synthesis
community	HRD	management	
customers	HRM	shareholders	

CHAPTER TWO

HR Dichotomy: Do We Serve the Staff or the Shareholders?

OBJECTIVES

By the end of this chapter, the reader will be able to:

1. Understand the relationship of human resource practitioners to members of the stakeholder groups.
2. Differentiate among each of the stakeholder group segments.
3. Articulate the concepts of internal marketing and productivity enhancement.
4. Understand the concept of balance in stakeholder services.

In the Real World . . .

You are a human resource manager for a small chain of restaurants with 3 stores and about 150 employees. Most of your time is spent in recruitment and selection activities, as well as training. Because your department is small, you don't have a specialist to handle compensation practices. You did, however, participate in a wage and salary survey with the local hospitality HR chapter, and learned that you are paying your culinary and kitchen staff at rates below corresponding rates at other restaurants. This explains why you have high employee turnover and difficulty recruiting people for these positions. You dutifully bring this to the controller's (Dick) and district manager's (Sarah) attention. You explain to them that you would like to propose an increase in wages for these positions to make you competitive with the labor market. They arrange to meet with you in Sarah's office the next day.

You arrive armed with your survey data. You begin the meeting: "You know, our high turnover and unsuccessful recruitment efforts for staff positions have been driving me crazy. Now I know the cause. We are paying below the rest of the market in this county for these jobs. We need to increase our hourly wages."

Dick looks up from his spreadsheet at Sarah and says, "This would take us over budget for labor dollars."

Sarah glances at you with concern. She takes a moment to collect her thoughts, then says, "I understand your dilemma. But we made a promise to the owners with this budget. We can't go back to them and say we projected the wrong figures for these wages. They just wouldn't understand. I'm afraid you will just have to do the best you can with our current pay structure . . ."

INTRODUCTION

We are familiar with the traditional business management functions of accounting, sales, marketing, and production. In the late 1970s, the strategic approach to managing human capital created the human resource function. Today, the implications of technology systems in the overall strategic positioning of organizations bring new challenges to the practice of human resource management.[1]

HUMAN RESOURCE MANAGEMENT VS. PERSONNEL ADMINISTRATION

The difference between personnel management and human resource management is that the latter denotes the impact of HR practices as a strategic force in the planning and operation of the organization. Managers must possess a basic level of knowledge in all of the business functions. This is why human resource management is provided as part of management training in all academic and corporate training programs. All managers are human resource practitioners (individuals who plan and allocate people resources). Also, managers make decisions regarding allocation of resources used as **inputs** to develop organizational outcomes. Finally, most managers will be responsible for developing human resource strategies at various times in their careers. These are all compelling reasons for having a basic knowledge of human resource management.

inputs—Resources required to generate products or services.

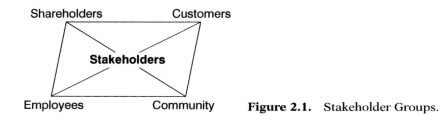

Figure 2.1. Stakeholder Groups.

We identified the members of the stakeholder group in part of the last chapter. The individuals who are members of this group are considered to be **internal** to the hospitality organization. They are members of the organization because of their affiliation as stakeholders. Figure 2.1 reviews the stakeholder group members identified in the last chapter.

internal—Factors inside the organization.

CONSTITUENCIES

Let's begin with the shareholders. If the hospitality organization is part of a publicly traded corporation—one that is traded on the stock market—the shareholders are referred to as stockholders. With privately held firms the shareholders hold titles of owners, partners, or investors. Whether public or private, the affiliation of the shareholders is to gain a return on their financial investments. Stockholders purchase stocks, which provide capital funding for the organization. Their expectation is that the price of the stock will rise above the purchase price to provide a **return on investment (ROI)**. These individuals possess no emotional ties to the organization and are often not even sure of how the company operates.

return on investment (ROI)—Money that is paid to investors.

Private investors have an interest in the organization's operating profits as well as the financial **appreciation** of the assets valuation. For instance, investors in a hotel are seeking a short-term ROI from the operational profits of the property in some cases, as well as hoping for appreciation in the real estate value of the property as an asset. Like the stockholders in a publicly traded company, the investors usually have a limited understanding of the business of the hospitality organization, but feel there is a financial gain to be had through their affiliation with it.

appreciation—An increase in financial value; a way of showing thanks for a job well done.

Senior managers spend a good deal of time "educating" the shareholders about realistic expectations for the performance of a hospitality organization. If the investors are willing to learn the nuances of the business and be patient with regard to the return on their investments, a good relationship will prevail. If, however, the investors are solely interested in **short-term gain** (as is the case with stockholders), there may be conflicts between the managers and the shareholders. The challenge here for human resource managers is the potential misunderstanding on the part of the shareholders concerning the labor-intensive aspect of our business. Hospitality is perhaps the most **labor intensive** of service entities and manufacturing enterprises. With no knowledge of industry management, shareholders have difficulty in understanding the large payroll expenses affiliated with most hospitality operations.

short-term gain—Financial returns over a period of one year or less.

labor intensive—Requiring large amounts of labor dollars due to many worker positions.

The lifeblood of the hospitality enterprise is the guest, as those of us in the business like to refer to our customers. While the shareholders are responsible for capital investment in the business, the guests are the ones who purchase services at respectable pricing levels. It is the guests who are responsible for operational **revenues**, profits, and asset appreciation. Every resource (including human resources) is ultimately paid for by the guests. The marketing department is primarily responsible for the acquisition of guests for the hospitality enterprise. This is an external function, as the focus is on consumers (potential guests outside the organization) for the purpose of conversion into customers (guests) who use the services of the organization. While the guest is interacting with the organization, it is the internal members (employees) of that organization who provide the services that the warrant the guest's business. Hence, there are two types of marketing for a hospitality organization: external marketing performed by sales and marketing personnel, and internal marketing provided by the service **(line employee)** and support **(staff employee)** workers. Since the function of the human resource department is to acquire and maintain employees, HR practitioners comprise the internal marketing function for the hospitality organization. Thus, human resource managers have a direct internal impact on guests through the organization's employees.

The purpose of an employee-employer relationship is best described by the term **quid pro quo**: something of value exchanged for something else of value. In this case, the worker is hired to provide services to an **internal customer** or **external customer** in return for **compensation.** While the term compensation conjures images of financial remuneration, the experienced HR practitioner knows that psychological payment for organizational performance and membership are also important factors.

Employee acquisition is accomplished through the functions of **recruitment** and **selection** strategy implementation. Employee maintenance

revenues—Income earned through the sale of products and services.

line employee—An employee who produces products or services or generates revenue.

staff employee—An employee who supports the line workers.

quid pro quo—Something of value that is exchanged for something else of value.

internal customer—Workers who serve the customers/guests who are customers of support workers.

external customer—A customer or guest who purchases products or services.

compensation—Direct payment to employees.

recruitment—The process of generating a pool of qualified applicants for a position.

selection—Choosing the most qualified candidates for positions.

retention—Keeping productive employees within the company.

employee relations—Maintaining rapport with workers by satisfying their needs.

social responsibility—Duty to the community stakeholder group and society.

value-added manager—A manager who enhances productivity.

(retention) is the outcome achieved through effective **employee relations** strategy execution. These strategies produce compensation, training and development, recognition, performance management, communication, and leadership practices, all discussed in later sections of the book.

The final constituency within the stakeholder group is the community in which we do business. The community includes individuals who are external to the organization, but maintain some form of familiarity with it, usually due to logistics. Vendors, suppliers, neighbors, competitors, travelers, friends and relatives of our guests, financial institutions that support our shareholders, families of our employees, and any other member of society who may indirectly interface with our business is a member of this constituency group. Our duty and responsibility to this group is summed up by the term **social responsibility.** Social responsibility is the duty to act as a good corporate member of society by doing business in a manner that avoids harm, and if possible, contributes good things to our neighbors and constituents. This topic is discussed in detail in Chapter 6 of the book.

At this point we have considered the needs of each segment contained within the stakeholder group and discussed the ways in which we provide service to each segment. Figure 2.2 depicts the constituents that we serve and how we serve them.

The diamond service model has many connotations. A diamond is a valuable gemstone, which reminds hospitality managers that the purpose of their existence is to add value (**value-added manager**) to the organization. What is value? Many closed-minded individuals equate value with fiscal (financial) performance. But at what cost? If an organization chooses to meet the fiscal demands of the shareholders at the expense of appropriate employee relations or customer service, or even social responsibility, the cost

Figure 2.2. The Diamond Service Model.

may be too high. It is certain that the shareholders will be content in the short term, but over time, the value of the employees, customers and social perceptions of the organization will become diminished. How capable will an organization with substandard employees, poor service, and alienated social reputation be of providing future financial returns to the shareholders?

PRODUCTIVITY

As mentioned before, an organization must maintain balance. So it is with the diamond that is precariously perched on one angle, easily tilted to one side or another, if the managers are unable to keep it balanced; hence, the potential predicament of the human resource manager. She is charged with the responsibility for maintaining corporate balance for the hospitality organization, which means contributing to fiscal performance by acquiring and maintaining proficient workers who provide excellent guest services in a community-friendly environment. To the casual observer, this is an environment in which the fiscal needs of the shareholders may be in conflict with the welfare of the employees. Obviously, lower wages, decreased benefits, stark working conditions, and minimal training and development expenses will enhance the **bottom line**, which will surely make the shareholders happy. The unskilled HR practitioner truly would feel a bit schizophrenic in such an unbalanced environment. However, the human resource manager with the right training will know how to add value to each of the four sides of the service diamond equally, if the shareholders are patient enough to provide such an opportunity. The only way for a human resource practitioner to become a value-added manager is through **productivity** enhancement, which is a balancing act in itself. Figure 2.3 depicts the productivity model for hospitality organizations.[2]

What is productivity? In accounting equation terms, productivity is **outputs** divided by inputs to deliver a positive outcome. For instance, if we spend \$2 to provide a service and charge \$3 for the service, our productivity outcome is \$1, which is also called **profit.** Achieving that outcome is not as easy as accountants would have us believe. In actual practice, we must make

bottom line—Net profit or loss.

productivity—The relationship of resource expenses and revenue as connected by a transformation process and encircled by meaning and learning loops.

outputs—Products or services produced by the company to earn revenue.

profits—Revenues less expenses that yield a positive balance.

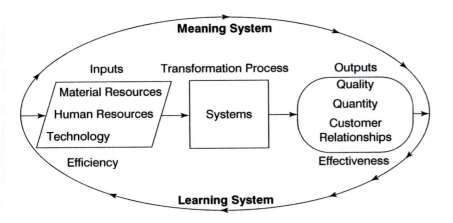

Figure 2.3. Productivity Model.

transformation process—The conversion of material resources into products and services.

meaning system—A driver loop that reinforces values and purpose throughout the organization.

learning system—A feedback loop in which members of the organization gain knowledge about productivity.

efficiency—Doing things right. Minimizing costs for quality resources.

effectiveness—Doing the right thing. Measured in quantity and quality of products and services. Also measured in revenues.

one-dimensional—Focus on a single side of the productivity model.

two-dimensional—Balanced focus on inputs and outputs to enhance productivity.

decisions on how to spend our $2 wisely to maximize its contribution to the conversion of resources **(transformation process)** into outputs (products and services) that are perceived to be worth $3 in the perception of the buyer (guest). To further complicate this process, there are invisible human factors such as perceived values **(meaning system)** and perceived experience **(learning system)** that add an emotional dimension to our chances of producing a productive outcome.

In this model, resources (materials, money, technology and people) serve as inputs to a transformation process that yields outcomes (products/services) for distribution to customers (guests). **Efficiency** refers to the responsible use of resources, while **effectiveness** refers to the quantity and quality of outputs. People provide activities as a means to enhance both efficiency and effectiveness within organizations. Therefore, managers work with people to provide business applications that improve productivity. This requires human resource practitioners to be familiar with the business of the organization to contribute to productivity enhancement. Similar to the diamond service model, the productivity model is carefully perched in the center, requiring balance from both sides of the equation. The earlier example of appeasing the short-term profit motives of the shareholders at the expense of the employees, customers, and community is not an example of productivity enhancement because it is **one-dimensional**, by focusing on one side of the model, as opposed to **two-dimensional**, which considers both sides of the equation. That is to say, it maximizes the right side of the equation while destroying the left side of the equation. Operational and accounting managers have a tendency to make one-dimensional managerial decisions, which ultimately result in organizational suicide. It is the task of the HR manager to caution these managers (who usually lack training) and educate them in the workings of value-added management by influencing both sides of the productivity model in a fashion that maintains a balance between efficiency and effectiveness.

Historically in all industries, accounting and finance managers have tended to be efficiency oriented. Contrarily, marketing managers have tended to possess an effectiveness orientation. In good times, marketing managers were promoted to the position of CEO, which would cause a firm to spend ridiculous amounts of money to increase sales. When times became lean, the finance manager would be placed in charge, resulting in cost cutting beyond

HOSPITALITY NEWS *Whose Job Is It?*

This is a story about four people named everybody, somebody, anybody, and nobody.

There was an important job to be done and everybody was sure that somebody would do it. Anybody could have done it, but nobody did it.

Somebody got angry about that, because it was everybody's job. Everybody thought anybody could do it, but nobody realized that everybody wouldn't do it. It ended up that everybody blamed somebody when nobody did what anybody could have.

—*Anonymous*

Source: Hospitality News, May 2003, p. 23.

reason, which made it impossible for the firm to produce the appropriate quality and quantity of products and services. This see-saw effect would continue back and forth, creating organizations that were either too efficiency oriented or too effectiveness oriented. The untrained shareholders and general public came to believe that this was a natural cycle for business economics. This is not true! Some firms have realized the error in this belief system and have begun to place human resource executives in CEO positions. The reason for this is that the training provided to the human resource practitioner is based on organizational balance, through two-dimensional decision-making processes. One business economic factor that is true is the dynamic nature of the external environment surrounding the hospitality business enterprise.

Technology and other external factors are responsible for dramatic changes in the demographics and psychographics of the workforce. With these advances, individuals are shifting from process work to knowledge-based work. In this millennium we are becoming a workforce of knowledge workers, we are requiring more highly skilled workers than ever before. Unfortunately, however, our industry is behind the technology curve relative to non–service-oriented industries.[3] This factor is contributing to a labor crisis in our industry. Present-day human resource practitioners must embrace technological innovations to reduce the amounts of unskilled and semi-skilled labor in our industry in response to this crisis. This is certainly one of the mandates for the human resource manager of the future.[4]

HR MANAGEMENT FUNCTIONS

There are three basic HR management functions. Because of the increase in service-based production, customer service is a major issue. Secondly, quality (effectiveness and continuous improvement) initiatives remain as important factors in all organizations. But perhaps the most important issue is productivity, which is the tool of the value-added manager, as mentioned earlier in the chapter.

It is widely known that service-based enterprises drive the economy. The service professional is now a knowledge worker in that they collaborate and communicate for the purpose of creating, using and distributing information. Executives, managers, supervisors, and professionals are all knowledge workers.

SUMMARY

This chapter has presented an overview of the hospitality resource function from the viewpoints of our constituents (the individuals that we serve). It has been established that the needs of all members of the stakeholder group are important to the long-term welfare of the hospitality organization. We discussed value-added management through productivity enhancement as the means by which we may accommodate the needs of all the constituent

In the Real World . . . (Continued)

Immediately upon hearing Sarah's words you start to become angry: "If you are so concerned about the owners, what will they say when our turnover costs force our recruitment and training expenses through the roof? Do you know that each position that turns over costs about nine months' wages to replace an hourly job?

Sarah smiles slightly and says, "Well, those are your budget items. If that happens, I am afraid you won't meet your budget; that won't look good on your annual performance review."

Dick, sensing your vulnerability, chimes in: "That's right—the figures are the figures. You should have asked to change them when we developed the budget."

Now you are beginning to seethe at the thought that these two are holding you hostage for trying to do the right thing for the company. Finally you say, "Well, Dick, looking at these budget figures, it seems to me that you understated the tip credit figures for the servers."

Dick stares at you in disbelief. "What are you talking about?" he puffs, as his face turns red.

You give him a slight smile. "That's right, the tip credit for servers is off by a quarter per hour per server." You continue: "I wonder what the owners will say when they find that out."

"Why didn't you tell me that before?"

"You never asked me, Dick."

As they both stare at you, you continue. "Seems to me if we correct this little error by the controller's office, we should have more than enough for a little wage increase. Any objections?"

---

parties. It is the task of the HR manager to be a "manager's manager" by knowing all there is to know about the business operation. The HR practitioner is the balance mechanism in the firm, with the mission to maintain organizational balance through two-dimensional decision-making processes. This information should dispel any myth that human resource departments are supply-side cost centers. Through internal marketing and the education of operating managers, the human resource practitioner contributes to the "bottom line" of the organization, while protecting its assets and enhancing its overall economic health. While it is true that some human resource practitioners are deficient in the training necessary to make such contributions to organizations, the reader of this text knows better. Only untrained or partially trained HR practitioners feel like they are schizophrenics. The other practitioners have been cured of this debilitating malady.

DISCUSSION QUESTIONS

1. The In the Real World vignette shows how you as a human resource manager knew that the tip credit for servers was understated. This means that the amount the company is allowed to deduct from the minimum wage standard for tipped personnel was $.25 lower for each server per hour. This adds up to a sizeable amount, since the majority of the staff consists of service personnel. How do you feel about having to re-

sort to this strategy to give the kitchen staff a raise? What would have been the right thing for Sarah to do?

2. After having this experience, would you be looking for an HR job with another company? Why or why not?

KEY TERMS

appreciation
bottom line
compensation
effectiveness
efficiency
employee relations
external customer
inputs
internal

internal customer
labor intensive
learning system
line employee
meaning system
one-dimensional
outputs
productivity
profits

quid pro quo
recruitment
retention
return on
 investment
revenues
ROI
selection
short-term gain

social
 responsibility
staff employee
transformation
 process
two-dimensional
value-added
 manager

CHAPTER THREE
How the Government Got Involved in Our Business

OBJECTIVES

By the end of this chapter, the reader will be able to:

1. Understand the role of government as a regulator of business practices.
2. Consider the history that led to the current state of government regulations.
3. Identify the steps in the evolutionary development of management practice.
4. Understand the role of agencies in the practice of government regulation of commercial enterprises.

In the Real World . . .

You are a newly hired assistant manager in the food and beverage (F&B) department of a large resort. The F&B director holds monthly strategy meetings with all the managers in the department for the purpose of devising new ways of enhancing departmental productivity. At this, your first meeting, the F&B director has invited the controller and marketing director to participate in the meeting. You walk in with your manager, grab a cup of coffee, and take a seat. Since you are new to this operation you observe the dynamics of the following conversations closely.

The F&B director starts things off. "Ladies and gentlemen, I have invited Sheila (the controller) and Mark (the marketing director) to help us with our productivity enhancement initiative. They will provide us with some new ways of looking at our operation."

After a preliminary overview of the current status of the initiative, Mark starts to comment, "Look," he says, "You got to spend money to make money. If you want to enhance productivity, you need to drive revenues. The only way to drive revenues is to invest in advertising and promotional activities to increase business."

Sheila jumps in, "Hold on there, Mark. The budget is the budget. You don't enhance productivity by overrunning your expense budgets. That's ludicrous."

"Oh Sheila, not this again. If you had your way, you would be on the floor with a stopwatch conducting time and motion studies to reduce labor."

"You bet I would! Efficiency is the key to every operation. Our biggest single expense is labor dollars. So it makes sense to reduce those expenditures as much as possible."

"Increasing revenues is dollar wise and cutting costs is penny foolish. Put more bucks on the top line and that will take care of the bottom line."

"Mark, apparently you were asleep when they talked about scientific management in your school. If you had your way, we would be out of business."

This discussion continues to go back and forth for quite some time. After a while, you decide to go get another cup of coffee . . .

INTRODUCTION

This chapter takes us from where we were in the early 1900s to our current status in this new millennium. There is no question that there has been a good deal of evolution over the past 100 years. Some would argue that development in the United States has been mostly for the good of society. However, as is the case in any society, there are some aspects of evolution that have resulted from inappropriate activities in this capitalistic society.

The Industrial Revolution started what we call management today. Prior to the development of mass production, commerce consisted primarily of artisans. A young male would learn a craft by working as an apprentice under the tutelage of some master in the trade. A person who desired to learn carpentry would work along side an accomplished carpenter. The same was true for other artisans, craftsmen, farmers, ranchers, and merchants. The leading industrial nation prior to the 1900s was Great Britain. It was in this country that disputes occasionally arose among individuals who were engaged in commerce. Most of the arguments were between buyers and sellers of products. However, an occasional dispute would arise between an apprentice and his employer (craftsman or merchant).

The legal system in England during this time was also relatively sophisticated. The religious cardinals, who controlled the provinces back then, would appoint judges called chanceries to hear civil complaints, including those evolving from the engagement of commerce. The chanceries would notice similarities among certain disputes and decided to create court documents for applications to future court hearings. The chanceries concluded that a previous case would set a **precedent** for deciding future cases with similar content, which would preclude the judges from having to hear each argument as if it were presented for the first time. The result of this efficient system was that judges were actually making laws through court hearings that would be applied to future matters requiring legal decisions. Since this body of judge-made law applied to **civil** disputes among what was then referred to as "commoners," it became known as **common law**, which is also referred to as the law of **Torts**. The British carried these laws to the United States, where they are applied to this day.

After the American Revolution, our forefathers crafted the supreme legislation of the land to ensure that government would not interfere with the lives of individuals. This supreme law became known as the U.S. Constitution. At the time, it was never thought that companies would ever infringe on the rights of individuals, since corporations were yet to be invented. So, disputes among employees and employers were handled within the domain of a common law doctrine known as **employment-at-will** (EAW), which is still in existence; however, it has become greatly eroded from its original intent.

Basically, the employment-at-will doctrine states that an employer and an employee enter into a mutually beneficial relationship known as **quid pro quo**. The employer receives services from the employee and the employee receives compensation from the employer. Therefore, according to the doctrine, they are on equal ground. The employer may choose whoever it wants to employ, and the employee may choose any employer. Therefore, the employee is free to come and go, and the employer is free to start and end the employment relationship, **unilaterally**, at any time, for any reason, or no reason at all. At this time a small number of states in the United States uphold a current version of this doctrine and are known as employment-at-will states. This doctrine and its implications are discussed in greater detail in a later chapter.

MANAGEMENT EVOLUTION AND THE INTERNAL ENVIRONMENT

The dawn of the Industrial Revolution brought together large numbers of employees working on newly invented assembly lines in manufacturing environments. This created the need for individuals to supervise the work of groups. As the manufacturing environments grew larger, they became organizations or companies that required a hierarchy of managers to oversee the operations. It was in the 1920s that the practice of management began to evolve. Figure 3.1 describes the evolution of management thinking from that time to the present.

One of the first approaches to understanding the management of workers was called **scientific management**.[1] The father of scientific management was an engineer by training, Frederick Taylor.[2] Taylor used his engineering

precedent—A matter of law as decided in a court dispute that has applications for cases with similar facts.

civil law—A body of law that governs actions between and among the members of a society.

common law—Unwritten laws resulting from precedent-setting court decisions which are applied to future cases. Known as judge-made law.

torts—Another name for common-law doctrines.

employment-at-will—A common-law doctrine that is applied to the actions of employers and employees in disputes arising from the employment relationship.

quid pro quo—Something of value that is exchanged for something else of value.

unilaterally—An action taken by a single party to an agreement.

scientific management—The first formal doctrine of management that is focused on the best way to do tasks and is efficiency based.

1920s–1930s	1940s	1960s–1970s	1980s	1990s–2000s
Scientific Mgmt.	Mgmt. Science	Behavioral Science	Human Resource Mgmt.	Systems Mgmt.
Taylor			Situational Leadership	
Gilbreth				
Hawthorne Studies				
Human Relations				

Figure 3.1. Evolution of Management.

skills to conduct "time and motion" studies to determine the most efficient use of labor. For instance, if individuals were digging a hole, he would experiment with shovel sizes to determine the best output per shovel-load for a specific period of time. A husband and wife team who were also academics became interested in scientific management as well, Frank and Lillian Gilbreth.[3] Frank died some time before Lillian, who continued her work until 1972. The goal of scientific management was to find the "one best way" to do work. One of the Gilbreths' more popular studies involved bricklayers. They devised scaffolding to raise the bricks to the level being worked on by these masons. This precluded the workers from having to reach to the ground as the structure they were working on rose up. Scientific management may be referred to as a single-dimensional approach to management, as its sole focus is on worker efficiency measures, with no consideration for concept of effectiveness, which is at the opposite end of the productivity spectrum.

Another researcher, Elton Mayo, stumbled upon a surprising discovery in his experiments with worker output.[4] Mayo was researcher who was hired by a company that provided light fixtures to conduct experiments with workers that might correlate levels of lighting in the workplace with increased labor productivity. He is best known for two experiments that involved mostly female workers who performed somewhat redundant labor activities. Mayo appeared in these work areas as a scholar who was interested in learning about worker performance. As he began his experiments he found that worker productivity did actually increase as the lighting in the rooms was made to be brighter. However, he later found that worker productivity continued to increase as lighting levels were dimmed. As you can imagine, this did not make the light company happy, and they removed Mayo's funding for further experiments. However, he did conclude that the reason worker productivity was increasing was the attention he was paying to the workers, who were accustomed to working in a solitary environment. This conclusion launched the first behavioral approach to management, resulting in the development of the **human relations** philosophy of management thinking.[5] Unfortunately, the concept didn't take hold as a broadly accepted management philosophy until the 1960s, when behavioral aspects of management became

human relations—A management philosophy that considers the emotional needs of workers.

popular. Among other precepts, this school of thought suggested that the emotional needs of workers are factors for consideration in the practice of management.

management science—A management model that applies the scientific method to decision-making activities in organizations.

Management scholars faced new challenges during the 1940s, when the United States engaged in strategic maneuvers as part of World War II. The researchers were asked to provide probability models to solve complex strategic problems related to military deployments. This required the application of the scientific method to the practice of management, resulting in a new management approach, **management science**.[6] At this point, the practice of management was influenced by two task-oriented doctrines and one behavioral philosophy. After the war, an economic boom took place in the United States, resulting in more complex organizations employing a variety of **white-collar** and **blue-collar** workers. In 1950, the discipline of management was recognized as a bona fide academic field of study, with the appointment of Peter Drucker as the first professor of management at the New York University.[7] Drucker became one of the premier gurus who shaped the practice of management as we know it today.

white-collar—Professional and administrative positions in organizations.

blue-collar—Trades and labor positions in organizations.

As the country moved into the 1960s, new thinkers in the field of psychology began to discover human behavior models that posed relevant practices in the management of people.[8] It was at this point that the Hawthorne studies were revisited and the **behavioral science** approach to management became popular.

behavioral science—A management model that considers the "whys" of human behavior in the workplace.

Eventually, corporate leaders recognized individuals as more than just labor expenses by realizing that people in organizations were worthy of investments to enhance personal and professional growth. The new model applied to workers presented them in the category of **human capital**: assets worthy of investments to enhance corporate growth. This thinking created a second behavioral philosophy in the field of management, which became known as the **human resource philosophy**.[9] This is the thinking that eventually evolved into the practice of human resource management, which is defined as the accomplishment of organizational objectives through the management and development of human capital.

human capital—The philosophy that investments in the development of people result in increased value to an organization.

human resource philosophy—The philosophy that workers are human capital.

HOSPITALITY NEWS *Managing a Non–English-Speaking Workforce*

A dramatic statistic revealed in the 2000 census is that 49 percent of Hispanics in the United States are not fluent in English. In addition, Hispanics are the fastest growing minority in the United States, representing 12.5 percent of the population. This indicates a 60 percent growth in 10 years, and experts predict continued growth by the year 2010 and thereafter. In Arizona alone, Hispanics represent 25.3 percent of the population, which is an increase of 88 percent in 10 years, signifying an additional 600,000 Hispanics. However, their education level has not improved as exponentially as their growth: 11 percent have graduated from college, 56 percent have a high school diploma, and 28 percent have less than a ninth-grade education.

The legal picture for Hispanics is similarly astonishing. EEOC complaints have more than doubled in five years, and settlements have risen to more than $50 million. In June 2000, a class action lawsuit by 22 Hispanic females against Grace Culinary Systems, Inc. (a subsidiary of W.R. Grace) resulted in a $1 million settlement. In April 2001, a Texas university paid $2.4 million to Hispanic housekeepers due to discrimination.

An article by Stephen M. Paskoff and Lori J. Shapiro in the November 2000 issue of *Legal Times* stated, "In several recent cases, the U.S. Supreme Court has articulated its mandate to employers: A policy prohibiting harassment and discrimination in the workplace is not only required, but must be clearly and effectively communicated to company managers and employees so that they both understand the policy and can apply it in practice." They go on to say, "Without realizing that the most important outcome is an impact on behavior, some companies simply pass out materials about discrimination, sexual harassment, or employment issues to employees without any link to corporate culture, expectations, or standards."

Employers can no longer make superficial efforts to effect behavioral changes. These efforts must be substantial and comprehensive.

Additionally, they must be communicated in the employees' native language to be effective. Otherwise, we are not communicating clearly and effectively as recommended by Paskoff and Shapiro.

This information presents extraordinary challenges for human resource professionals. A comprehensive plan must be developed. Training is one key element. Another is that of developing a corporate culture that maintains a philosophy of bridging the cultural gaps within their employee population, and enacts systems and programs to support that belief.

This philosophy must start at the beginning and continue throughout the life of a Hispanic employee. Since the hiring process is the first experience a Hispanic applicant will have with an organization, providing an employment application in Spanish and having a bilingual interviewer in human resources will speak volumes about your commitment to diversity. Once hired, all employee memos, policies and procedures, and signage should be translated into Spanish. New employee orientations, all employee meetings, and coaching and counseling sessions will need to be conducted in Spanish.

Within the Hispanic culture, the immediate and extended family play an integral role. The more a company can integrate a family atmosphere, the more success it will have in retaining this workforce. For example, Lucent Technologies bridges the cultural gap by providing an employee business partner group that helps African Americans, Hispanics, and Asians with their unique challenges. This group devises its own business plan that addresses such issues as language and family. It provides a family atmosphere where everyone feels accepted and supported, as well as a recruitment and retention tool for the organization.

Finally, training programs with bilingual trainers and training videos in Spanish with Hispanic actors that are not dubbed or subtitled are critical to the success of an organization's training efforts. Companies that are enacting this philosophy are experiencing added benefits, such as lower turnover rates due to increased loyalty from their Hispanic workforce, higher productivity, and enhanced job banks due to increased employee referrals. And their recruitment efforts have been more successful due to communicating this training philosophy to applicants. These companies have learned that it's simply the right thing to do, *and* it's good business.

Source: Maureen E. Harrop, *Hospitality News,* March 2002, p. 3.

contingency model— A management philosophy that suggests management decisions should be tailored to the situation at hand.

situation—The environment within an organization at a specific place and time.

internal environment—Factors that comprise the internal infrastructure of an organization.

external environment—Factors from outside the organization that influence the organization and its people.

systems model—A management model that all parts of an organization and its external environment exist as patterns of relationship to each sub-part.

While the human resource approach to management was a quantum leap forward in modern thinking, more holistic models of managing organizations began to emerge in the 1970s and 1980s. One model involved an organizational leadership approach that became known as the **contingency model** of management.[10] This framework provides a three-way approach to management that involves the needs of the managers, the workers and the organizational environment or **situation** at hand. Contrary to scientific management, which seeks the one best way to do work, the contingency approach suggests that the situation determines the best management decisions in the workplace. Hence, there is no one best way to do work, as it all depends on the situation at hand.

The contingency model is holistic in that it considers factors in the **internal environment** as an influencer of worker-manager relationships, which makes this a three-factor theory. However, that model has been taken one step further to consider the environment outside the organization as relevant to the management within the organization. This outside environment contains factors that influence the organization and the people within the organization and is referred to as the **external environment**. The paradigm that considers the external and internal environments in addition to the relationships between workers and managers is called the **systems model** of management.[11] One of the factors that influences organizations from the external environment is the legal environment as prescribed by government regulation of business enterprises.

THE GOVERNMENT AND THE EXTERNAL ENVIRONMENT

Organizations in this new millennium have become quite complex during the time that has elapsed since the beginning of the Industrial Revolution, as evidenced in the evolution of management thinking that has occurred. The same is true for world societies, which represent the macrocosm that reflects upon the microcosm levels of local governments and organizations. We live in a complex world.

Complexity brings about new types of social problems that create uncertainty among the people who comprise the population. Uncertainty brings about risk, which results in social fears. In democratic nations such as the United States, the people are theoretically empowered to influence the legislators. Fearful masses will encourage the legislation to place regulations on those entities that represent sources of social fear, such as criminals, for instance. Business enterprises have given individuals living in the United States many reasons to be fearful, which is why today's corporate environment is highly regulated by government agencies. At question is what the business organizations have done to warrant state and federal government regulation.

Perhaps one down side to capitalistic economies is the creation of incentives for the exploitation of workers on the part of those who engage in the practices of commercial enterprises.[12] Historical accounts are full of stories about the exploitation of immigrant workers, slavery, and indentured servitude. Included in these accounts are incidents of abusive child labor practices, workplace deaths due to unsafe conditions, company-owned towns, intimidation tactics deployed against organizing workers, share cropper arrangements, sweat shops, mining accidents and others. Ironically, these actions were indirectly perpetrated by some of the nation's most prestigious capitalists, including Carnegie, Mellon, Rockefeller, Rothschild, Flagler and others.[13] For this reason the government turned a blind eye toward the abusive practices occurring within the commercial enterprises in this country for a number of years. Finally, as these incidents became matters of common knowledge among the nation's citizens, the government was forced to respond to protests against exploitive business practices aimed at the working class.

When the government took notice of the unethical employment policies of corporations, the legislature began to develop federal and state statutes aimed at the regulation of workplace practices. The practice of government regulation of business functions began slowly in the early 1900s and escalated to the level of regulatory legislation that exists in the current day, which imposes complex requirements for compliance on the part of corporate managers. Business regulatory practices translate into the lessening of freedom to do business on the part of enterprise practitioners, which results in additional expenses that are passed on to consumers via the pricing of products and services. However, most individuals in this country feel this is a small price to pay in the process of protecting workers from the exploitive practices of managers who represent the financial interests of corporations. At question is whether this current state of affairs could have been avoided. Why did the early capitalists engage in these practices? Could they have rewritten history to result in much lower levels of regulatory infringement on the practice of businesses at the current time?

Reflection upon historical business practices from today's perspective produces the recognition that our business forefathers acted in unethical ways in the conduct of their employment practices. The purpose of these actions was likely to be the quest for profit maximization. It is apparent that in those historical times choices were made to disregard the human rights and needs of workers in efforts to maximize returns on investment for the shareholders, which were often in the form of sole proprietorships in those years. These unethical actions created higher returns in the short term, as the shareholders of that time were evidently enjoying rich financial rewards at the expense of the workers. However, in the long run, a look at today's regulatory practices leads us to the conclusion that our forefathers created a business environment in which returns to the shareholders are marginalized as a result of the magnificent costs associated with legal compliance issues. This leads us to the conclusion that unethical business practices may yield short-term profitability, but they will ruin that business in the long run. This is the basis of our discussion concerning business ethics that is addressed in Chapter 6.

To paraphrase Patrick Henry: Those who choose to use their freedom unwisely shall inevitably forfeit their liberty. In the practice of commerce, the loss of freedom equates into increased business expenses on the part of the commercial enterprise. This adversely affects not just the shareholders, but also the consumers, who absorb the costs of doing business through the pricing of products and services. The current legal environment surrounding business practices is considered to be in a dynamic state; it is continually changing, with more legislative acts passed in each upcoming year. While business regulation includes aspects of the law such as interstate commerce, taxation, generally acceptable accounting practices, product advertising and disclosure, product safety and other areas relative to commercial practices, the employment practices of companies are the focus for this text. As will be discovered in the next chapter, the legal environment concerning the employment relationship is in itself an extensive area of the law. The regulatory laws governing the practices of business are within the legal domain known as administrative law. Administrative law is that body of law that oversees the practices of federal and state government regulatory agencies. For instance, one federal agency called the Equal Employment Opportunity Commission (EEOC) provides governance in matters relevant to a number of civil rights or anti-discrimination statutes. All regulatory agencies such as the EEOC fall within the jurisdiction of that body of law known as administrative law, which possesses parameters that are quite different from other applications of legal practice.

You may recall from your college classes that the U.S. Constitution provides for a balance of powers among its three branches of government. Figure 3.2 provides a depiction of the balance of powers among the legislative branches.

The legislative branch creates law, the executive branch enforces the law, and the judicial branch adjudicates or interprets matters of law.[14] The intent of this provision was to preclude any single branch of government from being all powerful, to ensure a system of checks and balances in the governance of the citizenry. However, when Congress (the legislative branch) created regulatory statutes, it was noted that these matters of law were quite complex and required the empowerment of technocrats, individuals familiar with these intricacies, to manage the implementation of each statute. In response to this need, legislators created administrative agencies consisting of empowered

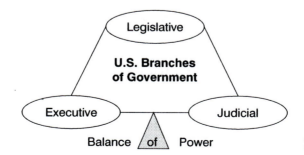

Figure 3.2. Balance of Power.

technocrats to oversee the management of each newly created regulatory statute. In their zest to create such agencies, Congress overlooked the constitutional concept of balance of powers by making these agencies all powerful to practice the administration of regulatory statutes. Hence, an administrative agency such as the EEOC possesses the power to legislate administrative orders, enforce those orders, and adjudicate perceived violations of the agency's mandates.

It is obvious that relative to the balance of powers restricting the activities of governmental branches, the commissioners of administrative agencies are totally empowered to govern matters of administrative law within their appointed jurisdictions. For instance, the EEOC has the power to make rules of law, which is the creation of law, a power reserved exclusively for the legislative branch of government. It has the power to enforce its law, similar to the restricted power of the administrative branch of government. And it may adjudicate (or judge) the law in matters of dispute, a right only reserved for the judiciary branch of government known as the courts. So you see that administrative agencies such as the EEOC enjoy very high levels of empowerment. Of course, members of Congress rationalize that they have the power of creation over administrative agencies. Theoretically, according to this construct, they are the "givers of power" to the agency, and they may restrict the actions of the agency by removing agency funding, referred to in legal circles as the power of the purse. Thus, it is the contention of Congress that any abuse of power on the part of an administrative agency may be addressed through congressional authority to prohibit and even disband such an agency. This poses an interesting argument; however, it is yet to be known as to when such an action has been taken in matters of administrative law. It may be argued as well that members of Congress who oversee an agency with the powers of legal creation, enforcement, and adjudication are overstepping their appointed power of legal creation by managing the other two powers (enforcement and adjudication) in agency administration. These arguments are better reserved for administrative law courses. However, it is important for the practitioner of human resource management to be familiar with the power wielded by administrative agencies in matters of employment law.

Perhaps some of the earliest legislation created to directly regulate the actions of commercial enterprises pertaining to employment practices includes those laws that protect the rights of workers to engage collectively in an effort to establish bargaining units that possess the intent to negotiate in good faith with a specific employer or its agents over working conditions. These laws began to emerge in the early 1900s and comprise an area of law known as labor relations law. Labor relations law pertains to the rights of individual workers to form and join labor unions, which are third party entities that lead the unionized workers in a process to articulate working conditions referred to as collective bargaining. The purpose of this process is to establish a collective bargaining agreement, which is a contract between employers and employees that specifies matters of working conditions for collective groups of individual workers in a specific organization. Just as the EEOC is one agency empowered to oversee the administration of civil rights legislation, the agency that administers matters of labor relations law is called the National Labor Relations Board (NLRB). One thing that both agencies have

right—Something that a person is entitled to from nature or law.

privilege—Something that is given as a gift to a person or is earned by a person based on performance.

in common is that they fall within the jurisdiction of administrative law. Thus, the NLRB is a very powerful agency, just as is the EEOC, although each has a different mission relative to safeguarding worker rights. Labor unions are discussed in detail in a later chapter.

Human resource management is largely concerned with the protection of the rights of individuals in the workplace. So, it is necessary to identify the nature of a right, as opposed to a privilege. A **right** is something that a person is entitled to by nature or law.[15] On the other hand, a **privilege** is something granted to an individual that may be rescinded by the granting party. The key difference between these two concepts is the premise of entitlement. A right is an entitlement. A privilege is not an entitlement; instead, it is a gift that is granted to a person or a status that is earned by that person.

For instance, most laypersons misunderstand the concept of a right-to-work state. Many untrained individuals believe that this means that a worker and an employer may choose to enter into a working agreement or end a working agreement at will. We know from earlier discussions in the chapter that this description identifies the employment-at-will doctrine. The concept of a right-to-work state has nothing to do with employment at will. Instead, right-to-work refers to the right of employers to hire permanent replacements for those union workers who choose to engage in an action of work stoppage, such as a labor strike (which provides a right to work for an individual who is outside the organization). However, most individuals (correctly) understand that both doctrines have something to do with a person's rights as determined by the law. On the other hand, nature provides us with certain rights, such as the right to live, breathe, and engage in personal relationships. There are situations in which the legal law will remove a right provided by the natural law, or nature. For instance, the courts may impose a death sentence on a convicted criminal. While this person was in possession of a natural right to live, the society removes that natural right through the legal doctrine of capital punishment. Democratic nations produce laws to safeguard the natural right for individuals to live in freedom from governmental constraints. Evidence of this thinking exists in the Bill of Rights attached to the U.S. Constitution in which the natural freedoms of individuals are construed to be inalienable rights.[16] meaning that the government shall not impinge on nature's granted right to live in freedom.

Workers' rights, in the view of human resource practitioners, involves the implementation of practices designed to treat every employee in a fair, uniform, and consistent manner regarding all terms, conditions, and privileges of the employment relationship. At the same time it is the charge of the HR practitioner to safeguard the assets of the organization by ensuring legal compliance and that appropriate managerial practices exist throughout the corporation. Therefore, the protection of employee rights in the workplace comes down to knowing every aspect of the legal environment and providing solid managerial practices in all aspects of workplace governance. For these reasons, excellent human resource practitioners are referred to as managers' managers, since they know everything there is to know about management in organizations. The mission for every HR practitioner should be to maximize the development of management skills for every person in a position of authority throughout the organization. This is a proactive approach to human resource management, as solid managerial practice reduces the need for reactive HR interventions. These concepts are discussed in detail in a later chapter.

SUMMARY

This chapter has provided information that describes how the government became involved in the business of businesses. The choices made by early business leaders showed disregard for the needs and rights of workers. The result of these choices is the regulatory environment surrounding business enterprises in existence today. Prior to becoming matters of law, the treatment of workers in organizations was left to the ethical propensity of managers and business owners. It has been made clear that those authority figures made incorrect ethical choices in those times. When individuals choose to act unethically, the legal environment is enhanced to right the pre-existing wrongs that may have occurred. The result is that government regulation is a permanent part of the business landscape, which creates employment and promotion opportunities for human resource practitioners, as well as other professional positions.

In this chapter we reviewed the internal environment of business operations by a look at the evolution of professional management throughout the years. The external environment of organizations was also examined from the perspective of the legal aspects of common and statutory laws. Part of our legal discussion included the rights of individuals to form labor unions designed to bargain in good faith with employers concerning the activities of individuals in the workplace. We concluded with a discussion concerning employee rights and provided an overview of proactive human resource management. Each of these topics is discussed in detail in the next section of the book.

In the Real World . . . (Continued)

As you sit down with your second cup of coffee, you begin to realize that this meeting is getting out of control, and that this is not the first time that Sheila and Mark have had this argument. The F&B director rolls his eyes as the two continue to go back and forth with their managerial philosophies. You realize from your training that both Mark and Sheila are correct in their philosophies, and that they simply need to put the two concepts together.

Since this is your first meeting, you are a little shy. But after this prolonged debate, you finally say, "Couldn't we reduce labor costs and increase revenues by developing the talents of our people?" A hush fills the room as everyone turns to stare at you. "Well," you continue, "that would be the human resource approach to enhancing productivity." The F&B director smiles at you with approval. "Next week," he jokes, "we will invite Sheila, Mark, and the HR director to be their referee."

DISCUSSION QUESTIONS

1. Since the government is already regulating our businesses, there probably is no need to ensure the rights of workers beyond what is prescribed by law, right? Why or why not?

2. As the profession of management evolved, leaders seemed to shift from task-oriented approaches to people-oriented approaches. Does this mean that the focus should be solely on the people aspects of management? Why or why not?

3. If there is a balance of power among governmental branches, why is this not the case with administrative agencies? Should this be the case with the EEOC, for instance? Why or why not?

4. Do you think there are people in positions of power in organizations that think the same way that our capitalist forefathers thought? Do you think they would exploit people if they could? Why or why not?

KEY TERMS

behavioral science	external	management	situation
blue-collar	environment	science	systems model
civil law	human capital	precedent	torts
common law	human relations	privilege	unilaterally
contingency	human resource	quid pro quo	white-collar
model	philosophy	right	
employment-	internal	scientific	
at-will	environment	management	

CHAPTER FOUR
The Legal Environment

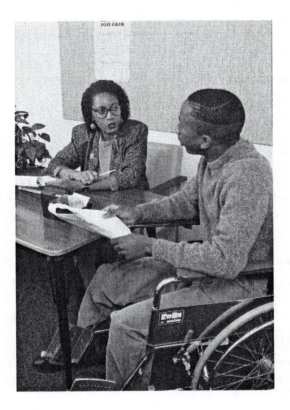

OBJECTIVES

By the end of this chapter, the reader will be able to:

1. Understand the provisions, coverage, and exceptions of major statutes.
2. Comprehend the four theories of discrimination as applied to the laws.
3. Recognize legal exceptions to discriminatory practices.
4. Understand the role of the EEOC and the courts in processing claims of discrimination.

In the Real World . . .

You work in a human resource office for a large resort as a clerical assistant. You are assigned to work with various managers in the specialist departments. Sometimes you work with the training manager, employment manager or compensation manager. When you arrive at work, the director assigns you to work with her on a big project. It seems that an employee has filed a claim of discrimination against the resort. The EEOC is investigating the allegations and has sent a notice of findings of fact to the human resource office.

You enter the director's office to find that she has already cleared a work space for you. You ask about the nature of the complaint. She replies, "You name it: sex, race, color, national origin, and religion."

"What? How can it be all those things?"

The director smiles at you and says, "This is how it is. Once a person becomes a complainant, the EEOC has them complete a checklist of all the factors of discrimination. By the time a complainant leaves their office, he or she has filed a claim based on every form of coverage that exists."

You continue to stare at the legal notice in disbelief. "So what do we have to do?"

She replies, "Oh, about 100 hours of fact-finding work. We will give the database a workout to pull all of the statistics and reports we will need to defend the organization. It will take us about two weeks to prepare the response. Actually, this will be very good experience for you, since you haven't done this type of work yet. So, if you are ready, let's get down to work."

INTRODUCTION

A large portion of the human resource manager's time is spent to ensure compliance with the many statutes that exist for the protection of individual rights that are applicable to the employment relationship. As we discussed earlier, this is the responsibility of the human resource practitioner as part of the responsibility to protect the assets of the organization. In this case, legal actions against the organization for improper employment practices could be quite costly and ultimately put a company out of business. At the same time, there is a significant cost associated with legal compliance activities aimed at precluding legal action against the organization, as we will discover in this chapter. We have discussed the dynamic nature of business regulation as an external force that impacts organizations; when it comes to the employment aspect, regulatory forces are in the form of civil rights and anti-discrimination legislation.

While most people are familiar with the Civil Rights Act of 1964, as amended, the first legislation to protect against race and color discrimination was enacted in the 1860s. These laws continue to be invoked in the courts. However, the civil rights movement didn't start to take hold until the 1960s, with numerous statutes entering the law books from then through the 1990s. It is likely that newer laws will be created during this millennium. Table 4.1 identifies the major statutes that contain applications to employment scenarios, listed in chronological order.

Table 4.1 Civil Rights Statutes

Act	Year	Provisions
Equal Pay Act	1963	Requires equal pay for men and women performing substantially the same work
Title VII Civil Rights Act	1964	Prohibits discrimination in employment on the basis of race, color, religion, sex, or national origin
Executive Orders 11246, 11375	1965, 1967	Require federal contractors and subcontractors to eliminate employment discrimination and prior discrimination through affirmative action
Age Discrimination in Employment Act (ADEA)	1967	Prohibits discrimination against persons over age 40 and restricts mandatory retirement requirements, except where age is a BFOQ
Vocational Rehabilitation Act	1973, 1974	Prohibits employers with federal contracts over $2,500 from discriminating against individuals with disabilities
Pregnancy Discrimination Act	1978	Prohibits discrimination against women affected by pregnancy, childbirth, or related medical conditions; requires that they be treated as all other employees for employment-related purposes, including benefits
Immigration Reform and Control Act (IRCA)	1986, 1990, 1996	Establishes penalties for employers who knowingly hire illegal aliens; prohibits employment discrimination on the basis of national origin or citizenship
Americans with Disabilities Act (ADA)	1990	Requires employer to accommodate individuals with disabilities within "reason"
Civil Rights Act of 1991	1991	Overturns several past U.S. Supreme Court decisions and changes damage claims provisions
Congressional Accountability Act	1995	Extends EEO and Civil Rights Act provisions to U.S. congressional staff
Family and Medical Leave Act (FMLA)	1993	Mandates employers to provide eligible employees with up to 12 weeks' leave during any 12 month period.

FEDERAL EMPLOYMENT LAW STATUTES

The Equal Pay Act

The Equal Pay Act (EPA) of 1963 prohibits disparity in pay between genders. For example, a male host in a restaurant may not be paid more than a female host in that same restaurant. This is because the two individuals are performing jobs that are equal in skill, effort and responsibility, performed under the same or similar conditions. If the male has been working at the establishment for a period of time that warranted an increase in hourly pay, that is fine, as long as the female host has the same opportunity when she has worked for that period of time.

As is the case with most statutes, there are exceptions to the provisions of the EPA. One exception has to do with bona fide seniority or merit systems. In the host example, the male host was further along in the seniority system than the female host. If the establishment provided pay increases based on performance, that would be considered to be a merit system. Another exception involves quantity- and quality-based earnings, such as sales commissions.

Table 4.2 EPA Provisions and Exceptions

Statute	Provisions	Coverage	Exceptions
Equal Pay Act (EPA)	Equal pay between the sexes	All FLSA covered employees	Seniority; merit; output related compensation; non-gender differentials

Fair Labor Standards Act (FLSA)—This law was enacted in 1938 and has provisions for overtime payment and child labor protection. It is the law that provides exempt and non-exempt status and is also responsible for the federal minimum wage.

Differentials based on factors other than sex are also exceptions. For instance a host may make less than a maître d', because the maître d' does more than just work the door of a restaurant. The host may be a female; if she were promoted to the position of maître d', she would receive the appropriate pay.

All employers that fall within the jurisdiction of the **Fair Labor Standards Act (FLSA)** of 1938 must comply with the EPA. We will discuss the FLSA later on in the book. Also, some employers may be inclined to reduce pay rates to make them even. This is not permissible under the act. Hence, the employer would have to increase pay rates to achieve equality. Table 4.2 provides a summary of the provisions and exceptions regarding the EPA.

As discussed in previous chapters, discriminatory practices have existed throughout the history of the United States, in the workplace as well as other areas of civil interaction. In the late 1950s and into the 1960s, the U.S. Supreme Court (the highest court in the land) heard a small number of significant cases that tested the constitutionality of inequities waged upon certain civil groups. This significant activity encouraged the legislative branch (Congress) to enact legal statutes aimed at equal treatment among groups engaged in civil activities. These laws became known as civil rights statutes. Among the most popular of these is the Civil Rights Act of 1964, which was amended in 1972 and reframed in 1991.

HOSPITALITY NEWS *Gender Discrimination*

You could have legal trouble of you're discriminating in pay on the basis of gender. Under both the Equal Pay Act and Title VII of the U.S. Civil Rights Act, it is illegal to pay male and female employees differently for equal work in jobs that require equal skill, effort and responsibility and that are performed under similar working conditions.

The only way you can justify a salary difference is to prove that it is based on prior experience, education, seniority, or salary history—not gender. You must have ironclad proof that men are earning more because of merit. You can, however, compensate supervisors beyond their base salary—regardless of their gender—for superior performance.

Source: Hospitality News, March 2003, p. 36.

The Civil Rights Act of 1964

The Civil Rights Act of 1964 as amended took a three-prong approach to guaranteeing civil rights by including provisions for housing, employment, and education. Title VII of the act addresses the protection of civil rights in employment and is the focus of this discussion.

Title VII of the Civil Rights Act prohibits discrimination in all employment decisions on the basis of race, color, sex, religion, and national origin. The courts have interpreted the provision relating to sex as including pregnancy, childbirth, abortion, marital status, stereotyping, and harassment, which are referred to as sex-plus issues. The law applies to both private (commerce) and public (government) sector organizations, agencies, unions and apprentice committees that involve at least 15 employees engaged in 20 weeks or more of annual operations.

The Civil Rights Act is enforced by a federal regulatory agency called the **Equal Employment Opportunity Commission (EEOC)**. The EEOC was established on July 5, 1965, and was vested with the powers of enforcement, rulemaking, and adjudication. It is the EEOC that gave immense power to the enforcement of Title VII in the workplace. Since 1965, a number of civil rights–related statutes were added to its jurisdiction. Interestingly, however, while the CRA prohibited discrimination in all employment practices, the statute failed to define the specific actions that constitute a discriminatory practice.

As we will see in the next section, the matter of definition was left to the courts. For now, let's take a look at Table 4.3 to review the highlights of the CRA of 1964, as amended.

Equal Employment Opportunity Commission (EEOC)— The federal agency that enforces, administers, and adjudicates for most discrimination statutes.

Table 4.3 Civil Rights Act (1964) Highlights

Statute	Provisions	Coverage	Exceptions
Civil Rights Act (CRA)	Prohibits discrimination based on race, color, sex, religion and national origin	Public and private sector with 15 or more employees working 20 or more weeks per year	BFOQ and business necessity (BN) (to be discussed in the next section)

FOUR THEORIES OF DISCRIMINATION

Definitions of what constitutes discrimination were determined through case law. Case law consists of those court decisions that establish precedents to be followed in future similar cases, as you may remember from the last chapter in our discussion concerning common law. One landmark case defining aspects that determine discriminatory activities was *Griggs* v. *Duke Power*.[1] To this day there remain four theories of discrimination in the view of the courts relative to employment relationships.

Prior to discussing these theories, it is important to note who is who in an agency complaint and a civil court case. A person who files a complaint with an agency (the EEOC, for instance) is referred to as the **complainant**, or the complaining party. The employer in such matters is referred to as the respondent, charged with responding to the complaint before the agency. If a matter goes to civil trial, that trial will take place in **Federal District Court (FDC)**, since the matter involves federal civil rights laws. When the parties go to trial, the complainant becomes the **plaintiff**, since that person is petitioning the court for a decision and the respondent becomes known as the **defendant**, since the employer is in a position to defend itself against the claim in the view of the court. So, when a complaint is first filed with the EEOC, the employee or prospective employee (for instance, an applicant who did not get a job) becomes the complainant and if the matter goes to court, that same person becomes the plaintiff. The employer that the claim is filed against becomes the respondent, and if the matter proceeds to court that employer becomes the defendant. Each party to a dispute concerning discrimination has a duty to prove certain aspects of the complaint, which is referred to as **burden of proof**.

The burden of proof begins with the complaining party (complainant) then shifts to the responding party (respondent), with the same being true for trials involving plaintiffs and defendants. It is important to note that there are two basic types of trials that take place in a courtroom. Criminal trials involve crimes against the state, in which the burden of proof for a prosecuting attorney is "guilty beyond a reasonable doubt" in order to get a verdict against a party (defendant). Civil trials involve wrongs committed between members of society and are non-criminal in nature. An EEOC complainant who goes to court (becoming a plaintiff) is a party in such a civil trial. The burden of proof in a civil case is a **preponderance of evidence**, which means that the slightest extra weight in the evidence will result in a judgment that is favorable to that party. This is a much lighter burden relative to that which is levied upon a prosecuting party in a criminal matter.

Finally, it is important to define those individuals who are covered under a specific anti-discrimination statute. Back in 1964, the intent was to protect

complainant— Designation of an individual who has filed a claim of discrimination with an agency.

Federal District Court (FDC)— Area courts with jurisdiction over federal statutes to include discrimination cases.

plaintiff—The filing party in a legal dispute.

defendant—The party against which a civil claim is filed in a court of law.

burden of proof—The duty of a party in a claim or charge to provide evidence of legal standing.

preponderance of evidence—The balance of evidence in which a court decision is made on the slightest weight in one direction. This rule is applied in civil cases. Beyond a reasonable doubt is the rule of evidence for criminal cases.

those individuals who consisted of a smaller portion of the commonly referred to members of society. Thus, the term used for those requiring protection from discrimination was referred to as a **minority**, or collectively as minorities. In today's parlance these terms are inappropriate when referring to those covered under provisions of the law, particularly since all individuals are covered under at least one anti-discrimination statute. Hence, the term used for those individuals and groups who fall within the provisions of a statute is **protected class**.

Disparate Treatment

The case of *Griggs* v. *Duke* did an excellent job of defining intentional discrimination, referred to as **disparate treatment**. In such a case, the complainant or plaintiff has the burden of proof to show the intent to discriminate through some form of unfavorable treatment. A person might say, "The employer fired me because I am hispanic." At this point the burden of proof shifts to the employer to articulate a non-discriminatory reason for the action. For example, the employer might say, "It is true that we fired him. But it was not because he is hispanic; it was because he was stealing from the company." Now the burden of proof shifts back to the plaintiff to demonstrate that the defendant's testimony was a mere **pretext** for discrimination. To do this the plaintiff would say something like, "I didn't steal anything. Yes, I was in possession of what the company calls **contraband**, but the items were given to me by someone else. Non-hispanics just receive disciplinary warnings for contraband possession, but I got fired because of my national origin."

In essence there are three elements of a disparate treatment claim. First, the complainant must have incurred harm resulting from a decision by the employer. Second, the complainant must show that the employer intended to discriminate. Third, in the event that the respondent articulates a non-discriminatory reason for the employment action, the complainant must show that the reason was a pretext to discrimination. It would seem from this discussion that the complainant possesses a heavy burden in the matter of a dispute. However, in actuality, all the complainant must do is to articulate the allegations. It is the employer or respondent that must show physical evidence that the allegations are not true. Hence, the burden of proof for a complainant is very shallow, since he or she needs only to make allegations. This level of proof is called **prima facie** or first glance proof. Despite the legal nuances associated with shifting burden of proof, the burden always remains with the employer in matters of dispute regarding discrimination. This is true because the employer must demonstrate its case with physical evidence and is charged with proving a negative, in that it must prove that it did not discriminate.

Disparate Impact

A second theory of discrimination sounds very similar to disparate treatment, but is quite different in actual application. This theory is known as **disparate impact**. It is similar in that a complainant does incur hardship due to a decision on the part of an employer or prospective employer. However, the key difference between disparate impact and disparate treatment is the element of **intent** (discriminating on purpose). While disparate treatment required a demonstration of the intent to discriminate, disparate impact has no such requirement, making the case for a complainant easier to establish.

minority—A label attributed to individuals who fall within a protected class as defined by civil rights statutes.

protected class—Those who fall within the jurisdiction of legal protection.

disparate treatment—A theory of discrimination in which a protected class individual is intentionally treated in an adverse manner that results in harm.

pretext—A seemingly legal excuse to engage in discrimination.

contraband—The possession of materials that are in violation of a company policy.

prima facie—"First face" evidence, or the evidence at first glance. Those facts that are readily apparent.

disparate impact—A theory of discrimination in which members of a specific protected class are treated adversely, as demonstrated by a statistical imbalance that may occur unintentionally.

intent—A knowing and willful action of illegal discrimination.

In a complaint of disparate impact, the complainant demonstrates standing as a member of a protected class and identifies an action (such as an applicant who is denied a job) that was discriminatory. An example of this would be a fine dining establishment where a female applies for a server position and is denied the job. She files a claim with the EEOC stating that she is a protected class (based on gender) and that she was denied a server position because the restaurant hires male servers only. At this point, the burden of proof shifts to the restaurant (employer) to demonstrate that it hires enough females relative to the population of females within the local vicinity (*Wardscove* v. *Antonio*, 1990). For instance, if the population comprises 50 percent females and the restaurant has 10 servers, then in proportion to the population, the restaurant should have 5 female servers. However, in such a matter known as *Wardscove* v. *Antonio*, the court held that the employer needs to demonstrate that it employs 80 percent of the represented class in the population to be in compliance. This is referred to as the **four-fifths rule**. According to the four-fifths rule, the restaurant would be in compliance if it had 4 female servers and six male servers.

Claims of disparate impact always boil down to the statistical representation of protected classes within an organization. This is why human resource practitioners collect applicant flow data and maintain statistical counts of employees who represent protected class status, to ensure that 80 percent of each protected class within a geographical area of the organization (usually 100 miles, or county jurisdiction) exist within the group of employees. If a complaint of disparate impact is substantiated, the employer may be required to announce publicly the discriminatory practice and invite members of that protected class to receive reparation (Daniels Lamp, Marriott, Joe's Stone Crabs). Figure 4.1 displays such a publication.

Accommodations Theory

A third theory of discrimination is known as the **accommodations theory**. This requires the employer to accommodate an employee based on protected class status at a level that courts deem to be within reason, thus the term

four-fifths rule—A 20% margin of leeway resulting in a requirement of 80% of statistical representation within categories used to establish a legal defense against allegations of disparate impact.

accommodations theory—A theory of discrimination that requires employers to reasonably accommodate the practices of specified protected class members under certain circumstances.

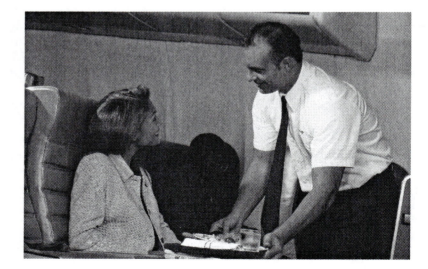

PUBLIC NOTICE

You can check out any time you like. . .

If you applied for a position with the company listed above between January 1999 and December 2002, you may have been discriminated against.

As part of a settlement with the Equal Employment Opportunity Commission, the company has reserved an account in the amount of $12 million for reparations to those who file claim.

Please contact the Law Firm of Dewey, Cheetem, and Howe at 555-1313 to file a claim of discrimination.

Figure 4.1. Notice of Discriminatory Practice.

reasonable accommodation. This pertains to the coverage of religion under the CRA. An employer must reasonably accommodate the religious practices of an individual, which includes scheduling preferences and payment of overtime to another party to cover a shift. As we will see later in the chapter, some of the more recent statutes such as the Americans with Disabilities Act and the Family Medical and Leave Act are based totally on the theory of reasonable accommodation.

Perpetuation Theory

The fourth and final theory is referred to as the **perpetuation theory** of discrimination. This theory is concerned with righting the wrongs of discriminatory practices that existed in the past and is the basis of **affirmative action** programs. Affirmative action gives underrepresented protected classes opportunities to advance in employment to level the playing field of representation in response to prior advancement restrictions that may have existed against such advancement. An example of this would be an organization that has a policy of promoting individuals based on seniority, where the senior individuals are absent a certain protected class due to prior discriminatory hiring practices. An affirmative action program would provide those members of the underrepresented class early advancement opportunities to right the wrong of prior discrimination.

LEGAL EXCEPTIONS AND DEFENSES FOR EMPLOYERS

While the courts assumed the responsibility of defining the actions that constitute discrimination, they also provided two defenses for employers to justify seemingly discriminatory practices. The first defense is known as a

reasonable accommodation—The burden of responsibility placed on an employer that determines the legal level of accommodation, usually measured in dollar amounts relative to the resources of a given organization.

perpetuation theory—A theory of discrimination that precludes employers from perpetuating past discriminatory practices that may have existed prior to the enactment of a statute.

affirmative action—A process for righting the wrongs of past discrimination through goals aimed at balanced representation of those protected classes that are underrepresented due to past discriminatory practices.

business necessity—
Job-related reason to
discriminate based on
the safe and efficient
operation of an orga-
nization.

business necessity reason to discriminate. A business necessity is defined as
that which is necessary to the safe and efficient operation of a business. The
courts adopt a narrow interpretation of this statement. The word efficient is
construed by the courts to mean normal in terms of the business operation.
Also, the employer must show no other acceptable alternative to discriminating based on business necessity as supported by objective data. Of course,
safety is a better argument than efficiency in such cases. For instance a pregnant x-ray technician could be precluded from working for safety reasons,
while requiring a male sales representative in South America because people
in that region prefer to do business with men would not be acceptable in eyes
of the courts. The x-ray situation is a matter of safety, while the sales representative scenario is simply a matter of client preference, which is not considered by the courts to be a reason to discriminate.

**bona fide occupa-
tional qualification
(BFOQ)—**A character-
istic providing a legiti-
mate reason for
excluding certain indi-
viduals in a protected
class from considera-
tion for a position.

    A second defense for an employer is called a **bona fide occupational
qualification (BFOQ)**. This is a scenario in which the employer must discriminate based on a characteristic associated with the nature of a job. For
instance an attendant in a men's locker room could require that the position
be filled by a male. It is important to note that race and color can never be an
acceptable BFOQ or business necessity, as there is no good reason for a job to
require a specific race or color.

SEXUAL DISCRIMINATION UNDER TITLE VII OF THE CRA

Matters of sexual discrimination have gained a large share of popularity in
the news media, as well as the attention of the courts. This is mostly due to
sex-plus discrimination issues that have arisen since the early intent of the
legislators. A sex-plus issue is a form of sexual discrimination in which females are treated differently than males based on marital status, medical condition (pregnancy, for instance) and other matters. Sexual harassment was
originally considered to be a sex-plus issue until recently, when it was determined that men and women are protected equally from such harassment.

**sex-plus discrimina-
tion—**Gender-related
factors resulting in
discriminatory prac-
tices in the workplace.

    In the view of the courts there are two types of sexual harassment. A di-
rect form of harassment is considered to be **quid pro quo sexual harassment**, in which a person seeks a sexual favor from another in exchange for a
favor or based on the threat of some negative action. For instance, a supervisor approaches a clerical worker and requests an intimate date, while men-
tioning an opportunity for a promotion and further notes that rejection of the
request could result in a poor schedule. This is an example of quid pro quo
(something of value exchanged for something else of value) harassment.

**quid pro quo sexual
harassment—**Direct
harassment by one
person (usually a su-
pervisor) which in-
cludes preferential
treatment or avoid-
ance of adverse treat-
ment in return for a
sexual favor.

**hostile
environment—**
Anything deemed by a
person to be offensive
in nature by any per-
son of a protected
class.

    The second form of sexual harassment is subtler than quid pro quo and
is referred to as **hostile environment** sexual harassment. In the interest of
providing broad protection to potential victims of sexual harassment, the
courts permit a very subjective definition of a hostile environment to be any
aspect of the environment that is deemed by an individual to be sexually offensive. It is clear that this form of subjectivity leads employers to take a very
conservative approach to prevent the appearance of a hostile environment.
For instance, a coworker may tell a joke containing sexual content to five
other workers. One of those workers may deem the joke to be offensive,
hence the existence of a hostile environment as far as that one person is

HOSPITALITY NEWS *Failure to Properly Address Employee Complaints Costly*

In times of economic uncertainty, the number of employee concerns and complaints often increases, especially where the employer has been forced to lay off employees or otherwise cut costs. While managers often feel inundated with employee complaints, it is important to recognize that left unanswered, these complaints may fester and result in a dispute that takes twice as much time and money to resolve as the complaint would have at its initial stage. While a manager cannot always give an employee the desired answer or result, a timely, considered response is critical.

Let's consider an example. This incident takes place in Oregon. An employee who wants to know why he is not being paid overtime for "extra" work confronts a supervisor. The supervisor responds that he assumes the employee is not receiving overtime pay because he is not eligible, but that he will look into it. The supervisor then checks with a relatively junior human resources employee, who reviews a list of employees in the particular department and notes that the employee is classified as exempt from overtime. The supervisor then reports back to the employee that he checked with human resources and that the employee is not being paid overtime because he is not eligible.

As far as the supervisor is concerned, this is the end of the story, and she does not think twice about whether the employee should be receiving overtime or whether the information provided by the human resources person is accurate. As you might imagine, however, this is not the end of the story. The employee thinks the company is trying to cheat him out of overtime. Frustrated, the employee calls the Oregon Bureau of Labor and Industries (BOLI) and explains that he works in a warehouse where he receives and checks freight under loose supervision. The BOLI representative tells the employee that she believes the employee is entitled to overtime pay based on his job duties. The employee then calls an attorney and explains that he thinks he is being cheated out of overtime pay, and that someone from BOLI told him he should be getting overtime. The attorney asks for additional facts and then states that she will take the employee's case and write a demand letter to the employer regarding the unpaid overtime.

Assuming the employee has been misclassified and is entitled to overtime pay, and assuming the employer does not pay the unpaid overtime within 48 hours of the attorney's demand, what was hypothetically a $1,500 problem has just become a problem that could cost the employer $5,000. The reason is that Oregon law provides that in any action for the collection of wages, the court shall award reasonable attorney fees in addition to the unpaid wages. The employer also will be required to pay a civil penalty equivalent to the employee's regular eight-hour daily rate up to a maximum of 30 days. The monetary cost of this issue does not take into account the time spent by the supervisor, the supervisor's manager, and the human resources department in responding to the attorney's demand. Nor does the price tag include any legal fees incurred by the company in consulting its employment counsel.

Although the supervisor in this scenario probably was not expected to question the accuracy of the information provided by human resources, the supervisor's manager (and the human resource manager) is responsible for ensuring that employees are correctly classified for wage and hour purposes. In addition, managers must ensure that their supervisors are educated and trained in the fundamentals of employment law so that the supervisors understand potential legal issues and how to deal with such issues.

Most aspects of the hospitality industry are highly regulated, including many aspects of the employer-employee relationship. The following is a brief summary of just a few areas of your business that are or may be regulated by local, state, and/or federal laws: wages and hours of work (Federal Fair Labor Standards Act); family and medical leaves of absence (state regulation as well as Federal Family and Medical Leave Act); disability discrimination (Federal Americans with Disabilities Act); immigration/employment of aliens (Federal Immigration Reform and Control Act of 1986); discrimination for reporting a safety or health violation; discrimination against "whistle-blowers"; discrimination on the basis of sexual orientation.

Source: Anne E. Denecke, *Hospitality News*, September 2001, p. 23.

concerned. Additionally the EEOC, under the direction of former commissioner Clarence Thomas (who was later accused of the blatant sexual harassment of a law clerk during his Supreme Court justice nomination hearings) and the courts, has taken a stern approach by articulating a number of requirements for employers the absence of which will automatically result in the assumption by the authorities that the organization actually condones sexual harassment in the workplace. It is important to note that claims of hostile environment sexual harassment have been filed against employers based on actions of co-workers that include calendars, posters, copy machine art, emails, jokes, innuendo, pranks, cartoons, comments, compliments, and gestures. Anything that may be seen, heard, felt, or read could be deemed by an individual to be offensive, resulting in a claim of hostile environment harassment. In order to protect the organization from a potential claim of hostile environment, the employer must comply with the workplace requirements listed in Table 4.4.

As stated earlier, the exclusion of any item listed in Table 4.4 will result in the assumption that the organization actually condones sexual harassment, including hostile environment harassment in the workplace.

Table 4.4 Workplace Requirements to Defend Against Sexual Harassment Claims

Activity	Description
Policy	The employer must have a thorough and concise policy articulating its posture against sexual harassment to include hostile environment harassment.
Sanctions	The employer must have an articulated policy noting disciplinary action based on evidence of sexual harassment to include hostile environment harassment that provides for progressive sanctions based on the severity of the action.
Postings	The employer must post notification of sexual harassment and remedies for perceived sexual harassment prominently on bulletin boards and other communication media throughout the workplace.
Education	The employer must document continuous training and educational meetings with all members of the staff on a periodic basis.
Due process and protection from retaliation	The employer must clearly communicate the process for filing a complaint about sexual harassment with third parties in non-supervisory functions that consist of both a male and female individuals to hear complaints based on the preference of the complaining party and must demonstrate an appropriate response to each allegation, while precluding retaliation against the complaining party.

FEDERAL LAWS

Age Discrimination in Employment Act

The Age Discrimination in Employment Act (ADEA) (1967, as amended) is enforced by the EEOC to protect discrimination against workers over the age of 40 years. It applies to both private and public sectors with 20 or more workers. It prohibits any discriminatory decisions based on age and requires equal benefits for protected workers. It mostly prohibits mandatory retirement, although a few positions are exceptions to this rule. A position in which there is a safety BFOQ would be an exception to compulsory retirement, while a flight attendant could not be forced to retire. Also, policy-making executives may be required to retire, while such a requirement could not be imposed on middle managers.

One unique aspect of the ADEA is that it authorizes jury trials in court cases. Also, the law provides for remedies to include **compensatory** (compensation) and **punitive** (punishment to the perpetrator) **damages** in cases of willful bad faith discrimination or reckless regard of the plaintiff. Remedies also provide for **liquidated damages**, which is twice the amount of regular damages (*Rawson* v. *Sears Roebuck*). Table 4.5 describes the features of the ADEA.

compensatory damages—Court awards to compensate those who have been wrongfully harmed in the opinions of a jury or a judge.

punitive damages—Additional awards designed to punish a defendant for willful harm to a plaintiff.

liquidated damages—Punitive awards that are double the amount of regular punitive damages.

Vocational Rehabilitation Act

The Vocational Rehabilitation Act (VRA) (1974, 1975) applies to federal contractors and recipients of federal financial assistance. It is enforced by the Office of Contract Compliance and Policy (OFCCP), a division of the Department of Labor (DOL). The law prohibits discrimination and requires an affirmative duty on the part of all contractors. Since the passage of the Americans with Disabilities Act, the VRA is a somewhat outdated piece of legislation.

Pregnancy Discrimination Act

The Pregnancy Discrimination Act (PDA) (1978) stipulates that pregnancy must be treated the same as any other medical condition in the workplace. This was originally intended to address leaves of absence, but has been extended to include work assignments during conditions of pregnancy. The courts conclude that the matter of appearance is not a factor for assigning work duties. A class action suit brought by servers against a crab house restaurant in Fort Lauderdale, Florida demonstrated the fact that appearance may not be used as a legal defense.[2] The law also provides for reassignment to a similar position upon the return from a leave of absence. A pregnant

Table 4.5 Features of the ADEA

Statute	Provisions	Coverage	Exceptions
Age Discrimination in Employment Act (ADEA)	Prohibits discrimination based on age	Public and private sector with 20 or more employees; protects individuals over age 40	Safety-related BFOQ and business necessity (BN), and policy-making executives

individual would also have standing under the Family and Medical Leave Act (FMLA) (1992).

Immigration Reform and Control Act

The Immigration Reform and Control Act (IRCA) (1986) is designed to mandate employers to document that prospective employees possess the right to work in the United States. It is enforced by the Department of Justice. The law contains a clause that prohibits the refusal to hire or the discharge of an individual based on citizenship or national origin. It only prohibits intentional discrimination on these bases, while requiring employers actually to discriminate against undocumented aliens in the workplace.

Americans with Disabilities Act

The Americans with Disabilities Act (ADA) (1990) requires the reasonable accommodation of individuals with disabilities in the workplace. It also has provisions for public buildings and transportation. The doctrine of reasonable accommodation has been redefined in the courts as a result of disputes related to the act. Organizations now spend thousands of dollars annually on reasonable accommodation activities. While some workers take advantage of the law through frivolous claims and requests, employers have mostly been the beneficiaries of the statute by providing opportunities for highly productive workers who contribute a great deal to their organizations.

Civil Rights Act of 1991

The Civil Rights Act (1991) is really a modified version of the CRA 1964 as amended. For a period of time during the 1980s, the U.S. Supreme Court rendered mostly conservative rulings on matters within the jurisdiction of the Civil Rights Act of 1964. In response, the then-liberal Congress rewrote the law and entitled it the CRA 1991, to overturn the decisions of the high court. All of the provisions of the CRA 1964 as amended are included in the 1991 version, plus a few additional aspects. For instance, the law increased the employers' burden of proof in disparate impact cases. It also increased the employer's burden of proof in disparate treatment cases relative to the discriminatory intent provision, in which the employer must prove a lack of a motivational factor based on protected class status to establish non-discrimination in such cases. Finally, the CRA 1991 added compensatory and punitive damages to be awarded to prevailing plaintiffs to a limit of $300,000, where no monetary damages were available under the 1964 act. In the scheme of balance of powers among governmental branches, the establishment of the Civil Rights Act of 1991 is a clear case of the legislative branch creating a new law in response to disagreement with the interpretive style of the judicial branch of government.

Family and Medical Leave Act

The Family and Medical Leave Act (FMLA) (1993) was established to guarantee that workers are granted leaves of absence from the workplace to care for themselves and family members, while ensuring they return to their positions upon the conclusion of the leave. This law is a step forward in one respect, as it includes males under the provisions for childcare leaves of absence. On the other hand, most medium to large organizations had leave of absence benefits in place that were more generous than the provisions of the law, and subsequently reduced those benefits to be in compliance with the law, which works to the employees' detriment. The law was administered and enforced by the Department of Labor (DOL) shortly after its passage.

The Congressional Accountability Act

The Congressional Accountability Act (CAA) (1995) was established to include members of federal and state congress under coverage of the antidiscrimination laws. Prior to its enactment, members of Congress were exempt from the provisions of the laws that they mandated for all other parties. There was one case in which a Florida state congressman engaged in flagrant acts of sexual harassment with young female aides in public during the early 1980s. While the news media created a widely publicized scandal regarding the numerous accounts of impropriety, the congressman was not held accountable under the law, as members of congress were exempt from coverage until the passage of the CAA.

STATE AND LOCAL LAWS

In addition to the many federal antidiscrimination laws, there exist state and local laws and ordinances that replicate the federal statutes. In most cases, the state and local laws expand the provisions of the federal laws. For instance, in the state of Florida, the law that replicates a number of federal statutes is known as the Florida Human Rights Act (FHRA) (1978). The wording of this law is inclusive, and notes the following:[3]

> . . . [It is] unlawful to discharge, fail or refuse to hire or otherwise discriminate against any individual with respect to: compensation, terms, conditions,

or privileges of employment due to race, color, religion, sex, national origin, age, handicap, or marital status.

Human resource practitioners must be intimately familiar with legislation and case law on a federal level, as well as those provisions that exist within the state and locality of the organization.

statutory law—A federal or state law that is written by the legislature.

tort or common law—A law that is not written by the legislature that results from the interpretation of a judge, and is applied to other similar court cases.

SUMMARY

This chapter presented a number of civil rights and anti-discrimination statutes that affect the employment relationship within organizations. It is clear that there exists a complex web of intricate legislation that requires compliance on the part of human resource practitioners. It is important to note that the body of law presented in this chapter contains only the major federal **statutory** provisions that exist within the legal environment of human resource management. There are numerous other statutes and matters of **tort or common law** that fall within the domain of human resource

---

In the Real World . . .

Since you began to assist the director of human resources with the response to the EEOC claim, you have learned quite a bit about an employer's burden of proof. It took about two weeks to prepare the Respondent's Report, which consisted of about 100 pages of facts, figures, applicant flow data, statistical representation of protected classes, copies of policies, documentation of training sessions, and confidential records of internal investigations.

You are sitting with the director reviewing the completed report. You say to her, "Is this the end of the matter?"

She replies, "Actually, it is just the beginning."

You look surprised as you ask, "Well, what happens next?"

She sits back; looks upward, as if recalling the last time this happened, and says, "They will take about one month to review our statement. They will call from time to time with questions, which are really ploys to corroborate what we wrote with how we answer the questions verbally. Then we will receive a notice of an on-site investigation. An EEOC investigator will arrive about one hour before the agreed-upon time and wander the halls reading our bulletin boards and talking randomly with the staff members. The person will finally enter my office and request information to, again, corroborate the information in our report. If that goes well, we will be requested to appear at an informal finding of fact hearing at the EEOC office. The complainant will be there and will contest our facts. At the conclusion of that hearing, there will be about another month of review and we will eventually be notified about the status of the claim. The complainant will be issued a Notice of Right to Sue . . ."

"What?" you interrupt her. "After all of that, the complainant receives a right-to-sue notice?"

The director smiles at you, "Yup" she says, "It's really no big deal, it is just a notification that the EEOC won't pursue a court trial on the complainant's behalf, but if the complainant wants to proceed to court, that is her legal right."

You sit there, just shaking your head as you listen to the director. Finally, you say to her, "I guess that is why we are so careful around here." She smiles and says, "I think you get it. This was a great experience for you, huh?"

practices, as will be discovered in remaining chapters of the text. Hence, one requirement for effective human resource management is a thorough knowledge of all statutes and tort law applications that may have anything to do with the terms, conditions, rights and privileges of employment. In order to stay current, HR practitioners must monitor case law decisions on a continuous basis, as the temperament of the courts must be contained within the wording and practice of human resource policies and strategies. It is not uncommon for HR practitioners to retain legal counsel with expertise in matters of employment law. However, it should be cautioned that legal professionals are not trained in the practice of management for the most part. Additionally, legal professionals are overly conservative regarding legal prevention issues. Hence, it is recommended that human resource professionals be thoroughly trained in the practice of management and temper the advice of legal counsel with sound managerial policies. As we will discover in future chapters of the text, the primary right of individuals in the workplace is to be professionally managed.

DISCUSSION QUESTIONS

1. Now that you know what you know, do you think that most individuals file worthwhile claims against their employers, or do they file claims to retaliate against the employer or to make life difficult for them?

2. How much money do you think an organization spends in legal compliance issues per year? Is it worth it to the organization? Why or why not?

3. If the legal aspect of human resource management is so complicated, why don't organizations hire attorneys to run the HR department?

4. Do you think most practicing operations managers know much about the legal environment surrounding organizational practices? Why or why not?

KEY TERMS

accommodations theory
affirmative action
bona fide occupational qualification (BFOQ)
burden of proof
business necessity

complainant
contraband
defendant
disparate impact
disparate treatment
Federal District Court (FDC)
four-fifths rule

hostile environment
intent
minority perpetuation theory
plaintiff
preponderance of the evidence

pretext
prima facie
protected class
reasonable accommodation
sex-plus discrimination

CHAPTER FIVE
Employee Relations and Labor Relations

OBJECTIVES

By the end of this chapter, the reader will be able to:

1. Understand the role of employee relations in the practice of human resource management.
2. Describe the sourcing, purpose and applications of employee handbooks.
3. Recognize the differences between employee relations and labor relations.
4. Understand the employment-at-will doctrine and the nature of labor unions in the workplace.

In the Real World . . .

You work in a human resource office for a large resort as a management trainee. Lately you have been assisting the employment relations manager by working as an employee relations representative. In this capacity, you spend most of your day listening to employee complaints about the way their supervisors treat them or interpreting policy issues that they didn't bother to look up in their employee handbooks. You find the work to be emotionally draining, since most of the time you are dealing with negative scenarios. However, it is rewarding from the aspect of being in a position to help solve disputes and answer employee questions.

At about 3:15 p.m., Bonnie storms into your office, apparently in a fit of rage. Bonnie works as a dispatcher in the Room Service department on the second shift that begins at 3:00 p.m. She takes over for the morning shift dispatcher, a guy named Bif.

Bonnie slams her hand on your desk and screams, "I've had it with this job! I'm walking out right now. This Bif is a total idiot and if you don't fire him, I quit! It's him or me: You decide!" she shouts.

You look at her calmly. "What seems to be the problem?"

"What's the problem, what's the problem? I'll tell you the problem. Bif is a creep, a nerd, an S.O.B., a slob, a derelict, a lazy bum, a stupid idiot, and an ugly, egotistical jerk, that's the problem!"

Sensing a potential employee personality conflict you ask Bonnie, "Have you discussed this with your manager?"

She laughs. "My manager? I haven't even seen my manager in three days . . . my manager—what a joke!"

"I see," you say empathetically. "I'll tell you what. Bif is gone for the day by now. Would you be willing to go back to the Room Service department and start work to give me an opportunity to look into to this for you?"

Bonnie replies, "I'll go back there now, but after tonight I'm outta here if you don't get rid of that bum." She leaves your office in a huff.

INTRODUCTION

At first glance, it would appear that **employee relations** and **labor relations** are the same thing. In fact, they are two very different concepts. Employee relations is a very broad practice that influences all terms, conditions, rights, privileges and interactions of employment. It is the essence of the employment relationship with the organization and its agents. Human resource practitioners spend most of their time engaging in employee relations activities.

Labor relations, on the other hand, consists of a very narrow practice that is applied to interactions among management, workers, and labor unions in an organization that has union representation of its employees. Labor relations specialists are usually attorneys who practice an area of administrative law that includes contract negotiation, mediation, arbitration, dispute resolution and union relations. So employee relations is a very broad practice, as opposed to the narrow approach that is the focus of labor relations.

employee relations—Every aspect of the relationship between workers and managers from the time of hire through the time of separation from the organization.

labor relations—The specialty involved with establishing and managing collective bargaining agreements.

EMPLOYEE RELATIONS

integrity—Actions
and statements made
by the organization
are consistent.

From the time a candidate accepts and offer of employment through the entirety of the employment lifecycle, there exists a relationship between that employee and the organization. The organization is represented by all of its agents, which include co-workers, supervisors, and managers. It is the prime directive of a human resource manager to guard the **integrity** of that relationship with every single worker in the organization. The integrity of that relationship means that the organization and its agents behave in good faith and fair dealing that is consistent with its employment standards with every individual in the workplace. In other words, the organization must be "its word" with the staff.

As is the case with every management practice, employee relations begin with mutual expectations on the part of both the employer and employees concerning the terms and conditions of the relationship. These expectations must be specifically planned by the managers and then thoroughly communicated to every employee. In a complex organization this is no easy task, as every manager and supervisor must know, talk, and most importantly, act in accordance within those expectations.

EMPLOYEE HANDBOOKS

employee
handbook—A document that provides information about the company, its history, mission, structure, benefits, objectives, strategies, policies, standards, procedures, and rules.

The primary document used to articulate the expectations for the employer and the employees in an organization is called the **employee handbook**. An employee handbook contains all of the information that a person needs to know about being a member of the organization. Handbooks are usually authored by the human resource practitioners, reviewed by legal counsel, and approved by the executive managers of the organization. The handbook is presented to an employee on the first day of work. A thorough orientation program walks the new hires through the document in a stepwise manner to familiarize new workers with the expectations that lie ahead of them as members of the organization. Orientation processes are discussed in detail in Chapter 9.

An employee handbook may seem overwhelming at first glance, since it contains a great deal of information. This is not to say the handbook is lengthy, as each item is covered in a single paragraph for the most part. However, the handbook should contain every possible scenario that may occur within the employment relationship. It is commonly known that these are complicated relationships; hence, the handbook appears to include a vast array of topics.

It is not the expectation that any individual should memorize the employee handbook, except perhaps the human resource practitioners who wrote it. Instead, the bulk of the handbook is intended as a reference manual for questions that may arise in the course of the employment relationship. As a matter of fact, the employee orientation facilitator introduces the handbook to the group by saying:

> This is our employee handbook. It has everything you will need to know about being a staff member with our company. Yes, it does look like a lot of

information. I will review just the highlights and point out those areas of information that are available as references when you need them.

Most human resource managers learn how to write inclusive employee handbooks after years of having experiences that were not covered in previous handbooks. When an issue arises outside the handbook, the organization must make a policy concerning how to handle it. Figure 5.1 provides an example of the contents included in a typical handbook.

The first section of an employee handbook includes items of topical interest about the organization, its parent corporation and a history of the company's origins. Later in the section a brief, concise mission statement is listed. A corporate mission statement should be a broad description of the organizational purpose and philosophy. It should be simple enough for employees to memorize, especially if that organization claims to be mission driven. An organizational chart describes the structure of the organization by providing a diagram of functions. The final portion of the first section describes the purpose of the handbook. In this description, employees are told about the value of the manual for future reference concerning most issues involving employee relations. Employees are also advised that it is their responsibility to review policies as needed and that ignorance of a policy is not an excuse for failure to meet with expectations. This may sound harsh, coming from a company representative on the first day of employment. However, it is much kinder than to say nothing up front and hold the employee responsible later on. It is important to remember that sound management practices are more about clarity than kindness, as they represent a business entity in which everyone is expected to pull their own weight.

The second section of the employee handbook should include a thorough review of the benefit packages available to members of the employment group. Many employee handbooks save this information for the last section, which is okay; but it is a nice touch to emphasize the good things about employment with this organization in the beginning of the book.

Table of Contents
Welcome to the Hotel California

The Hotel California Resort and Marina
About the Corporation
Our History
Our Mission Statement
Our Organizational Chart
Purpose of this Handbook

Employee Benefits
Benefit Highlights
Leave of Absence
Insurance
Bounty Bonus

Employment
Work Hours
Wage and Salary Administration
Introductory Period
Schedules
Performance and Salary Reviews
Payment of Salary and Wages
Gratuities and Tipped Employees
Workers' Compensation
Employee Responsibilities in Case of an Accident
Safety
Radios and Musical Equipment
Solicitation and Distribution of Literature
Grooming and Dress Code
Employee Uniforms
Guest Areas
Jury and Witness Duty
Suggestion Program
Employee Relations
Sexual Harassment
Employment at Will
Personnel Files
Keep Us Informed
Employee Assessment and Testing
Employment Screening
Security Background Checks
Employment Classifications
Right to Work in the United States
Job Postings and Transfers
Offenses, Infractions and Other Incidents

Resort Policies and Rules
Progressive Discipline
Conflict of Interest
Problem-Solving Procedure
Employee Clearance Process
Lockers
Resort Property
I.D. Cards
Name Badges
Employee Entrance and Exit
Package Pass
Payroll Discrepancies
Confidentiality
Employee Use of Resort Facilities
Parking
Smoking
Employment of Relatives
Telephones
Health Monitoring
Call-in Pay
Lost and Found
Absenteeism and Tardiness
Termination of Employment
Rules of Conduct

Figure 5.1. Sample Handbook Contents.

A third section includes information concerning the employment process. Newly hired employees have just completed most of the employment steps. The reason this is documented in the handbook is to document a **declaration of rights** on the part of the employer. In private sector employment, the employer must declare its rights involving the employment relationship. If an employer fails to do so, it is relinquishing certain activities that are required to safeguard the workplace and other employees. These rights include, but are not limited to, security functions such as search, seizure, contraband, for-cause testing and other investigative practices.

declaration of rights—A declaration of the rights of an employer relative to relationships with employees in the workplace.

As you can see from Figure 5.1, the bulk of the information in an employee handbook is about policies and rules for the workplace. In this section, the human resource manager attempts to list every possible scenario that may arise through the employment relationship; for this reason, there are a number of headings within this section. Each description is concise and brief, so as not to create a large written volume for employees to read. It should be noted that every policy, procedure, and rule is documented in precise detail in three other documents:

1. The policy manual is issued to each manager in the organization. It details each company policy and expectations for managing the implementation of each policy.
2. The standard operating procedures (SOP) manual is available to all employees and contains standards for performance and procedures to meet those standards.
3. The manager's manual is a document that lists how to handle each policy issue; it is distributed to all managers in the organization. Newly appointed managers should attend a training program on using the manager's manual shortly after being hired or promoted.

Figure 5.2 describes the documentation flow of manuals and handbooks for an organization.

Prior to the development of documents such as manuals and handbooks, human resource practitioners must engage in strategic planning activities along with other managers in the organization. **Strategic planning** results in organizational objectives, strategies, policies, standards, procedures and rules. Once this work is completed, the HR manager creates documents to communicate the expectations for performance and the parameters of employee relations to all members of the organization. Notice in Figure 5.2 that the strategic plan document flows from the organization's objectives and strategies. The **managers' manual** is a blend of strategies and policies, while the **policy manual** combines policies with standards. The **standard operating procedures (SOP)** manual combines standards and procedures to provide step-by-step directions for meeting standards for performance. The employee handbook is a condensed summary of all of these documents that flow from the strategic plan.

strategic planning—A process of developing plans based on factors in the external and internal environments associated with the organization.

manager's manual—A document of objectives, strategies and policies for managers to follow when acting as agents of the organization.

policy manual—A document that explains company policies.

standard operating procedures (SOP)—A document that lists standards for performance and action steps to be followed to meet with the standards.

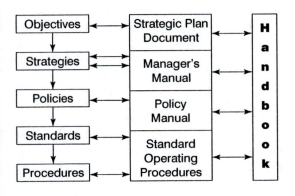

Figure 5.2. Human Resource Document Sources.

It is important to construct employee handbooks in a fashion that includes continuous notices that the document is for informational purposes. Also, the organization should reinforce its status in the employment relationship. For instance, if the organization is an at will organization, it will mention this status at various intervals throughout any documentation used for employee relations purposes. At will employment subscribes to the doctrine that the employer and employee engage in the employment relationship on their own free will, which precludes the existence of a contractual obligation on the part of both parties.

implied-in-fact con-tracts—Contracts that are not of an express nature, but have wording from which an individual may construe an intended agreement.

In some states, employee handbooks are construed to establish **implied-in-fact** contracts of employment from a legal perspective. An implied-in-fact contract is the establishment of a contractual relationship by communication that is not formatted as a contract per se. In such cases, legal counsel would advise to avoid the development and distribution of handbooks altogether. Unfortunately, while this is good conservative legal advice, it is terrible management advice. It is the duty of the managers in an organization to clearly communicate the expectations for performance; the failure to do so is a breach of management. At the same time, the organization should not place itself in a position where it is construed to possess contractual obligations that were not intended. The solution to this dilemma is to find an alternative information delivery method that is not construed by the court system in that state to establish a contractual relationship, if such a relationship is not intended by that organization.

EMPLOYMENT-AT-WILL DOCTRINE

employment-at-will (EAW)—A common law doctrine that prescribes the freedom of employers and employees to engage in employment relationships.

As we discussed in Chapter 3, the **employment-at-will (EAW)** doctrine is established through common law and is intended expressly to address the employer-employee relationship. In essence the doctrine states that an individual is free to work for any employer of his choosing and the employer is free to employ any individual of its choosing. Since the employer and employee make this choice freely, the employee may leave the employer at any time, by unilateral (individual) decision, for any reason, or no reason at all, with or without notice. Since individuals acting as agents (employees) for employers enjoy this right, the same rights are attributed to the employer. Hence the employer may end the employment relationship at any time, by unilateral decision, for any reason, or no reason at all, with or without notice. This is a description of the employment-at-will doctrine in its pure and original form.

At present, EAW is an eroding doctrine. It no longer exists in its original and pure form, as there are numerous exceptions to the doctrine. One exception is the existence of another common law doctrine known as a covenant of good faith and fair dealing that is, as we discussed in Chapter 4, applied to the employment relationship. This doctrine precludes the portion of the EAW provision allowing for discharge for "no reason at all." It is incumbent on an employer to provide an honest and legal reason for the discharge of an employee. Another portion that is overridden by the good faith and fair dealing covenant is the "no notice" aspect. Technically, the employer should provide one pay period in lieu of notice, which equates to one hour for an hourly employee. So, at this point we should reword the employer's rights under EAW to state that "the employer may end the employment relationship at any time, by unilateral decision, for an honest and legal reason, with sufficient notice." These restrictions do not apply to employees, who retain the rights of EAW under its original wording. As for employers, there are numerous other exceptions that inhibit employment-at-will status.

Public policy exceptions occur when the organization discharges employees for refusal to engage in activities which are contrary to the welfare of the public, such as price fixing or perjury activities. Also, an employee who notifies officials concerning activities by the organization that are contrary to public policy is engaged in the activity of **whistle-blowing** and is protected from discharge under EAW. Any employee separation arising for a purported state of federal statutory violation is also prohibited within the purview of employment-at-will.

An employer may only adopt employment-at-will in the absence of any other from of agreement that may be applied to the employment relationship. Hence the existence of a **contract** would preclude EAW standing. Contracts are agreements between at least two parties. Contracts may be established in writing (written contract) or verbally (oral contract). A contract may be **express**, which is the definitive establishment of an agreement, or **implied**, as established through a handbook or some common recurring activity. For instance, if employees are paid small bonuses for timely arrival for scheduled shifts, it may be construed over time that this activity constitutes an implied contract of remuneration for timely arrival. When this occurs, the contract is implied through continuous activities that may be construed to establish a **binding past practice**.

Express contracts are relatively straightforward, in which the only potential disputes that may arise would be with regard to terms and conditions of the agreement. This is not the case with implied contracts, in which the disputed issue that is inevitable would be the actual existence of contractual obligations. The courts have considered the establishment of implied contracts in cases concerning employee handbooks, employment offer letters, employment-related conversations, policy statements, and many other forms of employer/employee interactions. In contractual employment relationships, the employer must demonstrate **just cause** as a reason for termination of an employee who is under contract. This burden is in place to ensure the employer is not acting in a manner that might be considered to be a **breach of contract**, in which a party does not honor some aspect of the agreed-upon terms. It is apparent that the defense against breach of contract in a case involving an implied contract would be difficult, since the terms of such a contract are not expressly stated.

Organizations that choose employment-at-will status must work diligently to safeguard that designation. This is done by taking every precaution to guard against a charge of public policy, contractual, and statutory exceptions to EAW standing. Also, EAW employers wisely practice beyond the expectations of the covenant of good faith and fair dealing to substantiate that their employee relations practices are at a level above those required by restrictive employment requirements. In actuality, the prevention of EAW challenges simply requires the implementation of sound managerial practices. Figure 5.3 provides a list of these employment relations practices.

---

public policy—Those factors that are in the interest of the general public within a society.

whistle-blowing—Disclosing matters that violate public policy to third parties.

contract—A legally binding agreement between at least two parties.

express contract—A contract that expressly identifies the terms of an agreement.

implied contract—A contract that may be construed to exist through implications associated with the content of communication.

binding past practice—A practice that establishes a precedent to be applied to future practices of the same or similar circumstances.

just cause—A justifiable reason to take an action that is not a breach of any term or condition contained within a contract.

breach of contract—Failure by a party to adhere to terms and conditions of an agreement.

HOSPITALITY NEWS *"You're Fired"*

One of the least desirable responsibilities for any manager is to have to fire an employee. Here are a few tips that should be considered prior to notifying your employee:

Make sure you have a paper trail, showing that you have given fair warning to your employee.

Do it in a quiet area—not in your office.

It's best to do it early in the day and never on an employee's special day.

Have a script and be prepared. Have the facts and don't criticize.

Convey the message that your decision is not negotiable.

Give the employee the dignity of doing it in a professional manner: no big discussion, threats, or accusations.

Keep it simple. The less said, the better.

Give the employee all wages that she or he has coming.

Source: Hospitality News, April 2003, p. 8.

Strategic planning and thinking set the tone for the organization as a successful business entity. This drives every aspect of organizational performance including the practice of employee relations. As depicted in Figure 5.2, the strategic plan is the driver for plan documents, managers' manuals, policy manuals, and SOPs. These documents are distributed freely to members of the organization to establish expectations for performance. When incidents and infractions occur, the managers within the organization deal with them swiftly and appropriately, while carefully documenting their actions. Progressive disciplinary policies include warning processes to individuals that include declarations of further disciplinary actions, as discussed in Chapter 4. All disciplinary actions are reviewed and decided by multiple individuals at higher levels within the organization, including an executive representative in most cases. There must be due process that includes a mechanism for employees to appeal disciplinary decisions in the workplace. Finally, all of these activities evolve around solidly valid and reliable performance appraisal processes to ensure objective evaluations of employee performance.

Implement strategic planning throughout the organization.
Document and distribute expectations for performance.
Document and investigate all incidents and infractions.
Give warnings on performance and conduct infractions.
Use multiple reviewers and decision makers in matters of discipline.
Provide an employee appeals mechanism.
Develop performance appraisals that are valid and reliable.

Figure 5.3.   Steps for Employee Relations.

LABOR RELATIONS

In certain organizations, the workers choose to engage the representation of formal associations that promote the welfare of its members, called **labor unions**. A labor union represents collective groups of workers in an organization by negotiating employee relations activities such as work rules, job descriptions, hiring practices, compensation structures and other work-related matters through written contracts known as **collective bargaining agreements**. These agreements usually focus on bread-and-butter issues that include wages, working hours, job security, and other working conditions. One advantage of labor unions is that they force **management** to carefully consider the impact of its actions on large numbers of employees. While proactive managers would rise above this standard through long-term approaches to employee relations, this is not the case for many organizations. Hence, labor unions are necessary for worker representation within reactive organizations.

Union representation of workers has been in a steady state of decline for a number of years. Currently, less than 15 percent of U.S. workers are **organized**, which means they belong to unions that represent their interests. There are two reasons that may be attributed to the reduced number of union memberships. First, the legal environment concerning employment practices has developed significantly to provide protection for all U.S. workers, which was not the case when labor unions first became popular. Second, the financial circumstances that affect organizations makes it difficult for unions to negotiate higher levels of compensation and workplace inflexibility. For instance, instead of negotiating large wage increases for represented workers, unions are currently forced to agree to **givebacks** to organizations in order to keep the majority of the workers employed. For example, the airline industry is reporting chapter 11 and complete bankruptcy among the carriers on a monthly basis. This could result in massive worker layoffs, the threat of which drastically reduces the negotiating power of the respective labor unions. Instead of fighting for large wage increases (which was the practice in the 1970s), unions are making concessions to keep the airlines from declaring bankruptcy in an effort to

labor unions—Formal associations that are engaged to negotiate collective bargaining agreements on behalf of employees.

collective bargaining agreements—Union employment contracts.

management—Used to refer to supervisory agents of an organization in labor relations discussions.

organized—A collective group that is represented by a labor union.

givebacks—Concessions made by labor unions to return previously negotiated benefits or work rules.

maintain the jobs for their remaining constituents, who include pilots, flight attendants, ground personnel, mechanics and other positions. This reduction in bargaining power on the part of unions reduces the incentives for new groups of workers to organize and pay dues to labor representatives.

Historically, workers were considered to be expendable and working conditions were deplorable, as we discussed in Chapter 3. The individual worker was powerless against the large company to assert the right for decent treatment in the workplace. Around the late 1920s, workers started to recognize the power associated with building a united front against the management of organizations to force better working conditions. To this day, unions consider themselves to be "brotherhoods" based on the premise of united we stand, divided we fall. In the beginning, government officials were not sympathetic to the plight of workers. Federal and state troops were commonly sent to disperse groups of protesting workers who were united in the cause of better and safer working conditions. Finally, the government did begin to recognize the need for the workers to have a say in their organizations and began to support the right of individual workers to develop organized fronts to leverage employers to listen to their concerns and demands.

Originally, there were two federal union organizations. One was called the American Federation of Labor (AFL), and the other was referred to as the Congress of Industrial Organizations (CIO). These two organizations were bitterly opposed to each other's ideology for a number of years, but eventually overcame their differences to merge into a single entity that is known today as the AFL-CIO. The AFL-CIO is not a specific labor union; instead it is an umbrella organization that supports labor unions through political lobbying and education programs. Individual unions such as the Air Line Pilots Association (ALPA), the Teamsters, the Hotel and Restaurant Workers, and others are usually members of the AFL-CIO. The unions, such as ALPA, are nationally registered and maintain local chapter offices in major cities throughout the United States. An elected president operates each chapter and hires **business agents** who act as liaisons with a number of locally represented business entities. The business entity or shop, in union parlance, contains those workers who are represented by the union. Certain workers within the shop are designated as **shop stewards** to act as liaisons with the business agents, who work for the local chapter. The shop steward may be a server or bartender in a hotel who also interacts with the business agent on a frequent basis to discuss **grievances** or other matters that may be inconsistent with the terms and conditions of the collective bargaining agreement, which is the **union contract** for workers in that specific shop.

The legal status of a shop varies among different states, based on the legal definition in that state of a worker's rights. As a general rule of thumb, industrial-based states are more favorable toward union worker status than agriculturally based states. One exception to this rule of thumb is the state of Hawaii, which is heavily influenced by union presence, despite its status as an agricultural and tourism-oriented state. The reason for this is the terrible exploitation of the Hawaiian people and immigrant groups on the plantations during historical times. It is important to remember that Hawaii did not become a state until 1958. Worker exploitation was just one small aspect of the many human and social atrocities committed by the early colonizers, who came from Europe and the United States. Native Hawaiians were historically

business agents— Full-time employees of labor unions who act as liaisons with organizations and shop stewards.

shop stewards— Employees of an organization that also act as liaison with business agents.

grievances— Perceived unfair treatment in the workplace that may include union contract violations.

union contract— Collective bargaining agreements between labor and management within an organization.

treated in a manner consistent with the early treatment of Native Americans in the continental United States. To this day, Hawaiians have yet to receive appropriate reparation for the travesties imposed upon them during the historical colonization of the Hawaiian Islands.

Labor unions are mostly favored among those states that possessed large factories that provide assembly line production of products. New Jersey, for instance, is an industrialized state that recognizes the existence of **closed shops**. A closed shop is a workplace in which workers must be union members to be considered for employment. This can turn into a catch-22 scenario in some cases. For instance, in the early 1980s as casino hotels were being built in Atlantic City, an individual could not work as a bartender unless she was a member of the local Hotel and Restaurant Workers Union. At the same time, a bartender could not be listed with the union unless she had a bartending job. So you couldn't get a job without being in the union and you couldn't have bartender status with the union without having a job. Some states permit **union shops** in which non-union members may be hired into a shop, but must join the representing union upon being hired. In the state of Florida, all shops are referred to as **open shops**, which permits the hiring of union and non-union personnel, with no requirement of any employee in a union classification to join that union. In the event that a worker chooses not to join the union, he does not have to pay union dues and still enjoys the protection of the union in matters of workplace grievances.

The reason Florida restricts union-represented businesses to open shop status is that the state believes that workers should have a right to participate in gainful employment regardless of union membership. This philosophy makes Florida a **right-to-work state**. In addition to permitting non-union employees to work in unionized job classifications, workers who engage in work stoppages such as **labor strikes** may be permanently replaced in unionized organizations. Florida, an agriculture- and tourism-based state, is not considered to be a union-friendly state, as opposed to Hawaii and New Jersey.

While the states possess the power to restrict union shop status, the overall right to organize for the purpose of union representation is within the jurisdiction of federal law. The primary federal law governing the right of workers to organize is called the **National Labor Relations Act (NLRA)**, which is also referred to as the **Wagner Act**. In the early 1930s, when the government finally shifted in its thinking to support union activities, it established the NLRA. This law articulated the right of workers to organize within the workplace under the representation of a third-party labor union. It also defined unfair labor practices and established an administrative agency called the **National Labor Relations Board (NLRB)** to enforce and administer the law. The enactment of this law dramatically increased the levels of union membership between 1935 and 1947, which provides evidence of the need for workers to seek collective protection from the workplace practices of their employers during that time.

ORGANIZING ACTIVITIES

Let's say that the employees in a given organization begin to feel it would be in their best interest to be represented by a specific labor union. The employees would seek the assistance of union organizers, who would hold campaign

closed shops— Organizations that require union membership prior to hiring.

union shops— Organizations that require union membership upon being hired.

open shops— Organizations with unions that do not require union membership as a term or condition of employment.

right-to-work state— A state that protects the rights of non-union workers to pursue gainful employment.

labor strikes—Work stoppage action in which union workers refuse to report for work shifts.

National Labor Relations Act (NLRA)— Federal law that protects workers rights to organize with unions.

Wagner Act—Another name used to apply to the National Labor Relations Act.

National Labor Relations Board (NLRB)—An administrative agency established by the NLRA to enforce and administer the provisions of that act.

meetings outside the workplace. At the conclusion of the organizing campaign, the workers would cast votes to petition the NLRB to hold a union election at the workplace. If the majority of the employees vote in favor of a petition, the NLRB will contact the employer and administer an election for union representation at the workplace. In the event that the majority of workers vote in favor of such representation, the labor union will be designated as the representative or **bargaining agent** of the employees in a given classification. At this point, the managers of the organization incur the responsibility to **bargain in good faith** with the union as part of a process to establish a collective bargaining agreement, which becomes the contract that stipulates the work rules for all represented workers.

The union will begin the bargaining process by submitting a list of demands about working procedures, compensation, scheduling, job security, and other work-related activities. The list of initial demands will become the content of negotiations between labor and management over a period of time. Since the organization must bargain in good faith, it must demonstrate continuous activities aimed at ultimately reaching an agreement with the labor union. It is possible during the negotiating activities that the two sides (labor and management) may reach an **impasse**, which means that all attempts at reaching an agreement have been exhausted. In this event, a third party will be brought in to perform conciliation or mediation activities aimed at getting the parties through the impasse to an agreement. At some point

bargaining agent— The role of a labor union in the negotiation of a collective bargaining agreement.

bargain in good faith—Demonstration of continuous efforts to come to an agreement to establish a union contract.

impasse—A breakdown in the progress of bargaining in good faith.

there will be a **settlement**, in which the parties will have reached an agreement. The terms of the agreement are then presented to the workers (new union members) for **ratification** (final approval) of the contract. Once the contract is ratified, it becomes a binding collective bargaining agreement that stipulates the work policies and rules for all individuals represented within that union classification.

A portion of the union contract will stipulate the steps to be taken by an employee who perceives unfair treatment in the workplace under the guidelines stated in the agreement. This perceived unfair treatment is referred to as a grievance. The employee will follow the grievance procedure outlined in the contract, which is a process for filing a formal complaint of treatment that is a violation of the terms of the contract. The grievance will be processed by the human resource practitioners (usually labor relations specialists), and may involve interaction with the shop steward and the union business agent. Ultimately a determination will be made as to the merit of the grievance, which would find it to be **legitimate** (a true contract violation) or **frivolous** (without merit). In the case of a legitimate determination of a grievance, the managers of the organization would provide reparation to the employee to make up for the violation of a term within the agreement.

settlement—An agreement that is reached somewhere between initial demands and concessions in the collective bargaining process.
ratification—Final approval of the majority of represented union members to an agreement.

legitimate—A grievance that possesses merit.
frivolous—A non-meritorious grievance.

SUMMARY

In this chapter we differentiated the practices of employee relations and labor relations. Employee relations involve the objectives, strategies, policies, standards, procedures and rules for maintaining a good relationship between the managers and employees within the organization. Human resource practitioners spend most of their time involved with employee relations activities. Proactive organizations seem to possess superior employee relations relative to reactive corporations. In the final analysis, employee relations is all about sound management practices, which include the development and distribution of clearly stated expectations for performance in the organization. The primary document used to articulate these concepts is referred to as the employee handbook. The employee handbook is a reference guide for all of the workers in the organization regarding company history, structure, mission, benefits, policies, standards, procedures and rules. The employee handbook flows from the strategic plan for the organization as documented in the managers' manual, policy manual and SOP manual. The employee handbook is a concise summary of the information presented in these documents that attempts to address any conceivable issue that may arise within the employment relationship.

The broadest doctrine involving employee relations is the employment-at-will doctrine, which is still recognized in a small number of states. The EAW is a common law doctrine that in its purest form articulated the freedom of employers and employees to engage in relationships. Today, employment-at-will is an eroding doctrine due to the enactment of state and federal statutes as well as other tort matters, which provide for exceptions to EAW status. These exceptions include public policy, contractual, statutory, and good faith and fair dealing precepts. Employers doing business in states that recognize EAW go above and beyond typical employee relations to safeguard their status.

In the Real World ... (Continued)

As soon as Bonnie leaves, you walk into the employment relations manager's office to describe the interaction you just had. The wise ER manager says to you, "So what do you think we are dealing with here?"

"Sounds like a personality conflict to me."

"Maybe," replies the manager. "How about the absence of the room service manager during a shift change; what do you think about that?"

"It seems like an important time for the manager to be around since one shift is closing and another is starting, while the phone keeps ringing. Maybe the manager was called into a meeting or something."

"Maybe," says the ER manager, "But your report says that Bonnie hasn't seen the manager in three days, which tells me he hasn't been available for three consecutive shift changes. What to you think about that?"

"I hate when you make me think."

He chuckles, "I know, but that's my job in training you."

"Well, I guess we need to find out why the room service manager hasn't been around for these shift changes."

"Sounds like a good start."

The ER manager picks up the phone and dials the room service manager. "Hi Bob, could you stop by here right away? I think there is a situation you should know about."

The room service manager arrives about five minutes later. "What's up?" he asks.

The ER manager explains the situation. After citing all the facts, he finishes with, "What disturbs me, Bob, is that when we asked if this complaint went to you, we were told you haven't been around during the shift changes, which is contrary to the policy in our managers' manual."

Bob replies, "Yeah, the F&B director has had me putting together a project for the past couple of weeks and I got so caught up in it that I forgot to check with the dispatchers during the shift change. I know exactly what the problem is. The cause is really not a personality conflict between Bif and Bonnie, it's the overlap situation. Normally I make sure Bif keeps the area neat for Bonnie's arrival. Then I usually have him close out in the service area so he isn't in the booth while she sets up. To give her a hand, I usually handle the phones for her for about 15 minutes. Whenever Bif thinks I'm not watching, he leaves Bonnie a sloppy area and makes snide comments to her during the overlap because he knows she has a short fuse." Bob finishes by saying to both of you, "I'll take care of this and let you know when it's fixed so you can check back with Bonnie to make sure everything is all right with her."

"Thanks, Bob," the ER manager says. After Bob departs the office the ER manager smiles at you and says, "Another day; another experience. Let me know when you get a tough one," he jokes with you.

Labor relations is one aspect of employee relations that includes a collective bargaining agreement as established by a labor union acting in the capacity of the bargaining agent on behalf of a group of employee classifications. The relationship established by labor relations is contractual in nature. Hence, all activities within the scope of labor relations come down to contract interpretation that is usually handled by human resource practitioners called labor relations specialists. The existence of labor unions is testimony to the historical practice of inappropriate employee relations that still exists in some organizations to this day. Unions provide checks and balances that remind managers of the impact of their decisions on large groups of employees. While the government did not initially support the right of workers to organize, it eventually realized that this activity is worthy of legal protection. While the federal government provides organizing activity protection via the NLRA, states determine the levels of impact that labor unions have on specific organizations.

DISCUSSION QUESTIONS

1. What are the major differences between labor relations and employee relations? If you were a human resource practitioner in a union organization, would you just practice one of these and not the other? Why?

2. Is it possible to have labor relations in an EAW organization? Why or why not?

3. Some states consider employee handbooks to be contracts. How would you respond to this situation, if this were the case in your state?

4. If you were a human resource practitioner, would you accept management advice from the attorneys you deal with? Why or why not?

KEY TERMS

bargain in good
   faith
bargaining agent
binding past
   practice
breach of contract
business agents
closed shops
collective
   bargaining
   agreements
contract
declaration of
   rights
employee
   handbook

employee relations
employment-at-
   will (EAW)
express contract
frivolous
givebacks
grievances
impasse
implied contract
implied-in-fact
   contracts
integrity
just cause
labor relations

labor strikes
labor unions
legitimate
   management
manager's manual
National Labor
   Relations Act
   (NLRA)
National Labor
   Relations Board
   (NLRB)
open shops
organized
policy manual

public policy
ratification
right-to-work state
settlement
shop stewards
standard
   operating
   procedures
   (SOP)
strategic planning
union contract
union shops
Wagner Act
whistle-blowing

CHAPTER SIX

Management Ethics

OBJECTIVES

By the completion of this chapter, the reader will be able to:

1. Understand the relationships among legal, ethical and moral laws.
2. Comprehend the professional responsibilities of managers.
3. Be able to demonstrate the benefits of ethical management for managers, as well as organizations.
4. Apply ethical tests to management actions.

In the Real World . . .

You are working as a clerical assistant in the human resource office for a large internationally recognized theme park complex. One month ago, there was a terrorist attack in New York City. Since that time the theme park has been under high alert as a potential terrorist target zone. The tourism industry in your town relies heavily on visitors that arrive by air. Since the attack, flight arrival passenger numbers have declined significantly in your city. As a result of this, visitor volume at the theme parks has dropped by at least 50 percent. Immediately following the attack, the corporate office issued a freeze on all position requisitions. Since then, all part-time workers have been laid off and full-time workers have had their hours reduced. The big fear among the workers is that a massive layoff of full-time workers might occur.

The human resource director called a department meeting first thing this morning. All of the human resource managers and workers were present. There is a somber mood, as everyone has an idea of what this meeting will be about.

The director addresses the group. "Well, guys, as you know, business isn't getting any better. We have tried every trick in the book to retain our full-timers, but we are getting heat from corporate to start downsizing. I was in the president's office all day yesterday and the bottom line is that we are being told to reduce the full-time hourly and supervisory staff payroll by 5 percent. I hate the idea of putting our people out on the street, especially now, when jobs are so scarce in this town. I called you together to see if there is some sort of creative solution we can come up with to avoid a massive layoff."

Everyone in the room is thinking about the ramifications of a layoff, including concerns about their own jobs.

INTRODUCTION

When inexperienced human resource managers preach the management ethics premises they learned in some workshop to operations supervisors, everyone just sort of smiles at the naïve perspective that goes hand in hand with inexperience. But when an experienced leader gets in front of those same managers to confess that she has actually done right and wrong things in her career, and then describes how the wrong things have hurt her and the right things have helped her, everyone listens intently. It is like a movie where with his last breath, the dying warlord implores his followers to avoid the lifetime mistakes he has made. The young generals grieve as their wounded leader passes, lifting their swords with vows to do the "right thing from now on." Okay, maybe this is a little melodramatic, but you get the point.

CAN ETHICS BE TAUGHT TO MANAGERS?

The laws of supply and demand sometimes influence the development and delivery of informational programs. Certainly, social issues are indicators of the temperament of the societal macrocosm that directly influences commercial enterprises, which represent social microcosms. This is the case with hospitality enterprises, which mirror society. There is an increasing demand for training in the field of management ethics for supervisors and managers, especially in training and education segments of the hospitality and tourism industry. The data suggest that industry leaders and educators believe there is a need to include some form of ethical training in programs of higher learning for managers.[1] Interestingly, this was a sentiment in the middle 1980s that has resurfaced due to the publication of scandalous business practices, suggesting the cyclical nature of unethical behavior in commerce.[2] As was the case earlier, schools and human resource departments are adding managerial ethics components to educational courses and development programs. The question that comes to mind is whether ethics can be taught to managers.

There have always been examples of questionable ethics in most industries, and the hospitality industry seems to be no exception; for example, overbooking is a common practice among hotels and airlines. False or misleading advertising occurs in the tour and travel operation business. The media often report accidents and illnesses resulting from worker negligence. Faulty patio railings, construction flaws, fires, thefts and swimming pool accidents occur at hotels. Bacterial infections, burns, slips and falls, as well as truth in menu issues are sometimes associated with food service industry practices. Physical assaults, poor sanitation, improper waste disposal, foodborne viruses and other epidemics become news items attached to the cruise industry. Incidents of poor mechanical maintenance, sabotage, and worker impairment are reported in the air travel industry. Other issues include unethical shareholder practices and incidents of employment law violations within segments of the hospitality industry. It is likely that many of the individuals engaged in these types of activities have had, at one time or another, some form of ethical training, but for some reason made the decision to act contrary to those precepts.

ETHICS TRAINING PROGRAMS

It is not the intent of ethics training programs to provide managers and students with values training; that is the job of parents and role models during the formative years of childhood. It is doubtful that ethics training programs will influence personal beliefs and attitudes to any great extent. These are mostly established through individual experience by making comparisons of experience with existing personal value systems.

So, what is the purpose of ethics training programs? To create awareness of the ethical issues that surround managerial decision-making. Decisions made by managers result in activities being performed by members of organizations. Polices and practices evolve from managerial decision-making activities. The resulting actions affect other individuals, specifically, members of the stakeholder groups. As managers progress in their careers and their scope of authority expands, their decisions affect increasingly larger numbers of people. It is assumed that managers wish to do the "right thing." When they focus on the big picture—potential good and harm resulting from their decisions—managers seem to use this awareness to guide them toward doing the right thing for all people in all stakeholder groups. But when they get caught up in the moments of stress and egoism, they make decisions that they sometimes later regret.

Another purpose of ethics training is to provide a paradigm for proactive management practices. Proactive management focuses on long-term thinking, as opposed to short-term problem-solving activities. As we will discover in

Chapter 7 and again in Chapter 10, this is the essence of professional management. The proactive organization focuses on those issues that are crucial to long-term success for all participants, as well as issues that are critical to daily operations. Proactive managers are mission driven and strategic in their planning processes. Ethics training programs emphasize strategic planning models that include social and moral audits, as well as ethical codes for behavior.

A final purpose of ethics training programs is to convince managers of the need to promote management as a profession. As managers become aware of the far-reaching implications of their actions, they realize the immense power associated with management positions. This power creates the need for professional responsibility. It is the duty of managers to possess specialized skills in their respective disciplines, as well as supervisory skills for interaction with others. Therefore, managers should complete rigorous advanced technical and supervisory training programs. Managers should also subscribe to codes of ethics established by their colleagues, to high levels of personal and professional conduct, and should contribute to society through the practice of management. Entry to the field of professional management could be restricted to those individuals who possess the ability and character to work in a professional capacity. Experienced human resource practitioners include these criteria in their management selection activities.

WHAT'S IN IT FOR THE MANAGER?

Proactive managers realize that meeting the interests of all the stakeholder groups is vital to the long-term success of the organization, as well as their own managerial careers. There is currently a level of distrust regarding the practices of business owners and managers among the members of American society, as we discussed in Chapter 3. That distrust might be warranted, given the activities of early industrialists and corporations throughout the last century. The reason this attitude is significant is that the people of this society empower legislators to regulate business enterprises. To paraphrase the words of Patrick Henry, when we fail to govern our freedom wisely, we lose our liberties. Hence, businesses have lost the liberty to do business that was once enjoyed in this free enterprise economic system.

HOSPITALITY NEWS *Are You a Fair Manager?*

Have you created a work environment where one employee can take away another employee's account? Have you created a work environment where rules and policies apply to all your employees? Do you give special treatment to one employee over another? If one of your employees is related to you, do you make excuses for their inappropriate behavior—where it wouldn't be tolerated by others in your organization? If you answered yes to any of these questions, then you may be at risk to lose valued employees. Think about it!

Source: Hospitality News, March 2003, p. 8.

Since managers are employees of the organization, they are member of at least one stakeholder group within that company. They may also be customers or shareholders, in which case they represent more than one stakeholder group. As such, they have a personal "buy-in" to the welfare of the organization, in addition to their own career aspirations. Unethical activities may negatively affect these managers on both personal and professional levels.

Most managers are motivated to some degree by status and prosperity. What goes around, comes around. By enhancing the practice of manager to a professional level, managers enhance their own status and prosperity.

The trade media frequently identify segments of the hospitality industry that produce lackluster financial performance. Further investigations of these segments often reveal incidents of mismanagement, shareholder greed, employee dissension, and community mistrust. Proactive organizations seem to have the ability to do well even during difficult times for their particular segment. These organizations also seem to display fewer cases of the negative symptoms associated with this discussion. Hence we may conclude that proactive organizations are economically healthy entities that are capable of weathering difficult financial events. If this is true, proactive management must make good business sense.

In the broadest sense, managers are members of society. They are also moral beings. Some believe that otherwise morally sound and contributing members of society become amoral individuals when acting in business management capacities. These amoral beings emerge from the workplace each day to resume their roles as responsible citizens. Managers who subscribe to amoral professional practices are really cheating themselves. Since managers are motivated by challenging and meaningful work, it is natural for them to practice in a manner that contributes to the social standing of their respective organizations. This is one reason why when proactive managers are running organizations, those firms seem to reach higher levels of success than their competitors. At the highest level, the manager is a human entity. There are five aspects to the human composite: the physical, the spiritual, the mental, the emotional, and the social realms. Self-actualized individuals seek balance among these aspects of the composite.[3] The proactive manager is a balanced individual who is passionate about the challenges and meaning of her work. These are the qualities that make her a respected leader.

AWARENESS AND PARADIGM SHIFTS

One aspect of management ethics training is to generate awareness of ethical issues and responsibilities associated with managerial decision-making activities. Once this awareness is created, managers sometimes choose to enact shifts in their own management paradigm. A **paradigm** is a model of a principle. For instance, consider a paradigm of public welfare that advocates providing assistance to those members of society who are in need by providing food and shelter. Now consider a second paradigm of job service, in which persons in need are provided with training to become self-supporting. This second paradigm makes no sense in the absence of the first. The first one provides a foundation (food and shelter) that permits the implementation of the

paradigm—
A model that drives the thinking processes.

second paradigm (self-sufficiency training). An awareness of the first paradigm is required before the second one may be realized. This is a **paradigm shift**. The first paradigm may be illustrated by the proverb: Give a person a fish and feed him for a day. The second paradigm might be stated this way: Teach him how to fish and feed him for a lifetime. Awareness of the first proverb gives credence to the consideration of a shift into the second one. In management application the "awareness" consists of who we are today and the "shift" consists of who we want to be tomorrow.

paradigm shift—
A change in the thinking model.

Why should there be paradigm shifts? The simple answer would be that we work and live in an evolutionary world. It is apparent that managers are faced with new problems that require creative solutions. For instance, the mentality that prevailed among managers and venture capitalists during the 1990s, and certainly during the 1980s, is no longer acceptable business practice in this society. At the same time, the policies and practices that existed during those times continue to be used in organizations today. In some cases, the thinking in the hospitality industry has not changed in 50 years. The current environment is dynamic. Proactive organizations are rethinking, restructuring, and revitalizing operations in efforts to respond to changes that exist in the environment.[4] These activities require major paradigm shifts to establish new principles to guide the changes in organizations. To paraphrase Albert Einstein, significant problems in current day cannot be solved with the same level of thinking that existed when the problems were created. This helps to explain the reason for adopting new paradigms for proactive hospitality and tourism management.

On a universal level there must be a shift from traditional to modern management thinking in hospitality organizations. In order to do this, managers must shift from crisis management to mission-driven management. Next, managers should shift from checklist management to strategic thinking. This will require managers to shift from "talk" mode to "listen" mode in their communication styles. Another shift for managers is from win/lose to win/win outcomes.[5] Managers must also shift from individual productivity to team-oriented productivity to attain outcomes that are greater than the sum of the parts. Finally, managers must shift from stress inducement to stress management mode to maintain employee energy levels. Are proactive managers ethical managers? Figure 6.1 provides a moral evaluation of proactive managers to help you answer this question.

Proactive managers . . .
1. Take charge of personal and professional destiny—they are not victims.
2. Are mission driven to align their personal goals with organizational goals.
3. Seek long-term outcomes, not short-term profits or other forms of gratification.
4. Are empathetic listeners who care about the needs of others, especially their staff.
5. Seek win/win/win for others, themselves and the organization.
6. Are synergistic by being team stewards.
7. Are spiritually, mentally, physically, emotionally, and socially balanced—hence they are holistic beings in search of self-actualization.

Figure 6.1.   Qualities of a Proactive Manager.

MORAL AND SOCIAL AUDITS

moral audit—
Internal audit of management decisions within an organization.

codes of ethics—
Guidelines for conduct created by a group of professional peers.

ethics committee—
A cross-section of individuals from various organizational levels who administer codes of ethics.

social audit—
An external audit of organizational practices affecting customers and the community.

The **moral audit** focuses on activities within the organization by evaluating the actions of workers, managers, and shareholders and comparing those actions with **codes of ethics** for the corporation. In proactive organizations, codes of ethics are designed by a cross section of managers from every level of the corporation. Once the code is established, it is communicated to the management team through training sessions. Every manager in the organization signs an agreement to abide by the code in all decision-making activities. An **ethics committee** is established to audit the code of ethics for relevancy on an annual basis and to act as a non-supervisory third party to hear ethical complaints from any organizational constituent about the questionable actions of managers who are perceived as violating the code.

The **social audit** focuses attention outside the organization. This audit provides information concerning the outcomes of decisions on the environment outside the organization. This would focus on the customer and community stakeholder groups. Both the moral and social audits are part of the annual strategic planning process for the organization.

PROFESSIONAL RESPONSIBILITIES OF HOSPITALITY MANAGERS

There are five primary responsibilities for professional management that should be adhered to by all hospitality management practitioners. The first responsibility is to carefully select the hospitality organization. Managers' reputations are essential in achieving industry credibility. Managers who choose to represent organizations that lack integrity damage their own professional credibility. Before accepting employment with a firm, the manager should conduct a thorough diagnosis of that organization's integrity level to ensure the corporation operates in a proactive and ethical manner. When managers are selective about the firms they choose to represent, a ripple effect occurs in which the best and brightest managers are affiliated with the high integrity organizations, which puts pressure on other corporations to enhance levels of integrity to attract and retain management talent. Those firms that continue to operate beyond the standards of integrity will ultimately cease to exist due to a lack of effective leadership resulting from an inability to hire competent managers.

A second responsibility for industry managers is to acquire and maintain levels of training and education to ensure competency. Managers must be technically proficient in their respective disciplines and, regardless of that discipline, they must be effective practitioners of management. This requires thorough knowledge and skills in the functions of management, which includes the effective supervision of people. The entire concept of management is based on the premise of accomplishing the objectives of the organization through the activities of others. Hence, managers should be proficient in the entire range of supervision skills. Additionally, managers must be adept in the functions of planning, organizing, staffing, evaluation, use of resources, fiscal responsibility, interpersonal relations, communication, counseling/discipline, productivity enhancement, training, development, leadership and teambuilding. These techniques require specialized skills and training. Managers who attempt to work without these skills are acting in an irresponsible manner.

A third responsibility for managers concerns a thorough technical comprehension of hospitality/tourism interfaces. Every segment of this industry is connected in some way. In most cases, other industry segments represent membership in the customer and/or community stakeholder groups. Managers must view this industry from a broad perspective in order to act proactively. Thus, comprehension of the workings of the industry as a whole is a requisite to meeting managerial responsibilities.

The fourth management responsibility requires the skills to establish and maintain standards designed to ensure the welfare of all stakeholder groups associated with a hospitality organization. Reactive managers often find themselves acting in the interests of one group to the detriment to members of other groups. A manager who compromises standards to attain short-term profits for shareholders at the expense of customers and employees might be an example of this. The manager is responsible and accountable to all the stakeholder groups. This is why the first responsibility of managers is to choose organizations that permit this type of professional management. In order to meet this responsibility, a manager must possess skills in creative and innovative decision-making that provide win/win/win outcomes. This type of manager is a real professional who is committed and trained to practice holistic stewardship in service to all the stakeholders.

The fifth responsibility for hospitality managers concerns personal and professional conduct. All citizens in a society are expected to adhere to the legal laws for that society. The manager, as representative for an organization and a profession, must comply with higher levels of conduct than the average citizen or worker. As far as the legal laws are concerned, the manager must be knowledgeable about the provisions, coverage, and exceptions associated with all laws pertaining to the regulation of business entities. But the manager must exceed the standards established by the law by subscribing to self-regulating standards, such as codes of ethics. Additionally, since the reputation of the manager is crucial to maintaining credibility within the community, the manager has a responsibility to adopt personal codes of behavior that are above the law. This responsibility is created from a duty to exemplify integrity as an industry leader and a member of the social community.

If hospitality and tourism managers expect to be treated as professionals, they must meet the standards associated with any profession. The five responsibilities discussed in this section are consistent with those expectations for all professions in every discipline. Figure 6.2 provides a summary of

---

Hospitality and Tourism Management Responsibilities Self-Questionnaire

Will this organization permit me to manage in a proactive manner?

Do I have the inventory of skills and advanced training required to manage effectively?

Do I have current knowledge of my industry segment and its interfaces with other segments?

Do I subscribe to standards that ensure the welfare of all stakeholder groups?

Do I subscribe to standards of professional and personal conduct that are above the law?

Figure 6.2. Management Responsibilities Questionnaire.

questions that every manager should ask of themselves before engaging in the practice of management.

CULTURAL DIVERSITY

culture—
Shared values, attitudes, and beliefs.

What is **culture**? The experts provide numerous definitions of this term. One simple definition is the shared values, beliefs, and attitudes among a group of people. Usually we think of cultures as pertaining to ethnic groups or regions of national origin. It is true that regional and ethnic cultures possessing shared values, attitudes and beliefs do exist. The values for one culture may be incongruent with those for another culture. When individuals disagree with or misunderstand the values of other cultures, conflict occurs. Some regions or ethnic backgrounds possess singular or **homogeneous** cultural norms. This occurs in areas that are isolated from external cultural influences.

homogeneous—
A group that is represented by a single ethnicity.

heterogeneous—
A group consisting of multiple ethnicities.

American culture consists of influences from many races, ethnic backgrounds, communities and global regions. Thus, American culture may be defined as having multiple influences, which makes this culture **heterogeneous** in nature. The hospitality industry is also heterogeneous, and for this reason individuals in our industry must learn to disregard cultural differences and embrace cultural similarities. This is the essence of cultural diversity training programs.

While social cultures are applicable to entire societies, there are also cultural systems that are established by small groups of individuals who are brought together by some common purpose. For instance, there are cultures for business organizations, social organizations, industry segments, and certain types of institutions. These cultural systems are similar to societal cul-

tures; however, they operate on much smaller levels. The culture for a company or corporation is referred to as the **organizational culture**, which is the collection of shared values, attitudes and beliefs for members of that organization. People join organizations and bring with them various backgrounds and cultural ideals. They assimilate into the organization as employees and begin to understand the unwritten core philosophies and rules for behavior in that organization, referred to as **norms** or acceptable behaviors. These norms include traditions, rites, rituals, ceremonies, and celebrations within the organization. Behaviors including dress codes, formality levels, inside humor, buzzwords, company acronyms, and others are symptoms of the organizational culture.

Some people confuse the term organizational culture with another label, **organizational climate**. The organizational climate is the mood, perceptions, opinions, morale levels, loyalty levels, enthusiasm and other attributes relative to the relationship of workers to the organization. The climate within an organization is a collective worker emotional response to the practices of that organization.

organizational culture— Shared values, attitudes, and beliefs among members of an organization.

norms— Standardized acceptable behavior.

organizational climate— The collective emotional temperament among members of an organization.

CULTURAL RELATIVISM

When individuals' behaviors are influenced by norms (expectations) of a specific culture, they are behaving in accordance the unwritten rules of **cultural relevance**. Remember that a culture has specific values, attitudes and beliefs. Therefore actions considered appropriate in one culture may not be condoned by the value system of another culture. This is true for societal as well as organizational cultures. The standard cliché, when in Rome do as the Romans, is a practical example of cultural relativism.

This is why some managers may be very successful with one organization and are considered mediocre after accepting a position with a new firm. In some cases, the rating has nothing to do with the manager's performance, but instead a conflict with the norms for managers within the new organization. For instance, consider a middle-level manager who is a department director with an independent luxury resort property. The culture at this property rewards risk-taking management decisions, innovation, creativity, and the occasional violation of the rules for constructive purposes. This culture will attract self-confident and entrepreneurial managers, who are commonly referred to as "maverick" managers. If one of these individuals accepts a position with a corporation that contains a culture of strict standard operating procedures (SOP), adherence to the rules, risk avoidance, and decision-avoiding behaviors, it is likely that her style of management will be considered to be a violation of the behavioral norms for that organization. In this case, the manager's decisive leadership was the basis of her success with the former property; that same characteristic may result in her failure with a new organization. Managers who do not understand the phenomenon of organizational culture are understandably confused when the same behaviors result in polar responses between two types of organizations.

The opposite of cultural relativism is a concept referred to as **universality**. While relativism is relative to individual environments, universality is the same in every level and every area. Legal laws are jurisdictional; hence they are relative. Codes of ethics, on the other hand, seek to be univer-

cultural relevance— Adapting to the norms of behavior in a culture.

universality— Unity in beliefs and behaviors beyond what is relative to a specific environment.

sal, since the same codes of correct behavior should prevail regardless of the immediate environment. This being the case, a manager who swears to adhere to a code of ethics (as is required in most certification programs) is affirming compliance with that code wherever the manager practices the profession. Morals are those personal convictions of correct thinking and behavior within an individual that are at the highest level of ethical thinking. Similar to ethical codes of conduct, morality is universal, meaning that it is the same despite the environment. Figure 6.3 depicts the relationships among the legal law, codes of ethics, and morality.

The figure describes the forces from the moral law that affect ethical codes for professional groups and the legal law for society. The body of civil rights law, for instance, is an attempt to legislate morality on the part of decision makers in the workplace. Historically, those decision makers chose to discriminate, which is an immoral and unethical action. Hence, the law imposed penalties to force decision makers into compliance with ethical and moral behavior.

At first, the former discriminators grudgingly complied with the legal code. As newer generations enter into workforce decision-making positions, the legal code seems perfunctory, as the thought of discrimination is morally and ethically in conflict with their personal convictions. If a young manager were to go to work for an organization and later discovered discriminatory practices at that workplace, that manager would be likely to seek work with another corporation, since the actions of the first organization violate the manager's moral and ethical value system.

self-egoism—
Acting in the interest of the self without regard for the harm caused to others.

ethical relativism—
Convenient or situational ethics used to justify unethical behaviors.

MOTIVATION TO COMMIT IMMORAL AND UNETHICAL ACTS

From a philosophical approach, two ethical concepts may provide insight as to what makes individual commit immoral or unethical acts. One concept is referred to as **self-egoism**, which most people consider to be personal greed. Another concept is called **ethical relativism**, which most people refer to as situational ethics or ethics of convenience. The person who practices this is often heard to say, "Everyone does it."

The actions of the self-egoist are motivated primarily by personal gain with little regard to the ramifications experienced by others. For instance, a person who steals will steal from anyone, with no regard for the losses in-

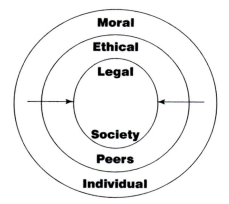

Figure 6.3. Legal, Ethical, and Moral Laws.

curred by the victims of the thefts. Shareholders who exert pressure on organizational managers to deliver short-term profits when doing so will cause long-term detriment to the value of the firm are acting out of self-egoism, aimed at an immediate return on investments. Managers who take advantage of other workers for personal gain and politicians who generate political favoritism for campaign donations are all acting out of self-egoism. Some self-egoists are referred to as narcissists—those individuals who care only for their own welfare despite the harm their actions cause to others.

Ethical relativism involves actions that are contrary to universality. For instance, an individual may raise funds for the impoverished and pay the employees in his company substandard living wages. Managers who impose employee layoffs justify their actions as meeting the needs of the shareholders. Other relativistic examples include employees cheating the time clock for extra pay and overbooking by travel and lodging firms. In each and every case, the perpetrators of these activities will justify their actions in some manner.

ETHICAL TESTS

There are two philosophical approaches to testing the correctness of an action from an ethical perspective. The first test is based on the **consequences** or results of an action. The most common type of consequential testing is referred to as **utilitarianism**. Utilitarianism focuses on the utility of the consequences of an action by measuring the harm or good inflicted on others as a result of the action. The purpose of utilitarianism is to maximize good and minimize harm through one's actions. For instance, a company is faced with having to lay off 5 full-time workers or cut the hours of 10 full-time workers. The harm of laying off 5 people would be total loss of income to the workers and their dependents. The other alternative would create only 50 percent as much harm. Therefore, the second option would be more appropriate from a utilitarian perspective.

Another viewpoint for ethical tests is considered to be the **formalist** approach. The formalists are not concerned with consequences resulting from actions. Instead they focus solely on the "form" or intent of the action. This thinking considers actions to be morally correct or incorrect in and of themselves, with no regard for the consequences of the action. One formalist process was established by philosopher Emanuel Kant and is called the categorical imperative.[6] This test has three categories (categorical); an action must pass all three categories to be considered morally correct. If it is considered to be morally correct then the actor has a duty to do the action (imperative). Table 6.1 provides a description of the three categorical imperative tests.

consequences— The results of an action.

utilitarianism— A consequential approach to testing the ethics and morality of an action.

formalist— A form-oriented approach to testing the ethics and morality of an action that focuses on the form of the action with no consideration of the results of that action.

Table 6.1 Categorical Imperative Tests

Test 1—Universality	The action must be universal, which means if everyone were to do this action, the action would continue infinitely and would not self-destruct.
Test 2—Beings as ends	The action must respect all rational beings as ends unto themselves. Therefore, the action may not treat beings as mere means to an end.
Test 3—Autonomy	The action must be acceptable to all rational beings, regardless of their involvement with the action.

Let's consider a few examples to clarify the categorical imperative tests. Test 1: Would the action continue, or self-destruct? Let's take telling a lie to someone. The reason people tell lies is that other people trust what they are saying. If everyone lied, then no one would believe what anyone says and the behavior of telling lies would cease to exist. But what if I lie to avoid hurting someone's feelings? you may ask. That is a good utilitarian argument, but the formalists don't care about consequences, just the form of the action.

Test 2, beings as ends—does the action use someone for an ulterior motive? Let's say two people are involved in a romantic relationship. The man wants to break it off. The woman dates his best friend to make him jealous. Is she treating the guy's best friend as a means to himself, or as a means to the end of making the boyfriend jealous?

Test 3, rational beings—if someone witnesses the action or hears about the action regardless of their personal involvement, would they condone the action? Consider lying behavior: Would anyone say it is the right thing to do, even if the consequences are in that person's interest, which doesn't count here anyway? Probably not. Would anyone condone using the best friend to make the boyfriend jealous? No.

Applications of the Tests

To understand the application of the categorical imperative, as well as the utilitarian tests, consider as an example the common practice of overbooking. Lodging and travel organizations frequently and intentionally overbook guestrooms and flights. If an individual is "walked" to another hotel or "bumped" from a flight, they are reimbursed to some extent for the inconvenience.

From a utilitarian standpoint, we need to identify the good and harm resulting from the action of overbooking practices. Overbooking certainly benefits the company, since it causes increased occupancy or passenger loads. It harms only a small number of people who are inconvenienced, and those people are compensated for the inconvenience, which mitigates the harm. Since the organizations only overbook by a small percentage, the majority of the guests or passengers have their reservations honored, so the vast majority of

those who choose to do business with the company receive what they paid for. In the longer run, higher occupancy and passenger loads enhance volume, which may be responsible for lower pricing that is passed on to the guests and passengers. So, you could say even the customers benefit from the practice of overbooking. Hence, it seems that intentional overbooking passes the utilitarian test.

From a categorical imperative perspective, remember that if the practice of overbooking fails even one of the three tests, it is considered to be immoral.

1. *Question:* If every travel and lodging company were to overbook reservations, would the practice continue infinitely, or would it self-destruct?

   Answer: Practically every company does overbook when the opportunity to do so exists. Overbooking has been going on for a long time and continues to be in practice; hence, it has not self-destructed. Overbooking passes this test.

2. *Question:* Does the practice of overbooking treat people as ends unto themselves who are worthy of respect and dignity? Or does it treat people as mere means to the travel and lodging companies' end of full occupancy and passenger load?

   Answer: The assumption of overbooking is that people will make reservations in "bad faith," that is, they will reserve a spot and not show up, thus leaving vacancies. Therefore, travel and lodging companies are treating people as though they are not trustworthy and are treating them as means to attain full occupancy and passenger loads, as opposed to treating people as ends unto themselves, who are deserving of a reservation that will be honored. Overbooking fails this test.

3. *Question:* Would an autonomous person who is a rational being, thinking rationally, condone this action regardless of participation in the action?

   Answer: A third party who witnesses individuals receiving compensation and incentives for their inconvenience upon being walked or bumped would probably condone the action, as the people seem to be satisfied with the compensation. Overbooking passes this test.

Overbooking as practiced by travel and lodging companies clearly passes the utilitarian test, as it generates minimal harm and mostly good for those doing business with the organizations. Also, the practice of overbooking passes two of the three categorical imperative tests; the practice does not pass the categorical imperative as being a correct action in its form. So overbooking passes on a consequential level, but fails on a formalist level.

This proves a point. It is possible for an action to pass one test and fail another. Also, it is possible for an action to be morally correct, yet ethically and legally incorrect. The opposite is also true. Therefore, there may be conflicts among various levels of tests concerning actions. In other words, there are no hard and fast rules for conclusively determining the correctness of actions. This is why the "masses" (uninformed majority) in a society prefer the closure associated with the law. An action is either right or wrong, with no in-between and certainly no thinking, which keeps all of the members of a society in line. However, if all matters were left to the domain of the law, what might eventually happen to our freedom? Thinking people rise above the law in the course of protecting their liberty, which was the original intent of the U.S. Constitution.

THE MYTH OF AMORAL BUSINESS

Myth of amoral business—
A philosophy that limits the responsibilities of a business entity to the payment of taxes and obedience of the law. This doctrine contends that when society views a business practice as harmful to society, the legislature should enact laws to regulate the practices of the business entity.

Economist Milton Friedman is credited with the publication of a definitive differentiation between the conduct of business and the duty to be socially responsible.[7] Friedman's contention was that the business of business is to do business. According to this doctrine, the only obligation of a business entity is to create products and services, as well as to pay taxes to the government. Friedman went on to declare that there is no duty of business to do good for society and that there is absent the duty to not harm society. These things, the doctrine notes, are the duties of the government, which is appointed by society. The natural conclusion to this thinking is that if society deems the practices of a business to be harmful, it should create laws to govern those practices. The business, he reasoned, does pay taxes to fund the government; hence, the government is in possession of resources to regulate the practices of businesses.

It is important to note that it was not Friedman's intention to advocate reckless business practices. However, the business practitioners of his day took license in this doctrine to do just that. As we saw in Chapter 3, the result is the current state of business regulations aimed at the conduct of companies and corporations.

THE LEGAL STATUS OF CORPORATIONS

Legal creation view—
An interpretation of legal law that views a corporation as an entity created by the state, which is created by society. As such, there is a legal duty for the corporation to act in accordance with the welfare of society, with a breach of that duty establishing grounds for the abolishment of a corporation.

Legal recognition view—
An interpretation of legal law that views corporations as free entities that merely register with the state, not an entity that is created by the state. Hence, there is no duty for a corporation to contribute to the welfare of society.

A definition of the American corporation was established in the landmark U.S. Supreme Court case of *Dartmouth College v. Woodward*.[8] In an opinion, then-Chief Justice Thurgood Marshall wrote, ". . . the corporation is an artificial being, invisible, intangible, existing only in contemplation of Law."

There are two legal views of corporations. One is called the **legal creation** view, the other the **legal recognition** view. The legal creation view states that the corporation is created by the state (government). The state and law are created by society. Therefore, when the corporation ceases to benefit society, society may destroy the corporation.

The legal recognition view notes that the corporation is a free entity. The state (government) merely registers the corporation. The corporation is not a state creation. Therefore the end of a corporation is not to serve the needs of society.

The two views represent extremes in philosophies concerning corporations. The legal recognition view is a conservative approach to defining the corporation. It is in line with the free enterprise system. As a result, individuals who embrace the doctrine of capitalism would subscribe to this viewpoint. Republican Party members would have a tendency to view businesses and corporations from this frame of reference. On the other hand, the legal creation view is a liberal interpretation of the status of corporations. Socialistic or highly liberal Democratic Party members might subscribe to this theory of corporations. The legal creation philosophy contains the type of thinking that contributes to the current trend of business regulation, which some individuals refer to as the **corporatization** of society, indicating that government places the burden of curing social problems on the business entity through regulation.

Corporatization—
The practice of establishing business regulations that place the burden of curing social problems upon corporate enterprises.

ETHICS AND HUMAN RESOURCE MANAGEMENT

It is becoming apparent that the human resource practitioner must be an eclectic manager. The HR manager is occasionally placed in the role of internal adjudicator within the company. Also, there is the duty for the HR practitioner to function as a manager's manager, hence the duty to be well informed in all areas of business practices. The human resource manager (and all good managers) should be well versed in matters of legal, ethical and moral law for the purpose of testing the actions of managers to ensure the prevention of harm on any member of the stakeholder groups. This is the means by which the manager protects the assets of the organization and enhances career potential.

SUMMARY

This chapter has considered the moral and ethical duties and responsibilities associated with management in organizations. This is a particularly timely topic, as the cycle of ethical business practices is dipping to another low point. Ethical business practices are good business, as they enhance the long-term financial viability of an organization. The overriding theme of this chapter is the consideration of management as a professional practice. Authority generates responsibility, and managers must possess advanced levels of training to manage people and organizations effectively. Mismanagement occurs when incompetent managers make decisions that harm individuals and corporations. Hence, individuals who subscribe to managerial careers must be fully competent to be proficient in their positions as managers. Human resource managers are responsible for training managers in ethical thinking, which includes proactive management, strategic thinking, ethical testing, codes of ethics, and social and moral audits.

DISCUSSION QUESTIONS

1. Affirmative action is a practice that provides special consideration to individuals to be placed in positions that may have been denied by previous discrimination. To this day, the implementation of affirmative action programs is a controversial topic. Do you think affirmative action should continue, or is it time to suspend these activities? Those who are advocates would argue from a utilitarian perspective, while those who argue against affirmative action would argue from a categorical imperative perspective. How would you use these to construct your argument?

In the Real World . . . (Continued)

After a long silence, the director chimes in with, "C'mon guys, I know this is not the best of times, but we have a chance to use our talents to do as little harm as possible to our cast members."

You figure there is nothing to lose, so you speak up, "I have a friend who works in General Services in the Cruise Division, who tells me that they are recovering quickly from the tragedy and that bookings are going through the roof. I guess the guests who would normally visit our parks are opting for cruises, since they seem to be safe vacation getaway options. The hiring freeze has been lifted over there, so maybe we could shift some parks personnel to shore-side and onboard cruise positions."

"Hmmm," the director murmurs, "I didn't even think of the cruise division. I'll bet they are doing more business than before the tragedy."

The employment manager jumps in. "We can notify everyone of the problem we are facing here in the parks and announce opportunities for temporary placement with cruise operations. I know that they schedule their onboard staff using three-month employment contracts. Usually, they fill the contracts from outside sources. We could offer these contracts to cast members who are flexible enough to work onboard positions. As far as shore-side jobs are concerned, they will just have to work in a different location on a temporary basis."

The compensation manager adds, "Since the cruise division revenues will be higher than budget, they will be able to afford a few extra benefits. We could outsource some of our janitorial and housekeeping staff to one of our vendors to provide housecleaning and lawn maintenance for those cast members who elect onboard temporary positions, and offer that service as a benefit. We can pay for it from one of the benefit accounts, which will be a small amount of the payroll savings due to the outsourcing of our own staff."

The training manager suggests, "We can shift our training resources to cruise operations and get everyone prepared with the necessary skills through "crash-course" training programs. Since our cast members already know our service basics, all we have to do is brush up on the technical job aspects. We can have them ready to do new jobs in a flash."

At this point, everyone is buzzing with great ideas. The director is enthusiastic. "This is a fabulous alternative to layoffs. I'm going to call the cruise division HR director right now."

2. Do you think ethics training for managers is a good idea? Why or why not?

3. Considering the news items about the accounting practices of certain organizations, do you think that most companies are acting unethically? Why or why not?

4. Does the practice of management qualify as a legitimate profession? Why or why not?

KEY TERMS

codes of ethics	formalist	myth of amoral	paradigm
consequences	heterogeneous	business	paradigm shift
corporatization	homogeneous	norms	self-egoism
cultural relevance	legal creation view	organizational	social audit
culture	legal recognition	climate	universality
ethical relativism	view	organizational	utilitarianism
ethics committee	moral audit	culture	

CHAPTER SEVEN

Protecting Employee Rights

OBJECTIVES

By the end of this chapter, the reader will be able to:

1. Understand the rights of employees to be professionally managed.
2. Comprehend the planning and expectations aspects of professional management.
3. Recognize matters of common law as applied to the employment relationship.
4. Understand the role of the human resource practitioner as a managers' manager.

In the Real World . . .

You have been working in the human resource office for a large resort for about six months now, performing clerical support functions. During this time you have witnessed the good, the bad, and the ugly with regard to the skills of various managers through their interactions with the office and, in particular, the human resource director. Since you came from working in operations, you already knew which managers had good and bad reputations with the staff. This has been reinforced through your observations of personnel replacement requisitions, disciplinary actions, and employee complaints. It seems that the managers you heard were bad, turn out to be really bad at managing their staff members.

One of the newly hired department directors is a recently retired Captain in the U.S. Coast Guard. He is in charge of marina operations at the resort. Prior to his appointment, an easy-going, nice guy ran the department for 20 years. In the view of the captain, the department was lax and required discipline. His self-appointed mission was to shake up the department by putting pressure on the managers and supervisors. After a few months on the job, the captain drafted a scathing performance review document for his inherited assistant director. In the comments section of the performance review, he noted that the assistant's demeanor toward the guests and hourly staff was "brusque and truculent." He went on to write the comment that the only salvation for the retention of this individual would be to send her to "charm school," to alter her behavior to reflect "civilized conduct," as opposed to her demonstrated actions which resembled the activity of an "untethered satellite." Additionally, the captain gave the assistant a "does not meet performance expectations" rating. Until that time, the assistant had been rated as "excellent" in each of her ten years of employment in the position. The woman became agitated during the performance appraisal interview with the captain. At one point she jumped up to leave the room and brushed hard against the captain's side, knocking against him, left the office, jumped into her car, and sped away.

That day, the captain stopped by the human resource director's office to notify her of the incident. The director advised the captain to contact the assistant by phone at home to inquire whether she planned to return to work on the next scheduled shift.

INTRODUCTION

The primary right of any worker in an organization is to be managed professionally. In the last chapter we discussed the complex legal environment that exists today as a result of historical incidents of prejudice that were applied to employment practices. Had those individuals with authority been trained to be professional managers, they would not have made decisions based on personal convictions. Management is not yet a legally regulated profession. One would not need to look too hard to identify individuals in management positions who do not have the training to manage people, as well as corporate assets and liabilities. Untrained managers have a tendency to practice "subjective management," which causes legal and morale problems in organizations. While a few organizations require managers to be certified by one of many professional management certification boards, this is not the case in most companies. Hence, as mentioned earlier in the text, it becomes the job of the human resource manager to be the managers' manager in the organization. This means that the human resource manager must train the operations and staff managers to become professional managers. In order to do this, the human resource manager must possess management training and experience.

This is one reason why seasoned operations managers become excellent human resource managers.

The focus of this chapter is twofold. First, there is discussion concerning professional management practice. Second, we consider the body of common law or torts as applied to managerial practice in organizations. While the last chapter considered federal and state statutes aimed at the protection of individuals in the workplace, common law provides generic protection of the rights of individuals in any social interaction to include the employment relationship.

PROFESSIONAL MANAGEMENT

Professional managers know that their job is to articulate clearly objective standards for performance up front and to reinforce those standards every day. This section demonstrates how those standards are developed. A simple definition for the practice of management is the accomplishment of the objectives of the organization through the activities of others.[1] **Management** is practiced in organizations and institutions. Hence, an **organization** is a collection of individuals who meet to accomplish a common objective. An **objective** is a target for performance as stated in an intended result of activities. The broadest objective for an organization is referred to as the **mission**, which is the purpose and philosophy of that organization. In essence, it is the reason that the organization is in existence. In some organizations, all decisions are prioritized based on the mission. These organizations are known as mission-driven organizations, in which the mission drives all of the important decision-making processes; items that are not related to that mission are considered to be minor issues. The mission values are communicated throughout the organization via the mission statement, which is a brief written description of the purpose for that organization. It is the responsibility of senior managers to establish and communicate the mission for the corporation. The managers audit the mission on an annual basis to verify its accuracy, given factors from the external environment, which exists outside the organization.

After the mission audit, the senior managers develop the objectives for the organization. Some organizations practice a method called **management by objectives (MBO)**, which is a process of top-down and bottom-up goal setting throughout the organization. In management, the term goal and objective are the same thing. The way MBO works is the senior managers develop objectives and they share these with the next level of management below them. That level uses those objectives as a basis to establish their own goals. They review and revise these with the senior managers and agree on a final version of objectives. Next, this level of management works with the next level and repeats the process. Eventually, every level of the organization has participated in setting objectives that feed into the level of objectives above them. Hence, all objectives are mission driven from the top of the organization, and every person in the organization has participated in the development of their own goals. While MBO is a time-consuming process, the final result is total participation in the development of each person's goals within the organization. Hence, there is total buy-in on the part of all the staff members who made their own goals, as opposed to having objectives imposed

management—The accomplishment of organizational objectives through the actitivies of others.

organization—A group of individuals brought together to accomplish a common objective.

objective—A target for performance.

mission—The purpose of an organization that includes its values and beliefs.

management by objectives (MBO)— Top/down, bottom/up shared goal setting at every level of the organization.

upon them from the level of management above. MBO, of course, is just one option in the goal-setting process. But regardless of the process, every organization must have clearly defined goals for performance throughout the organization.

Once the objectives are established, managers must break these down into factors that represent the expectations for performance in every department within the organization. Figure 7.1 depicts the relationship of objectives to performance expectations.

Since objectives are targets for performance, there must be action steps that are taken to reach each objective. These action steps are referred to as strategies. A single objective will usually have two to five action steps that articulate the steps to be taken to achieve the goal. Table 7.1 shows an example of an objective along with a listing of strategies.

Once the objectives and strategies are established for the organization, it is time to create **policies**, which are broad guidelines for performance. Some organizations call the collection of policies the policies manual, or listing of company policies for that corporation. An example of a policy statement is given in Figure 7.2.

Once the policies for the organization are established, it is time to convert those into **standards** and **procedures**. Standards take a portion of a policy that is applied to actual performance; procedures are the listing of steps required to satisfy the standard. For each standard, there must be listing of procedures for individuals to follow in order to meet the standard. Figure 7.3 provides an example of a standard and correlating procedures.

A comprehensive listing of standards and procedures should be available during employee training and as a reference tool for use in each department. In some organizations, the collection of standards and procedures is called the standard operating procedures (SOP) manual. Notice from the example in Figure 7.3 that the standard is a baseline for performance derived from the policy. The procedures, on the other hand, are listings of specific action steps to be taken to meet the standard for performance.

This completes the model described in Figure 7.1, in which the objectives lead to policies, which convert into standards and are broken down into procedures for performance. Organizations that do not possess objectively defined and clearly communicated standards and procedures infringe upon the rights of employees to know what the expectations are for performance in the organization.

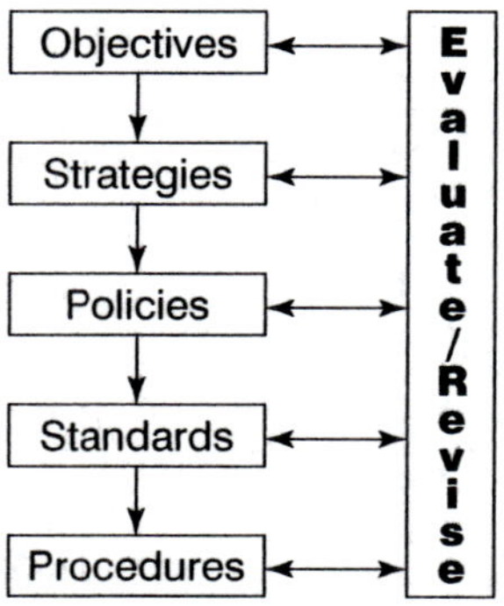

policies—Broad guidelines for performance.

standards— Acceptable levels of performance in an organization.

procedures—Action steps required to achieve standards.

Figure 7.1. Objectives and Strategies.

Table 7.1   Sample Objective and Strategies

Objective 1	Increase revenues by 10% over last year's total to be achieved by December 30, 2004
Strategy 1	Increase advertising and promotion budget by 5% over 2003 allocation to become effective January 2, 2004
Strategy 2	Add one new sales representative to cover missing territory by January 15, 2004
Strategy 3	Develop salesperson incentive program for rollout by January 30, 2004

HUMAN RESOURCE CONTRIBUTIONS TO ESTABLISHING EXPECTATIONS

Since the difference between human resource management and personnel administration is the strategic focus of human capital, the HR manager is an important participant in the entire strategic planning process that includes goals, strategies, policies, standards, and procedures. Once these are in place, the human resource manager focuses on **job** design activities for the organization. Job design is the practice of arranging tasks, duties, and responsibilities into **positions**. Technically, a job consists of the tasks, duties, and responsibilities contained within a position. A position consists of the job performed by an individual. This is why people refer to their positions as their "jobs" when speaking in slang terminology.

The primary function in the job design process is called **job analysis**. Job analysis consists of steps taken to identify knowledge, skills, tasks, duties, responsibilities and the working environment for each individual who holds a position. Figure 7.4 demonstrates the relationship of job analysis to strategic planning and development within an organization.

Job analysis activities should take place for every position in the organization at least once per year. Of course, there are many organizations that have never performed job analysis, but this doesn't mean the inaction is the correct way of doing business. The first result of job analysis activities is the creation of a document called a **job specification**. The job specification (job spec, for short) identifies the knowledge, skills, attitudes and abilities that

job—Tasks, duties, and responsibilities of a worker.

position—An individual who performs a job.

job analysis—A method of collecting and analyzing data resulting in job descriptions and job specifications.

job specification—A listing of knowledge, skills, attitudes, and abilities that collectively comprise the qualifications for a position.

Guest Service Empowerment Policy
It is the objective of the Hotel California to provide excellent guest services, as established in our Guest Service Index (GSI) rating system. One strategy to facilitate this goal is for all front line service personnel to be empowered to handle service recovery exceptions at the moment of occurrence. The following policy is applicable to front desk agents who have successfully completed the Guest Services Training Program (GSTP).

Empowerment Policy for Front Desk Agents
Qualified front desk agents are empowered to provide service recovery to guests of the resort by authorizing complimentary allowances in an amount not to exceed $250 per occurrence. Each complimentary allowance requires an entry into the guest services database to justify the exception. The appointed manager reviews all allowances within 24 hours of the occurrence of authorization. The reviewing manager shall respond to the authorizing front desk agent within the 24-hour timeframe to provide constructive feedback on the action taken.

Figure 7.2.   Sample Policy Statement.

determine the qualifications for a specific position. These documents are
used as part of the recruiting and selection processes. Another document resulting from job analysis is called the **job description**. This document articulates the tasks, duties, responsibilities, reporting relationships, and
sometimes the criteria for performance evaluation relative to a particular position. So the job specification identifies the qualifications of a potential employee in a specific position, while a job description articulates the activities
for the jobholder. The final outcome of the job analysis process is the criterion used to evaluate actual performance as compared to standards, which is
part of the performance management system. Evaluations of workplace performance are known as **performance appraisals**.

Standard

The standard for handling guest complaints at the Hotel California is to follow the procedure for complaint resolution and service recovery listed below.

Procedure

Listen carefully to what the guest is articulating in the complaint. Make eye contact and
acknowledge/paraphrase what is being said.

If the guest is in an emotional state, defuse the emotion by continuing to listen empathetically until the emotion is drained and the guest returns to a normal rate of speech.

Paraphrase your understanding of the nature of the complaint, and ask the guest for
permission to give you a chance to resolve the issue.

Use your knowledge of the operation to solve the guest's dilemma.

If the resolution involves financial remedies, refer to the standards and procedures for
guest service empowerment.

Confirm the resolution with the guest and document the situation in the incident database.

Figure 7.3. Sample Standard and Procedures.

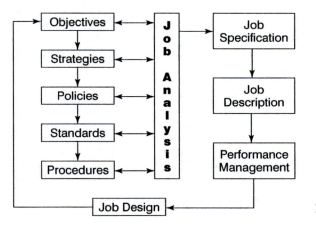

Figure 7.4. Job Design Drivers.

Job analysis is a key driver of almost every human resource strategy. For instance, job specs and job descriptions are used to provide qualifications and realistic job previews during recruiting and selection activities. Compensations plans are determined by qualifications and activities of positions, as well. Career planning and development activities are also driven by the job analysis function, as well as training, orientation, performance management systems and health/safety plans. Of course, there are safeguards to be taken in the design and implementation of job analysis activities. From a legal perspective, HR practitioners must ensure that any tests used are statistically valid and reliable for job relatedness. Also, the ADA has had an impact on the format of job descriptions, which must include essential duties listed in order of importance. Figure 7.5 shows an example of a job description.

A number of methods may be used to collect data for job analyses. These include observation, work sampling, interviewing, questionnaires, and combination methods. Work sampling is the collection of statistical samples of work being observed. In most cases HR practitioners use a combination of observation, questionnaires, and interviews for data collection. There are behavioral aspects of job analysis activities that require consideration on the part of participants. Any time an employee is being observed or asked questions about the job, it is a cause for anxiety. People are naturally creatures of habit and they fear those factors that may interrupt their routines by causing schedule changes or additional tasks and duties. Also it is natural, especially during times of the media reporting corporate downsizing, for employees to be concerned that their jobs will be eliminated. For these reasons, it is essential for the job analysis practitioner to take an honest and empathetic approach to collecting the data for analysis. Figure 7.6 provides the basic steps involved in the job analysis process.

THE RIGHT OF EMPLOYEES TO KNOW THE EXPECTATIONS

The information provided so far in this chapter concerns the primary right of individuals in the workplace. That right is to be professionally managed, which includes the processes presented here. The strategic approach to managing individuals begins with an audit of the corporate mission for the

Position: Executive Administrative Assistant   **Reports to:** General Manager
Department: Administrative and General   **Subordinates:** None

Basic Function: Provides administrative support to the General Manager by coordinating calendars, handling correspondence, receiving visitors, screening telephone calls and general filing and administrative area maintenance.

Essential Duties
Arrive at the work area at the scheduled time and prepare the executive offices for business within 30 minutes of arrival.

Handle all incoming phone calls using the standards and procedures for telephone etiquette.

Collect and distribute incoming mail items, place outgoing items in the mailroom.

Complete correspondence, filing, and other administrative tasks within prioritized timelines.

Prepare the office for closure at the end of the business day.

Additional Duties (as assigned)
Accompany the General Manager to specified meetings and client functions.

Make administrative decisions for the administrative staff in the absence of the executives.

Qualifications
Ability to process communications and computations at a level equivalent to the standards for a high school graduate.

Typing speed of at least 70 wpm.

Ability to solve administrative problems and prioritize tasks.

Diplomacy skills consistent with those required of an executive-level manager.

Working Conditions
Works in an ergonomically designed environment.

80 percent of working time requires sitting in an upright position.

20 percent of working time requires mobility to various areas within the organization.

Measures of Effectiveness
Measured to the standards articulated in the *Standard Operating Procedures Manual for Executive Administrative Assistants.*

Demonstrated willingness to make sound administrative decisions and show flexibility in work routine.

Demonstrated efficiency and effectiveness in the prioritization and completion of administrative tasks in a timely manner.

Figure 7.5. Sample Job Description.

organization. Next, objectives for performance are established. Objectives should be specific, measurable, attainable, challenging, and include "who" is responsible for "what" is to be accomplished by "when," which is the due date for completion of the objective. Each objective requires action steps called strategies. Strategies lead to policies, which are broad guidelines for performance in the organization. From those policies, standards are established to provide clear and objective expectations for performance. For each standard, there is a list of procedures that walk the worker through the process of meeting the standard.

Since the human resource practitioner acts in the capacity of managers' manager, it is incumbent upon the HR manager to ensure the practices presented so far actually exist and are communi-

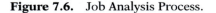

Identify existing positions and review documentation for each job.

Explain the job analysis process to subjects and supervisors in areas being analyzed.

Conduct the analysis in the most unobtrusive manner possible.

Prepare job descriptions and job specifications based on the findings of the analysis.

Revise performance management systems to reflect the changes made to job descriptions and job specifications.

Maintain and update job descriptions and job specs throughout the period of time until the next job analysis process.

Figure 7.6.   Job Analysis Process.

cated in every department and work unit in the organization. The absence of such practices in an organization is an indicator of mismanagement, which is a breach of management responsibility. Although it is seldom the case that legal challenges occur based on the breach of management responsibility, mismanagement does constitute a form of negligence in an organization.

THE RIGHT OF EMPLOYEES TO KNOW THE RULES

While standards and procedures articulate performance expectations, **rules** consist of the codes of behavior within the workplace. Failure to behave within the expectations set by the rules results in **misconduct** on the part of the worker. In some instances, the behavior may be of such a severe nature as to constitute **gross misconduct**. An issue of gross misconduct is usually grounds for employee termination from the company resulting from the first incident. So, while the SOP sets the guidelines for performance, the **rules of conduct** set the guidelines for acceptable behavior in the workplace. Once the worker has completed training, failure to meet the conduct or performance standards will result in **discipline**. Discipline has a negative connotation to most indi-

rules—Standards of conduct for individuals who are employed in the workplace.

misconduct—Failure to adhere to the rules.

gross misconduct—A severe infraction of the rules that warrants dismissal for the first incident.

rules of conduct—A listing of the codes of conduct for employees in the workplace.

discipline—A form of training to achieve desired behaviors.

progressive discipline—A process of disciplinary actions that include warnings concerning the consequences associated with future incidents.

viduals, due to its punitive applications. However, the definition of discipline is a form of training that redirects behavior to achieve desired performance and/or conduct. As is the case with all management practices, discipline must be administered in a fair, uniform and consistent manner for all individuals. Also, the organization should have a process of **progressive discipline** in place. This means that the process requires disciplinary warnings that result in appropriate consequences for repeated undesirable actions. This is where the "three strikes" analogy in organizations comes from. However, it is not as cut and dried as most organizations would like to believe. For instance, some companies have policies that state that the first incident of failure to perform or misconduct results in a verbal warning. This is misleading, as a manager never has a disciplinary interaction with an individual without creating a document of the incident and how it was addressed.

So in proper practice, there really is no such thing as a verbal warning. Instead, there is a "first warning," in which the incident is discussed along with required corrective actions on the part of the employee, ending with a notice further incidents will result in progressive disciplinary action up to and including involuntary separation from the company. Whenever this type of discussion takes place, it should be done in the privacy of an office, and a third party should be present to witness the interaction. Hence, there are three people in the room for a discussion of disciplinary warning: the supervisor, the employee being addressed, and a third-party manager to witness the discussion. All parties should sign a printed copy of the warning notice at the conclusion of the conversation. In the event that the employee does not want to sign the notice, the supervisor merely indicates "Refused to Sign" on the form, which is confirmed by the witnessing manager. Figure 7.7 shows an example of a corrective interview form used for counseling and discipline discussions.

Notice that the form requires a thorough explanation of exactly what was done wrong, the effect on the organization or other employees, the required corrective action on the part of the employee, and a space for the employee to list comments about the situation. You may ask, "Why have an area for employee comments?" This is a good question about a very important aspect of employee rights.

covenant of good faith and fair dealing—A promise to treat others fairly, uniformly, and consistently.

due process—The opportunity for an accused individual to provide a self-defense.

You may recall an earlier discussion about constitutional protection from the government, and that such protection does not exist for employees in the private sector. While there is no statutory protection for employees to voice their opinions, there is a common-law doctrine that implies that an employer possesses the duty to act fairly with customers and employees. This doctrine is called a **covenant of good faith and fair dealing**. The doctrine indicates that an entity that chooses to engage in a commercial enterprise is automatically bound by a promise (covenant) to act in good faith and fairness. For this reason, sound human resource management practices accord employees the opportunity to tell their side of the story during any disciplinary situation. This is referred to as **due process**. Those organizations that afford due process to their employees are going above and beyond what is legally required by statute. However, this practice is beneficial, as any adjudicator in a third-party hearing (EEOC, DOL, Unemployment Compensation, and others) will consider the due process accorded by the employer as an indication of good faith and fair dealing with employees, which weighs in favor of the employer.

Employee Name: **Date:**
Position: **Supervisor:**
Date of Hire: **Date of Incident:**

What was done wrong?

What was the adverse effect on the organization or other employees?

What must be done to correct the situation?

Employee comments:

Note: Any further occurrence of this nature will result in disciplinary action up to and including suspension from duties and/or termination.

Reason for Action	**Action Taken**
(check below)	(check below)
☐ Violation of policy	☐ Coach and counsel
☐ Job performance	☐ Disciplinary warning 1, 2, 3
☐ Misconduct or other inappropriate behavior	☐ Suspension (investigation)
☐ Other just cause	☐ Termination

Employee Signature/Date   **Witness Signature/Date**

Supervisor Signature/Date   **Executive Signature/Date**

DHR Signature/Date   **GM Signature/Date**

Figure 7.7. Corrective Interview.

Take notice of the statement just below the employee comment section of the corrective interview form in Figure 7.7. The key ingredient in a progressive discipline process is to warn the employee of potential consequences associated with further issues of substandard performance or misconduct. Looking further toward the bottom of the form, you will see check boxes to indicate the classification of the particular incident being recorded, followed by areas for multiple signatures. Every disciplinary action should include multiple party reviews, which should include individuals from the executive level of the organization. Sometimes this is called multi-tier review, indicating that reviewers represent upper levels of the organization.

Also, notice a check box for suspension. It is important to note that sound practice requires a thorough investigation of facts before deciding to terminate an employee. For this reason, upon the terminable offense, the employee is usually suspended for a brief period of time (not to exceed three days) to permit a thorough and comprehensive investigation of the facts. In the event that the facts do not substantiate the termination of the individual, that person should be paid for the time of suspension.

It is highly recommended that this be the only suspension scenario. Many employers practice suspension as a punitive measure. This is poor management practice. It forces the employee into a dependent situation, in which the manager has the authority to revoke earnings whenever that manager is displeased with the worker. Most seasoned managers will tell you, "Don't mess with people's pay." Instead, follow the progressive discipline process. When all avenues of correction are exhausted, terminate the employee from the company after a thorough investigation of the facts, giving that employee an opportunity to present his side of the story. Any experienced HR practitioner will tell you that there are three sides to every story: one side based on the supervisor's perception, the other from the employee, and a third from the perspective of those who witness the interaction between the supervisor and the employee.

COMMON-LAW RIGHTS APPLIED TO THE WORKPLACE

You may recall previous discussions of common law or the law of torts as law that is unwritten for the most part and is made by judges in the process of deciding civil cases. Common law comes from England and is interpreted individually by different states in the United States in current times. Common-law disputes between individual parties usually involve four factors of personal behavior. First is the concept of **responsibility**, or the duty to perform some action. The second factor, **accountability**, is defined as the duty to account for one's actions. Third, is the doctrine of **negligence**, which involves a breach of responsibility, for which an individual may be held liable. Fourth, there is the doctrine of **liability**, which is the duty to make things right in the case of a breach of responsibility (negligence). The test for negligence is that an individual knew or should have known that harm could result from a breach of responsibility. Hence, that person is held to be liable for the damages incurred from that negligence, which is usually in the form of financial payment to the party that was harmed. As mentioned before, in a matter of a court case brought under common law, the petitioner (party that was harmed) is the plaintiff and the party that is being petitioned becomes the defendant. The judge or a jury will award damages to the plaintiff based on the merits of the case, which may include compensatory and punitive damages. These matters are within the jurisdiction of the state courts.

The duty of a manager is to exercise **reasonable care** in the practice of supervising the activities of others. Reasonable care is defined as that which a person of sound mind would consider to be reasonable action in a situation.[2] The level of responsibility for an employer is the exercise of **due care**, which is that level of care that is reasonably expected of a person engaged in a position of responsibility, such as hiring employees. **Wrongful discharge** occurs when an employer terminates an employee for reasons that violate public policy (such as whistle blowing), implied or express contracts, or the covenant of good faith and fair dealing. Once again, this reinforces the practice of progressive discipline with multiple party reviews.

Constructive discharge occurs when the employee is not actually fired from a position, but instead quits the job due to unbearable treatment in the workplace by supervisors or coworkers. Constructive discharge commonly occurs in cases of sexual harassment where the employee resigns due to the harassment. Additionally, if the harassment included any physical contact by the perpetrator (such as touching, brushing against a person) or the intent of physical contact (such as blocking a pathway or standing in forced close proximity) **civil assault and battery** charges may be included in the harass-

responsibility—The duty to perform an action.

accountability—The duty to account for one's actions.

negligence—A breach of duty.

liability—The obligation to make reparations to others who are harmed from a breach of duty.

reasonable care—That which a person of sound mind would consider to be reasonable in a given situation.

due care—The duty to exercise reason consistent with the level of responsibility of the actor.

wrongful discharge—The discharge of an individual from employment for reasons that violate public policy, terms of an express or implied contract, or a covenant of good faith and fair dealing.

constructive discharge—Creating an uncomfortable work environment with the intent to encourage a person to resign from a position.

civil assault and battery—Any form of uninvited physical contact or the indication of the intent to make such contact.

ment complaint. If the treatment of the supervisor is deemed to be "outrageous" (particularly abusive), and the employee can demonstrate some form of hardship as a result of the treatment, the charge of constructive discharge will also include a claim under the tort doctrine of **intentional infliction of emotional distress**, which is commonly referred to as the "tort of outrage." If a person in authority prevents or coerces the victim from leaving an office, a charge of **false imprisonment** may ensue. The same could be true for security personnel during an interrogation interview of a suspect, for instance.

In matters where individuals communicate false information, either verbally or in writing, that casts a negative light upon the character of another individual, a civil charge of **defamation** by **libel** (written) or **slander** (verbal) could result. This charge occasionally results from unfavorable reference information that is shared about former employees seeking work with new employers. Even if the information attained by an employer about a current or prospective employee is accurate, it may be information that has no job-related implications; thus there is no "need to know" the information. For instance, an employer may conduct a credit check on a worker who does not engage in any form of financial transaction as part of the job. In this case the worker could have standing for a common-law case of **invasion of privacy**.

While there are numerous cases involving the legal doctrines just listed, the vast majority of disputes arises from direct or indirect negligence scenarios. Remember that negligence is a tort law in which a member of society knew—or should have known—that an action or inaction could have caused harm. It is based on the duty of a person to exercise due care in personal and professional matters. Hence, situations in which a person is harmed from some action within an employment relationship could make the employer liable for that action. For example: A licensed massage therapist (LMT) is employed in the spa at a resort. A guest files a criminal assault charge against the LMT for improper touching. Later, it is determined that the LMT had prior arrests, but no convictions, for sexual battery. From a common-law standpoint, the employer should have known this information by conducting a criminal background investigation prior to offering the LMT employment with the resort. Had the employer done this, it would not have hired the LMT, and the sexual assault would not have happened. Since the employer should have known about the propensity of this LMT to assault individuals, the resort is liable for the guest's harm resulting from the assault.

The premise for this liability is called **negligent hire**, a situation in which a person is hired into a position that facilitated their ability to cause harm to another, when the employer knew or should have known of the propensity for such harm. A similar case would be a culinary worker who has received disciplinary notices for violent behaviors in the workplace, including threatening a coworker with a knife. Later, the culinary worker enters into an argument with a sous chef and stabs him to death. This is a case of **negligent retention**, as the worker demonstrated a propensity for violent behavior with a knife and was not discharged from employment. Hence, the employer's decision to retain that employee in an area where cutlery is available contributed to the sous chef's death. They knew or should have known that this behavior would reoccur.

Since human resource practitioners are the "custodians of records" for the organization, they incur the responsibility for the security of the personnel

---

intentional infliction of emotional distress—The tort of outrage, treating an individual in a hostile manner with the intent to cause mental or physical distress.

false imprisonment—Prevention or the threat of prevention from permitting a person to move freely.

defamation—False information communicated to a third party with the intent to cast poor light on the character of an individual.

libel—Written defamatory comments.

slander—Verbal defamatory comments.

invasion of privacy—Accessing information concerning an individual in the absence of a need to know that information.

negligent hire—The employment of an individual that facilitates that person's ability to harm others, when the employer knew or should have known there was a propensity for that employee to inflict harm as part of the course of employment.

negligent retention—Failure to remove an individual with a propensity to incur harm to others from an employment position when the employer knew or should have known of the propensity to incur harm.

HOSPITALITY NEWS *Hospitality Employees—Check Them Out*

Business decisions in the hospitality industry are still affected by the aftermath of September 11th. Heightened security is not just for government agencies anymore. More hotels and restaurants are screening job applicants before sending them up to guests' rooms to clean, before giving them access to customers' credit card numbers, before bringing them into their facility and trusting them with the businesses' and customers' property.

Statistics show that 9.6 percent of job applicants have a criminal record. "One of our hotel clients just asked us to check an employee's social security number," says Robert Mather, President and CEO of Pre-employ.com. "The Human Resources Manager was shocked when we found her employee's social security number had nearly 200 aliases associated with it." Had she run the number the first time, she would have known before hiring the person.

Hotels and restaurants have good reason to check an applicant's background. Primarily it's to protect employees from violent felons, customers from sexual predators, and assets from convicted thieves. The secondary reason is legal—if a business gives someone access (say to clients' hotel rooms, credit card numbers) and that employee abuses their privileges, the business is held liable for negligent hiring. Managers inherently want to prevent workplace violence and theft, and knowing a person's past helps.

This information is the power to prevent disaster. Management can choose not to hire a dishonest person. They can also hire the person but place them where they don't put coworkers at risk for violence or customers at risk for theft. "We often have hotels and restaurants hire someone who has a misdemeanor," says Mather; "They just don't put them in the accounting department."

Judgments typically hold businesses accountable for employing people who committed crimes on the job or with information obtained through work. The businesses lost millions by compensating victims.

Somerset Auctions settled a multi-million dollar wrongful death lawsuit. Somerset hired convicted felon, Mesa Kasem, to deliver to customers. Kasem recruited a fellow gang member to help him rob the home of customer Kim Fang. On January 4, 2000, the gang members barged into Fang's home and pistol-whipped Fang's wife, her brother, and the nanny. Fang fired his own weapon, killing Kasem—then Kasem's accomplice fatally shot Fang twice in the back. The lawsuit claimed Somerset failed to use reasonable care to discover Kasem's violent criminal background, which included a conviction for shooting at a woman in a home (Hinton & Alfert, 2002).

A restaurant manager raped his 16-year old female co-worker. He had a history of sexual abuse. Judgment: $6.5 million.

A hospital employee murdered a co-worker. He had two previous convictions for assault. Judgment: $864,000 (National Institution for the Prevention of Workplace Violence).

The cost of a background check is a small amount relative to the potential loss.

Source: Kelly Smith, *Hospitality News*, May 2003, p. 27.

negligent maintenance—Failure to exercise due care in the security of items or information by a custodian.

files. They are also expected to prohibit any department from keeping replicated personnel files. The reason for this is in the event that an employee gains access to another person's file, the company may be held liable for **negligent maintenance** of records. This is why the only official personnel file exists in the human resource office in a separate locked room within the office, and in locked cabinets within that separate room. Let's say the person, who accessed the employee file, spreads rumors about that person based on the content of the file. In this case the company may be held liable for

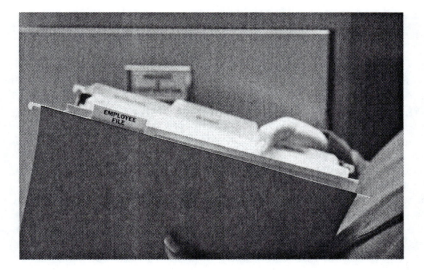

negligent disclosure of records. In both cases the employer is held responsible for the failure to exercise due care in the maintenance and disclosure of records, even though they did not condone access to the files.

negligent disclosure— Information that is disclosed to third parties arising from access to records that should have been secured with due care by a custodian.

SUMMARY

This chapter has focused on the rights of employees from both the managerial and legal perspective. An organization that chooses to hire employees incurs a duty to manage those employees in a professional manner. Unfortunately, there currently are no provisions to ensure the proficiency of a professional manager. The inability of most organizations to identify competent managers results in subjective management practices. The organization is clearly responsible for all activities associated with the employment relationship. Any failure of a manager to work with employees in a fair, uniform, and consistent manner creates a liability for the company. Professional management includes auditing the corporate mission, setting objectives, identifying strategies, creating policies, establishing standards, and articulating procedures for performance. The process for considering the jobs and position activities is called job design, which begins with job analysis. Numerous methods may be used during the job analysis process to gather and evaluate data. The outcomes of job analysis are job descriptions, job specifications and performance management systems. All of these are used to evaluate actual performance relative to standards for performance. Additionally, the employer is expected to communicate the rules of behavior to its employees.

DISCUSSION QUESTIONS

1. Do you think there should be a requirement for managers to be certified or licensed before they are permitted to practice management? Why or why not?

2. Have you ever had an experience where managers made decisions and supervised employees in a subjective manner? Why do you think these managers act this way?

In the Real World ... (Continued)

A month has passed since the incident between the captain and his assistant. The captain did call the assistant's house for three days in a row following the incident, and left messages asking her if she intended to return to work. She did not return the calls and never returned to her job. After three days, the assistant was considered to have abandoned her job. An employee separation form was completed and a personnel requisition was filed to replace the assistant's position. The captain promoted one of his supervisors to the position, and all was well in the marina operations department, except that the captain received a disciplinary warning for violating company policy by issuing a performance appraisal without the approval of the human resource director.

When you arrived for work this morning the director called you into the office to work on a project with her. She showed you a letter from an attorney demanding a settlement on behalf of his client, the former assistant to the captain. Attached was a deposition from the assistant noting several allegations of improper treatment toward her by the captain.

The claim noted that because of her size and weight, the captain personally disliked her. She went on to claim that she never intended to leave her job, but the treatment by the captain made life unbearable for her at the resort. In essence, she claimed it was a matter of constructive discharge. She went on to say that she was thoroughly embarrassed by the performance appraisal and was treated outrageously in that process due to the captain's intentional infliction of emotional distress. As a result, she has been unable to gain employment, as she feels faint every time she goes to apply for a new job. She claimed she was so traumatized by the captain's treatment that she is under the care of a physician and requires medication to prevent outbreaks of depression and anxiety. Further she claimed that the captain blocked her egress from the office during the interview, substantiating false imprisonment, and that when she tried to leave, he assaulted her. Additionally she claimed that the captain spread false rumors about her among the staff to cast her in poor light—a matter of defamation of character by slander. Her knowledge of these remarks further aggravates her medical condition, especially when she reflects on her co-workers sharing information about her poor performance that were found in the captain's office, constituting negligent maintenance and disclosure of records, as well as libel. Finally, her attorney concludes that the actions of the captain traumatized his client to the degree that she is unable to engage in gainful employment and that he is seeking damages in excess of $500,000 to compensate her for 20 potential years of lost earnings.

After you finish reading the documents, the director gives you one of her knowing smiles and says, "Here we go again. I will need you to put together information to establish evidence that we acted within our policies. This will require document searches and statements to be taken from every person in the department. This will take us a couple of weeks."

You say to her, "Is this going to be like that EEOC case we worked on?"

She replies, "Kind of, but not really. This is a matter of common law." She continues, "In this case, we have to demonstrate that we acted within reason and that she is being unreasonable." Then she glances toward you and says, "You are really getting a lot of experience in a short period of time here, aren't you?"

3. If you compare the beginning and ending In the Real World vignettes, can you see where the captain's former assistant got her story? Is it true? Do you think she has a good case? Were you surprised by the severity of her claims against her former employer?

4. Do you think it is easy to sue an employer? Why or why not? Do you think this is right?

KEY TERMS

accountability
civil assault and
  battery
constructive
  discharge
covenant of good
  faith and fair
  dealing
defamation
discipline
due care
due process
false
  imprisonment
gross misconduct

intentional
  infliction of
  emotional
  distress
invasion of privacy
job
job analysis
job description
job specification
liability
libel
management
management by
  objectives (MBO)

misconduct
mission
negligence
negligent
  disclosure
negligent hire
negligent
  maintenance
negligent retention
objective
organization
performance
  appraisals

policies
position
procedures
progressive
  discipline
reasonable care
responsibility
rules
rules of conduct
slander
standards
wrongful
  discharge

CHAPTER EIGHT
Recruitment and Selection Strategies

OBJECTIVES

By the end of this chapter, the reader will be able to:

1. Understand the strategic nature of recruitment and selection processes.
2. Comprehend the planning and execution of recruitment strategies.
3. Recognize matters of statutory and common law as applied to the employment process.
4. Understand the process of selection practices.

In the Real World . . .

You are working as a clerical assistant in the human resource office for a large casino hotel. You have been assigned to assist the employment manager during the recruiting season, which will last for about three months. The employment manager is responsible for all of the planning and implementation of recruiting and selection processes. While you have never worked directly with the employment staff, you have observed that they seem always to be working at a frenetic pace trying to process large numbers of applicants that appear at the door every day. To you it seems like a very stressful environment, with people scurrying to process all the applicants.

You remember that when you used to work in operations, some of the managers would speak poorly of the employment personnel. You recalled comments about how they just took their sweet time to replace vacant positions, and that they didn't realize how stressful it was to work without those replacements. Back then, you got the impression that the employment people were pretty lazy and didn't really care if a position was placed or not. After all, they always went home at 5:00 p.m., while the operations personnel were still working. But you also remembered your manager as not having any problem finding replacements for positions. In your recollection, your manager would visit the HR office frequently to work on manpower planning revisions and keep the employment people up to date on any changes in recruitment and selection needs. It seemed that your old department always had a sufficient supply of replacements for vacant positions. So, you wondered, why did these other managers have so many problems?

The employment manager invites you to lunch, to familiarize you with his operation. You are sitting together as he presents the stream of activities from recruitment, through selection, to placement of personnel. Afterward, he asks you if you have any questions at this point. You reply, "I am a little confused. When I was in operations there were managers who complained about how long it took to get a personnel requisition placed. Yet, my manager never seemed to have a problem with that. From listening to the other managers, I was under the impression that the employment people sort of dawdled in the process of placing new hires. Now, after watching you guys work, I see you are really stressed out."

The employment manager replies, "These are very good observations." He continues, "Employment is one of the most stressful areas of human resource management; that is why the director keeps a manager in the employment area for only one year, and offers another specialty after that. She knows that after a year, an employment manager is totally fried." "As for the opinions of the operating managers," he says, "Those that plan and communicate never have placement problems. This was the case with your former manager. However, most of them just don't get it, so it is easy to complain."

At the conclusion of the lunch, the employment manager says, "So, are you ready for a real HR challenge? If the employment office doesn't challenge you, no HR function will," he jokes, as you both head back to the office.

INTRODUCTION

The factor key to differentiating human resource management from personnel administration is the strategic nature of acquiring, developing and maintaining human capital. Since the break from personnel administration, human resource managers have been included in the overall strategic direction of a firm, which places the HR manager within the senior management of the organization. In some cases, the HR manager is selected to become the CEO or COO of the company. This is because a senior-level HR manager possesses balance of functions. For instance, a financial senior manager will have a tendency to emphasize efficiency, since that is the area of focus in financial and accounting managerial training. On the other hand, a senior marketing manager will emphasize effectiveness, since marketing is an optimistic science based on spending money to enhance revenues. Historically, in good financial times the marketing VP would become the CEO and in poor financial times the finance officer would be promoted to that position. In either case, there is an imbalance that pulls the organization in one direction or another, which keeps the company in a state of imbalance. You may recall the discussion in Chapter 1 about value-added management and the productivity model. That model is represented here again in Figure 8.1 to emphasize the necessary balance between efficiency and effectiveness in an organization.

Some organizations realize that human resource managers are trained equally in managing efficiency and effectiveness, which makes them appropriate candidates for CEO positions.

STRATEGIC PLANNING

Since HR managers are members of the senior management committee for an organization, it is essential that they are trained in the **strategic planning process**, which is a method used to plan organizational strategies from an open systems perspective. The open systems model indicates that its external environment influences the organization. However, the organization has no control over the factors that exist in the external environment. The organization does have control over the **internal environment**, which is the environment within that organization. Figure 8.2 describes the strategic planning model as an open system process.

Because this is an open systems model, the human resource manager must evaluate factors in the **external environment** by conducting an **external scan** of those factors. For instance, factors in the external environment that influence human resource functions could include the labor market, competition, economic factors, and other things that influence the levels of KSAAs (knowledge, skills, attitudes, and abilities) that exist outside the organization. At the same time, the managers look inside the organization at

strategic planning process—A systematic process using the open systems model to construct plans that include objectives and strategies for future performance.

internal environment—The factors contained within the environment of the organization.

external environment—The factors residing in the environment outside the organization.

external scan—The process of identifying opportunities and threats to the organization that exist in the external environment.

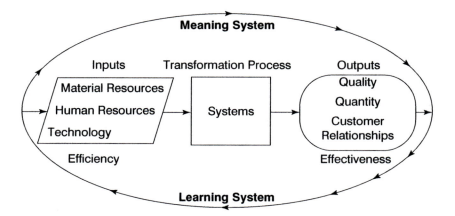

Figure 8.1. Productivity Model.

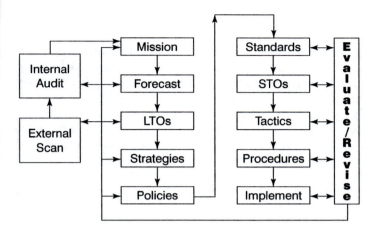

Figure 8.2.   Strategic Planning Process.

each department. This process is called an **internal audit**. In this phase, the managers are collecting data about management styles, resource allocation, work environment, interdepartmental relations, productivity and other factors. Once the data collection from the internal and external environments is complete, the manager analyzes the data. During the analysis, the data from inside the organization are categorized into strengths (things the organization does well) and weaknesses (things that could be done better). Also, the external factors are categorized into opportunities (things that could benefit the organization) and threats (things that could harm the organization). When the analysis is complete, the managers have a listing of strengths, weaknesses, opportunities, and threats. This is why this type of analysis is referred to as **SWOT analysis**.

  The next step in the strategic planning process is to audit the mission for the organization. You may recall that the mission is the overriding purpose of that organization. It also contains the philosophies and values of the organization. Every year the managers should revisit the mission statement to see if the existing mission still makes sense to the organization, or if it requires some form of modification. Once the corporate mission is audited, a separate mission for each department should be established to reflect how that department contributes to the overall mission for the organization. Figure 8.3 shows

internal audit—The process of identifying strengths and weaknesses within the organization.

SWOT analysis—The analysis of strengths, weaknesses, opportunities, and threats to the organization.

Corporate Mission
It is the mission of the Hotel California to acquire and maintain upscale guests by anticipating their every need and accommodating those needs during every moment of every visit with us.

Human Resource Mission
It is the mission of the Human Resource Department at the Hotel California to acquire and maintain staff members who possess excellent knowledge, skills, attitudes, and abilities to anticipate every need of our guests and to accommodate those needs during every moment of the every guest visit with us.

Figure 8.3.   Sample Mission Statements.

an example of a corporate and human resource department mission statement for a resort hotel.

mission-driven organization—An organization that retains the purpose and values of its mission in all decision-making activities.

If every department takes this strategic approach to managing their functions, the organization becomes what is known as a **mission-driven organization**. When faced with making a decision, every manager in such an organization would ask the question, "Does this situation affect the mission for the department and the organization?" If the answer to this question is yes, then the manager knows that this is an important decision that must be made immediately. It is the job of the human resource practitioner to convert the hotel, restaurant, theme park, resort, cruise line, airline—whatever—into a mission-driven organization. In a mission-driven organization, every individual marches to the beat of the same drum. The power of **synergy** in such an organization is amazing.

synergy—An outcome that is greater than the sum of its parts.

The rest of the strategic planning process involves establishing objectives, strategies and tactics, which are converted into policies, rules, standards, and procedures for each department throughout the organization. This process was covered in detail in Chapter 7. In the field of human resource management, there must be strategies for recruitment, selection, training, development, performance management, communication, and leadership within the organization. These strategies feed into the mission for the department, as well as for the organization.

If the mission includes the acquisition of great employees, then this model drives the strategies for recruitment and selection. If the mission claims to value the maintenance of employees, then there must be strategies for training and development to give the staff members current and growth-related skills. There must be strategies to evaluate the performance levels of

each worker to provide feedback and recognition for jobs well done. There must be effective communication strategies for articulating expectations for performance and to listen to the concerns and ideas of the employees. Finally, there must be a leadership strategy to convert all of the managers into leaders, which is no easy task. Every function within the human resource management domain is strategic in nature, which means establishing a plan and working that plan, while continually monitoring it through progress evaluation and plan revision.

RECRUITMENT STRATEGIES

The process of **recruitment** involves generating a pool of qualified applicants for positions within the organization. The external factors that influence recruitment strategies are all focused on the **labor market**. The labor market consists of individuals in possession of knowledge, skills, attitudes and abilities (KSAAs) that meet the standards for employment within the organization. Factors in the locality of the operation (such as education levels, personality types, unemployment rates, competitor recruiting practices, median age of the population, diversity levels and others) are external variables that must be considered prior to constructing recruitment strategies. For instance, a resort that is located in a metropolitan area possesses more local recruiting opportunities than one that is located 50 miles from the nearest major city. In one case, a major resort located in the Florida Keys (a chain of small islands beyond the southern tip of the state) finds it easy to acquire qualified tradespeople to do blue-collar work, but has to recruit administrative personnel from 50 miles away and service personnel on a national level from summer season locations. This location requires a very different strategy than one established at another resort located on the beach of Ft. Lauderdale (a winter resort town located in the heart of a south Florida metropolitan area), in which the population supports a labor pool for trades, administrative, and service positions. Both of these scenarios vary drastically from the recruiting needs of a large theme park located in Orlando that requires continuous internationally based recruiting methods to attract applicants for varied cast member positions. So it is clear that the composition of the external environment compared with the internal needs of the organization drives the strategic recruitment process.

How does an organization know which KSAAs it requires? The answer comes from our discussion in the last chapter concerning job analysis that yields job specifications. The job specifications list the KSAAs that comprise the qualifications for each position within the organization. This is the internal driver of the recruiting process. For instance, in the scenarios from the last paragraph, there was a sufficient number of individuals who possessed the KSAAs for work such as carpentry, plumbing, etc. However, individuals with the KSAAs to be accountants, IT workers, and administrative assistants were not available in sufficient supply in the local vicinity of the Florida Keys. In the recruitment planning process, the HR manager matches the profiles of the labor market with the KSAAs, as documented in the job specifications for each position within the organization. The collective number of individuals in a targeted population makes up the **labor force population**, while those in possession of appropriate KSAAs comprise the **labor pool** of individuals who

recruitment—The process of generating a pool of qualified applicants for a position.
labor market—The external variables that influence the labor pool.

labor force population—The population of individuals who are available for work.
labor pool— Individuals within the labor force population who possess KSAAs for positions within organizations.

manpower planning—A process of forecasting required position placement over a period of time.

turnover—The combination of voluntary and involuntary separation of employees within an organization.

voluntary separation—Employees who resign from positions in organizations.

involuntary separation—Employees who are discharged from positions in organizations.

promotions—Employees who are placed in positions that possess increased authority and responsibility within an organization.

sourcing—The process of locating potential qualified applicants to be added to the applicant pool for an organization.

succession-planning—Forecasting promotion and replacement personnel for planned management and professional positions vacated due to internal promotion or transfer.

may be attracted to apply for positions within the organization. So, the KSAAs represent the internal quality drivers of the recruitment process, with the remaining requirement consisting of internally generated quantity drivers.

The quantity driver for a recruitment strategy consists of a forecast of vacant positions that will require placement over a period of one year. This forecast is referred to as **manpower planning**. "Person power" planning would be a more politically correct term; however, many organizations still use the old terminology. Manpower planning involves calculating employment growth and attrition rates to project the numbers of positions to be placed in each category during each month over the next year. Employment growth figures come from the number of positions in each category that are added to the current number of positions. Attrition forecasts are derived from employee **turnover** statistics that are used to predict the number of position replacements in each category due to **voluntary separation**, **involuntary separation** and **promotions**.

Once the quality and quantity drivers are in place, the next step is to identify sources for recruitment. This practice is known as **sourcing**. External sources are those that exist outside the organization, while internal sources are those that exist within the company. Table 8.1 provides a list of a few internal and external sources for recruitment.

From an internal perspective, anyone who has access to those within the organization is considered to be an internal source for recruitment. Job postings are bulletin board and listserve notices announcing position openings and bidding systems are means for internal candidates to express interest in promotion and transfers. **Succession-planning** programs are also a means of identifying internal individuals for promotional opportunities. The goal of succession planning is to have a "person in the pocket" to be promoted to positions once the incumbent is promoted to the next level of management or professional status. This is a systematic way to generate internal promotions. However, it should be noted that a balance of internal promotions and outside hires for positions is the ultimate goal of the human resource practitioner, as this ensures open-minded decision-making at all levels of the organization. Companies with too many internal promotions become myopic in their thinking, known as "corporate inbreeding." Other internal recruitment sources include referrals from employees, vendors, and former staff and applicants. For instance, an individual may have applied for and was offered a position with the organization. That individual may have declined the offer to accept a position with another firm. The HR practitioner may ask that person if there is someone like her whom she would refer for the position.

Table 8.1 Recruitment Sources

Internal Sources	External Sources
Job postings	Competitors
Bidding systems	Schools, colleges
Promotions and transfers	Labor unions
Staff referrals	Trade associations
Vendor referrals	Agencies/executive search firms
Former staff and applicants	Media

External sources include competitors. Experienced HR practitioners are always on the lookout for talented individuals employed by other companies. An HR manager who visits the restaurant of a competitor and receives excellent tableside service may invite that person to apply for a position with her resort. Another external source of recruiting consists of schools (vocational and trade schools, for instance) and colleges (management trainee candidates, for instance) that train individuals with appropriate KSAAs for the standards of employment in an organization. Professional trade associations are excellent networking and referral sources, while executive search firms (headhunters) may be employed to refer executive applicants; agencies may be appropriate for temporary or administrative referrals. Media advertisements are widely used for recruitment; however, this practice is expensive and not very effective for finding individuals with the proper KSAAs. If this is true, one may ask why the media, including newspaper classified advertising, is used extensively. The answer is that HR practitioners must demonstrate the practice of announcing position opportunities to all segments of the local population to defend the organization against potential claims of disparate impact. Hence, the common practice is to use classified advertisements with newspapers that provide statistical data on the demographics of the readership. Copies of the advertisements are retained in the human resource records along with the statistical information as documentation of the continuous publication of job openings. On the other hand, trade publications media are sometimes very nice sources for certain specialized available positions.

EVALUATING RECRUITMENT PLANNING AND PRACTICES

A very large portion of the human resource departmental budget is allocated to the recruiting practices. As is the case with any evaluative process, the two items for consideration are effectiveness and efficiency.

The measure of recruitment effectiveness is how well the practices meet the recruitment goals of generating large pools of qualified applicants within minimal timeframes. All positions must be placed in a timely manner, as the longer a position remains unfilled, the more costly that opening is to the organization in terms of productivity. Hence, effectiveness metrics focus on the quality of applicant pools and timeliness of applicant pool generation.

Efficiency measures focus on the use of resources in the quest to be effective. Since the expenditures for recruitment are so large, it is important for HR practitioners to maximize bang for the buck in these practices. Efficiency measures focus on costs of resources such as advertising and networking, while effectiveness evaluates quality applicants acquired in a timely manner. The combination of efficiency and effectiveness measures is referred to as cost/benefit analysis. Human recruitment activities are evaluated in terms of cost/benefit analysis.

SELECTION PRACTICES

selection—The process of identifying individuals to occupy vacant positions within an organization.

Laypersons commonly think of recruitment and **selection** practices as a single process. This is not true. Recruitment has to do with the generation of a pool of qualified applicants. Selection, on the other hand, pertains to choosing qualified individuals for placement in positions within the organization. The task for HR practitioners in the selection process is to pick the most qualified applicant to join the organization, although we never admit this to the other applicants for legal reasons. If we say, "We chose the most qualified applicant" to one who was not chosen, this begs the question, "What does he have that I don't?" Now the organization is in a position to demonstrate the differences between the two individuals. Hence, we simply say, "We chose a qualified applicant to fill the position," when speaking with the public. All of the activities within the selection process are for the purpose of selecting a single person to fill an employment position. These practices are referred to as **pre-employment** activities. Figure 8.4 lists the flow of pre-employment activities that may be included in the selection process for an organization.

pre-employment—Activities that occur prior to an offer of employment.

application blank—A form completed by an applicant for a position with an organization.

The first step in the application process is the completion of an **application blank**, which is a standard form that is on paper or on line. The form is retained in the applicant records for a period of time and may be used for consideration for future positions, or the HR office may require an applicant to complete a new form for each position applied for. The structure of an application blank is crucial, as the purpose of the blank is to elicit as much information about the applicant as possible; however, the format must comply with legal requirements that vary by state. Figure 8.5 demonstrates a sample application blank for an organization.

The reverse side of the application blank provides areas for the applicant to complete information about employment experience by asking for information such as: employer name, location, type of business, address, phone number, start and end dates of employment, starting title, ending title, start-

---

1. Applicants submit resumes and complete application blanks in person or on line
2. Short pre-screening interviews with a human resource representative
3. HR rep eliminates unqualified candidates from the pool
4. Applicants are scheduled for screening interviews
5. HR rep selects three to five candidates from that pool for further selection
6. Pre-employment tests for ability, aptitude, personality, honesty or assessment centers
7. HR rep forwards pre-employment file to hiring department managers
8. Managers from departments conduct additional interviews with remaining candidates
9. Manager advises HR rep of selection for employment
10. HR rep makes a tentative offer to the candidate of choice pending drug or medical test results
11. Security office is authorized to conduct background investigation of selected candidates
12. A formal offer of employment is extended to the candidate indicating start date and orientation reservation
13. Applicants who were not chosen are advised of their status
14. Applications are retained in applicant files for one to three years

---

Figure 8.4. Pre-employment Activities.

ing and ending pay rate, and description of duties. There will be sufficient space for the applicant to list the last three positions. Below that section, there is space to list contact information of three references and an area to identify whom to contact in an emergency. At the bottom of the page there is a pre-employment statement that requires the signature of the applicant. Figure 8.6 provides an example of such a statement.

Next, the HR rep conducts a short pre-screening interview for the purpose of determining which candidates are clearly not qualified for the position. The remaining pool of applicants is scheduled for second interviews with the HR office. At the completion of this interview process, human resource representatives conduct reference checks with prior employers. Based on the results of these interviews, three to five candidates are referred to the hiring department for further interviews. In some cases, after passing the departmental interview process, candidates will be scheduled to meet with the executive committee, although this is not always the case.

Next there may be pre-employment tests, which include instruments to determine factors such as ability (keyboard tests for secretaries, for instance), aptitude (the capacity to learn accounting functions, for instance), personality (preferred response to environmental stimuli), honesty (propensity to be ethical), assessment centers (off-site testing of executive abilities), or psychological batteries (off-site testing to identify psychological profiles), as well as other forms of testing. The important aspect of testing is statistical **validity** (it measures what it is intended to measure) and reliability (it measures the same outcomes consistently). This is why Ph.D. psychologists should design all pre-employment and other test instruments used in the workplace, since these individuals are considered to be experts in statistical validity and **reliability**. This factor has two implications. First, is the ability of the Ph.D. psychologist to construct and validate the instruments, which may become the subject of legal scrutiny in the event of a disparate impact case involving **racial bias**, or others types of statistical flaws. Second, if the psychologist is acting as an **independent contractor**, she incurs the burden of proof via

validity—Statistical measurement of intended outcomes associated with variables.

reliability—Statistical measurement that demonstrates validity on a consistent basis.

racial bias—Instrument design that is not valid based on racial variables associated with subjects.

independent contractor—A third party who is contracted to perform a function that is not part of the regular employment relationship.

Hotel California
Application for At-Will Employment
This form must be completed by all applicants, even if you have submitted a resume

Personal Information

Name
Last   First   Middle   Other names
Address   Phone #   Message #
Street   City   State   Zip
Social Security #   Are you over 18 years of age?   How were you referred?
_____   ☐ Yes ☐ No   _____

Employment Information
Position(s) desired   Type of employment desired   Salary desired
_____   ☐ full time ☐ part time ☐ other $___per_____
Date available to begin work   Are you willing to work: ☐ Shift hours
_____   ☐ Overtime?   ☐ Weekends?

Business necessity or change of positions or responsibilities may require you to work overtime or different hours or tasks from those you have worked in the past. Is this acceptable to you? ☐ Yes ☐ No

Do you have the legal right to accept employment in the United States? ☐ Yes ☐ No All individuals who are accepted for employment must demonstrate proof of this before starting work.

Have you ever been employed by or previously applied to the Hotel California?
☐ Yes ☐ No
If yes, please describe.

Do you have any illnesses or physical condition that will require accommodation on the job? ☐ Yes ☐ No
Please describe.

Military Service
U.S. Veteran? ☐ Yes ☐ No
Branch of Service: Active duty from   to

Education and Training
School name   Graduated?   Degree or diploma   Major
                       ☐ Yes ☐ No
High school
College/university
Other
Languages—Specify languages in which you are proficient.

Security Data
Have you ever been convicted of a felony? (this information will be treated in a nondiscriminatory manner) ☐ Yes ☐ No
If yes, please describe.

Have you ever had adjudication withheld or pleaded no contest to a felony?
☐ Yes ☐ No
If yes, please explain.

Figure 8.5. Sample Application Blank.

Pre-Employment Statement

My signature verifies that all statements made on this application are true and no omissions or misleading statements exist regarding my employment history.

I understand that if any statements made on this application or during interviews are false or misleading, or if I have failed to reveal any prior employment, this may result in non-employment.

I authorize and release from liability all persons, businesses, schools, institutions, and other persons to provide the Hotel California with any relevant information that may be required to make an employment decision.

I understand that I shall be required to provide the Hotel California with documentation establishing my legal authorization for employment prior to commencing work.

I understand that if employed, my employment will be at-will and that no contract or guarantee of employment exists.

Applicant Signature _____ Date_____

Figure 8.6. Sample Pre-employment Statement.

chain of custody, which moves the legal responsibility for the instrument from the organization to a third-party contractor.

One form of honesty testing that was commonly used during the pre-employment process up until 1986 was called the polygraph (lie detector) test, conducted by a certified individual third party. The **Polygraph Protection Act** (1986) was passed by Congress, which for all intents and purposes excludes the use of the polygraph technique in private sector pre-employment processes. The polygraph is still used in the public sector; however, it is rapidly being replaced with voice stress analysis testing, which is considered to be a more valid and reliable indicator of honesty.

The department director has the ultimate decision-making authority concerning the candidate selected for hire. This determination is made during a round of departmental interviews and pre-employment testing. Once the

chain of custody—
The chain of responsibility that leads to the source of liability for a breach in the exercise of due care.

Polygraph Protection Act—The federal statute that prohibits the use of pre-employment polygraph testing for most employment scenarios, with certain exceptions.

HOSPITALITY NEWS   *Who's Left in Charge? Pick Middle Management Wisely*

Nothing undermines an organization like poor middle management. The greatest oversight by any employer is to allow poor supervisors to become dictators over your staff. If productivity is down and morale is low, the cause may be with who you left in charge. Here are a few common problems with managers who are really "manglers" instead of managers.

- Inconsistent changes in procedures caused by managers making personal decisions that do not always support company policy

- Favoritism
- Poorly delivered instructions, training, and requests such that employees aren't sure what is expected
- Big egos—supervisors wanting all the glory
- Discrimination and sexism

Source: Hospitality News, August 2002, p. 10.

department director makes a hiring decision, the information is forwarded to the human resource office and the candidate is advised that a tentative offer is on the table pending the outcome of additional testing. This type of testing may include drug tests via urine or blood (hair tests have been eliminated) and medical physical examinations. The reason the organization waits until the pending offer stage to conduct these tests is twofold. First, these tests are costly and are reserved for serious candidates only. Second, provisions within the ADA make it possible to scrutinize legally the administration of such tests as a pre-employment practice for all applicants, as the results could establish cause of discrimination based on disability in the hiring process. Remember that the ADA requires the reasonable accommodation of individuals with differing abilities in the workplace.

At the same time that the candidate is completing the drug and medical testing, the security department or other outside agency will be authorized to complete a background investigation of the candidate. This investigation will search public law enforcement records for arrests, driving record (if applicable to the job), and credit histories (if applicable). The thing for HR practitioners to keep in mind is that all investigatory information must be based on a "need to know," to avoid legal scrutiny under the law of torts for invasion of privacy, as discussed in Chapter 7. Also, the reason that the security or third-party investigation entity conducts the investigation is to separate that information from the pre-employment information, to avoid potential legal scrutiny of discrimination. The chain of custody is also a consideration here, as the security department will always use an independent contracting private investigation firm, so as to distribute the burden of proof associated with the process of investigation. Finally, the absence of such investigatory information could expose the organization to potential claims of negligent hire, as discussed in Chapter 7.

Notice the catch 22 scenario of this process. On one hand it is illegal to perform any discriminatory practice in the hiring process. A conservative approach would preclude accessing personal information for a job candidate to comply with this body of law. However, the employer has the responsibility to

guard against potential harm to another party arising from the employment relationship. If the employer hires a person with a propensity to incur harm, the organization could be held liable under common law tort of negligence, in this case negligent hire and negligent retention. The test for negligence in this case is that the employer knew or should have known that the employment relationship could result in harm to a third party. Hence the HR department would expose the organization to potential negligence law suits if it did not access this personal information, which could be considered by the body of civil rights law to be discriminatory. At the same time, should the employer access personal information about a candidate that is beyond the employer's "need to know" the information, a case of invasion of privacy could result. So you see that from a legal perspective, the human resource practitioner must very cautiously balance all of the legal responsibilities imposed upon the organization within the selection process.

Upon the completion of this entire process, the human resource office extends a formal offer of employment to the job candidate. This is usually done through an official offer of employment letter that is signed by the director of human resources, which clearly articulates the benefits, terms, and conditions of the employment offer. The HR reps compile a "start packet" for the first day of scheduled work for the newly hired individual. This packet will contain a number of forms to be completed and distributed. The start packet will include: completed application blank and original copy of the offer letter, payroll change notice form, job description, W-2 forms, benefits selection form, personnel requisition, relocation agreement (if appropriate), new employee checklist, parking permit, vehicle identification form, identification card, name badge, Employment Eligibility Verification (I-9 form), employee handbook and handbook receipt, notice of orientation, and any other documents necessary to fully process the person as a new employee with the organization. Next the newly hired individual is scheduled for an orientation session, which falls within the domain of training and development, a topic addressed in Chapter 9.

EMPLOYMENT INTERVIEWS

Notice that Figure 8.4 indicates a number of interviews with applicants that range from pre-screening, through screening, and into final departmental interviews. Interviewing is the most commonly used, yet least effective, form of job selection activity.[1] However, it is the least invasive form of eliciting information from the candidate to determine employment qualifications. One thing that affects interviewing effectiveness is that most managers are not thoroughly trained in interviewing techniques (addressed in Chapter 12). Individuals with hiring authority are not trained interviewers and there exists the potential legal scrutiny to be applied to the selection process. For these reasons, most organizations use the **structured interview** technique with job applicants. The structured interview is a listing of questions that is followed exactly by the interviewer without deviation. This ensures that all individuals involved in the selection process ask all applicants the exact same questions. Even though the interview is structured, it should be designed with **open-ended** questions, which are questions that require a non-programmed

structured interview—An interview that uses a questionnaire that does not permit interviewer deviation from the standard questions.

open-ended—A question that requires a response beyond a simple yes or no answer.

response form the person being interviewed. While the structured interview is safe and efficient, it is not an effective indicator of job performance potential; smart HR managers provide thorough communications training to hiring managers for them to develop skills in learning the most from a candidate despite a limited interviewing tool. This type of training includes active listening and observation skills used to process cues that lie beneath the spoken words of interviewees.

One of the first interviewing skills taught to operations managers is the importance of honesty in the interview process. Myopic managers sometimes have a tendency to be less than honest in describing the more difficult aspects of the work performed within certain positions. This a bad practice, as it sets up the newly hired individual for disappointment, once these unfavorable aspects of performing a job are realized. For this reason, human resource practitioners teach the interview technique known as the realistic job preview (RJP), in which the interviewer honestly and directly describes the good and less-than-favorable aspects associated with performing within a given position.

Highly trained interviewers may use a relatively effective technique called the **non-directive** interview. This is mostly reserved for executive and management position interviews, in which the questions are structured as to permit the interviewee to take the interview into various directions of conversation. This technique resembles an "if-then" decision tree, in which one question leads toward a tangent, and that tangent leads to another tangent, and so on. The advantage to this technique is that the process requires intense concentration on the part of the interviewee, during which the interviewer will have the advantage of observing unrehearsed non verbal and verbal cues.

Another form of interviewing technique that is reserved for trained interviewers is called the **stress interview**. The purpose of this technique is to

realistic job preview (RJP)—The disclosure of both favorable and unfavorable characteristics associated with a specific position.

non-directive—An interview process in which the answer to a previous question will determine the tangent of discussion in an interview.

stress interview—An interview process intentionally designed to determine how an interviewee reacts under stressful conditions.

HOSPITALITY NEWS *Three Sure-Fire Ways to Get More Revealing Answers during a Job Interview*

Getting a proper assessment of your job candidate is important during an interview. There are three sure-fire ways to get more revealing answers from potential employees:

1. Ask "Can you give me another example?" This question is always good to use, whether you're dissatisfied with the first answer and need more information, or you're fascinated by the answer and want to hear more.
2. Ask "What did you learn from that experience?" This question can give you a good

handle on a job candidate's judgment and maturity. And it buys you more thinking and planning time for your next question.
3. Be silent. Most people in social situations abhor silence and lulls in conversations. People will say a lot more just to fill the void. What they say could reveal a lot more about them.

Source: Hospitality News, August 2003, p. 7

observe the applicant's response to a stressful session of discussion. Security personnel may use this technique to test the ability of a candidate to decide courses of actions given scenarios that are posed in a stressful manner. The technique usually involves an interviewing panel of high-ranking individuals in an environment designed to replicate an interrogation scenario for the purpose of intimidating the interviewee. This is not a pleasant experience for most job candidates, but it is effective in eliciting programmed responses from previous intensive training during stressful situations. Interestingly, academic research institutions use this technique to interview prospective professors to determine their knowledge of the scientific method. They commonly use a panel of scholars, who will listen to a research presentation provided by the candidate and will proceed to challenge the scientific merits of the research for the purpose of witnessing how the candidate will respond to those challenges.

SUMMARY

This chapter has presented topics of information concerning the strategic approach to planning and executing recruitment and selection practices. It is clear at this juncture that both recruitment and selection strategies require a large investment of time and financial resources. However, the investment is worth while if it produces the result of hiring the most qualified individuals for positions within the organization. For this reason, the cost/benefit analysis is the means by which we evaluate these processes.

The process begins with planning for labor requirements in terms of positions that must be placed throughout the organization. Next there are recruiting strategies, which include the practice of internal and external sourcing. The purpose of this is to generate a pool of qualified candidates for each position vacancy. Once the pool is generated, the human resource representatives shift into selection mode by inviting applicants to engage in the preemployment processes. The result of these processes is a determination of the

---

HOSPITALITY NEWS *An Important Lesson on Hiring from a Major Airline*

More than any other industry, hospitality employees need to be individuals who care about others. How do you discover this quality in a job interview?

Here's an example of what is working for a major airline. When evaluating prospective employees, the airline brings all job candidates together in a room and asks each person to make a presentation. Everybody thinks that the company officials are evaluating the person making the presentation.

By evaluating the candidates in the audience to see who is attentive and supportive of the speaker, the company knows it would be getting someone who has the ability and disposition to care about others. If someone is self-absorbed or bored and has no empathy for the person who is up there struggling, then the company views that as a strong signal not to hire that person in the audience.

Source: Hospitality News, December 2002/January 2003, p. 20.

In the Real World . . . (Continued)

The past three months in the employment office has been a real eye-opening experience for you. You learned that while the activity levels of processing applicants were very hectic, the employment process actually follows a carefully constructed and constantly revised strategic plan. You learned that professional networking was the most effective recruitment tool for management and service-related jobs. You were also taught little tricks like watching the walking pace of a housekeeping candidate and leaving a pencil on the floor to see if the applicant would stop to pick it up. You found out that casino dealers actually auditioned for their jobs on the casino floor during live table games. You also learned that all background information other than reference checks was handled by areas outside the employment office, so that employment personnel would not have access to that information.

Perhaps the biggest lesson learned was that all that negative talk from the operating managers was the product of their own doing. The smart managers, like your former manager, communicated with the employment manager on a frequent basis. Those who chose to do that had no problems getting their employment needs taken care of. You couldn't help but wonder why those other operating managers didn't take the time to learn some of the tricks you had recently been taught. The other big thing you learned was the importance of balancing the legal requirements involved with the recruitment and selection process. The employment manager taught you about classified advertisement documentation and applicant flow tracking, as well as techniques for reference checks and chain of custody issues. You also noticed that the human resource director worked closely with the employment manager by meeting every morning and evening to revise strategies.

Finally, you realized that the past three months have just flown by because every day was filled with activity, from the time you arrived at the office until it was time to go home. Now you know why the director gives the employment manager the opportunity to switch to another specialty function each year.

One night, you are kicking back with a friend from an operations department. She says to you, "So how's the cake job in recruitment going?"

You reply, "You know, I always thought those guys had it easy, but now I not only know how hard they work, I also know why your manager never seems to have enough staff."

---

most qualified candidate for a position; however, the HR department conceals the specifics of the decision-making criteria to protect the organization from potential legal scrutiny and guards this information. The selection process concludes with a formal offer of employment, which begins the employment relationship between the newly hired individual and the organization.

DISCUSSION QUESTIONS

1. Consider the difference between a strategic approach to recruitment and selection vs. a reactive approach. Is there any way an organization can be effective and efficient in these processes by being reactive? Why or why not?

2. In your opinion, which function is more complex, the recruiting or selection process? Maybe you think they are equally intricate? Which is more important? Why?

3. Given the catch-22 nature of recruitment and selection, how would you choose to balance the statutory compliance issues with the potential negligence issues? Given your approach, is there any risk involved for the organization?

4. Why were a few managers able to replace all their vacant positions, while others sat around complaining about the employment office? What would you do if you were an operating manager with this organization?

KEY TERMS

application blank
chain of custody
external
  environment
external scan
independent
  contractor
internal audit
internal
  environment
involuntary
  separation
labor force
  population

labor market
labor pool
manpower
  planning
mission-driven
  organization
non-directive
  interview
open-ended
Polygraph
  Protection Act

pre-employment
promotions
racial bias
realistic job
  preview (RJP)
recruitment
reliability
selection
sourcing
strategic planning
  process

stress interview
structured
  interview
succession-
  planning
SWOT analysis
synergy
turnover
validity
voluntary
  separation

CHAPTER NINE
Training and Development Strategies

OBJECTIVES

By the end of this chapter, the reader will be able to:

1. Understand the needs analysis process preceding training activities.
2. Identify useful techniques for skills and knowledge training.
3. Recognize commonly used training terminology.
4. Understand the role of the human resource practitioner in the training process.

In The Real World

You are working in the human resource office for a large resort hotel alongside the training manager. The director of human resources enters the office to discuss a situation that recently came up in an executive committee meeting. She tells you and the training manager that the GM is concerned about declining scores in the Guest Service Index (GSI) ratings. She mentions that the GM is adamant that a new guest service training program is to be implemented immediately for all guest service personnel. The conversation goes as follows.

Tom, the training manager says to the director, "You know as well as I that there may not be a training need as the cause of the low GSI scores. So, we spend a portion of our budget to provide training to all the service personnel and then the scores will remain low, which means the GM will blame us for poor training."

"I know," replies the director, "I tried to talk some sense into the GM, but he is in panic mode and won't listen to me."

Tom responds with a little bit of anger. "This puts me in a bad situation, doesn't it?"

The director replies, "Look, take advantage of your new assistant here," as she points toward you. "You two can start to put together a training program, while conducting a needs analysis at the same time. If you come up with solid proof that this is being caused by some factor other than training, I will go to the mat for you. Will that work?"

Tom responds, "Oh, it will work all right." Then he addresses you. "You are about to learn the first rule about ways to keep your job as a training manager," he smiles.

INTRODUCTION

When we say the human resource manager is a manager's, manager, we refer to the role of the HR practitioner as a management educator. This may be one reason why we see so many active human resource managers teaching college management courses in addition to their regular jobs. Contrary to popular belief, the primary responsibility for training and development activities does not rest with the human resource department exclusively. Operating managers are quick to delegate this responsibility to HR practitioners, mostly because most operating managers are not well trained in training and development activities. For this reason, it is important for all managers to receive training in human resource management.

One area that is certainly the responsibility of the human resource practitioner is to be the "guardian" of workplace training budget allocations. This is done by continuously advising executive managers on the merits of training and development activities through cost/benefit analyses. Another primary responsibility for HR practitioners is to ensure that all training initiatives are based on learning gaps among the workers in the organization. This ensures that training programs are implemented only when training needs exist within the organization. There are too many examples of executive managers mandating training programs in response to perceived problems that are not real "training" problems. The result of this haphazard approach is the removal of training professionals from their positions, as well as lessened regard for the merits of training. The activity that ensures the implementation of training initiatives for the right reasons is referred to as needs analysis or needs assessment. This activity is described in detail later on in the chapter.

Providing appropriate levels of knowledge and skills is the essence of training in the workplace. The primary responsibility for technical and administrative training belongs to the immediate operating manager. In organizations where training managers are employed, the operating manager remains the person with ultimate responsibility for training workers. The objective of training is to provide a transfer of knowledge and skills to the worker. This means that the learning received during training is applied directly on the job. Effective training methods will have an impact on individuals' knowledge, skills, and behaviors. Modifying knowledge, skills, and behaviors is relatively easy when compared to the task of changing peoples' attitudes. It is not the purpose of training to change attitudes. Therefore, training should not be considered as a solution to solving attitude problems. In fact, the only time training is considered as a solution is when a training problem exists, such as hiring new employees without appropriate levels of technical skills. A training problem is defined as a negative gap between actual performance and standards for performance due to the knowledge and skills of a worker. This called a **learning gap**. A learning gap is identified through a process that is known as **needs analysis** or needs assessment.

learning gap—A negative gap between what the worker can do vs. what needs to be done in the job.

needs analysis—A process of assessing the existence of a training problem as defined by a learning gap through data collection and analysis. Also referred to as needs assessment.

problem—A negative gap between actual performance and standards for performance in an organization.

NEEDS ANALYSIS

The purpose of needs analysis is to determine whether or not a training problem exists in an organization. An examination of the symptoms of performance problems does this. The hardest part of the problem-solving process is to identify the root **problem** from a list of symptoms. Many top managers make the mistake of throwing training programs at problems that are either organizational or workplace engineering problems. The training program will inevitably fail to solve these types of problems, and the senior manager will often abandon all training and fire the training manager. When an appropriate needs analysis is performed, the analyst is looking for gaps between knowledge and skills on one hand and standards for performance on the other. This is called a competency gap (or learning gap). If a competency gap is identified, a training problem exists. Once the training problem is verified, trainers proceed to design, develop, implement, evaluate, and reinforce the training program.

THE ROLE OF THE TRAINING MANAGER

Any proactive human resource office will have a manager who is responsible for the oversight of all training programs. This individual should be a training professional, responsible for needs analysis, training design, training development, and training evaluation and reinforcement. This is not to say that the training manager conducts all of the training programs even though this person will facilitate many of the more sophisticated training sessions. Instead, the primary role of the training manager is to reinforce the value of training to the organization through cost/benefit analysis, as well as teaching training skills to operating managers, which is sometimes called "train the trainer" initiatives.

HOSPITALITY NEWS *The Benefits of a Structured Job Training Program*

Instituting a structured training program will help you run your business efficiently and ultimately keep more money in your pocket.

Studies show that employees not only need structure in the workplace environment, but actually want it. These same studies indicate that employees who have more structure in their jobs tend to be happier and remain longer with their company. Therefore, it is vital to institute a well structured training program as a solid foundation for employee-dependent businesses like those in the foodservice industry.

Carefully plan your training program. Throwing a new employee into the fire and expecting him/her to learn by doing creates numerous inefficiencies, which ultimately hurts your business. Prepare training programs so employees know exactly what is expected of them everyday. The program should be specific and include the time each task is to be started and approximately how long it should take. Training programs should clearly outline goals and expectations both for the teacher (experienced employee) and the student (new employee).

As part of your training program, employees hired to perform one specific job should also cross-train for other jobs so they can assist in other areas where workflow is experiencing a crunch. This makes you less vulnerable to staffing shortages and dependence on one employee, which ultimately keeps the power of control in the hands of you, the employer.

In addition, include as part of your training program (and regular job criteria) the mandatory use of daily and weekly task checklists which are vital for maintaining your company's high standards. Not only do checklists help maintain the standards of current employees, but they help during turnover when a new employee replaces an existing one. Without specific task checklists, job standards often slide, are improperly judged as unimportant and eliminated, or are just plain "forgotten" during employee turnover.

Finally, as part of a structured training program, a job description outlining specific requirements and expectations must be designed for each position. The new employee must read and sign a job description acknowledging comprehension, which will prevent any further misunderstandings about the job duties.

Instituting a properly structured training program is the key to developing an efficient labor force. As a direct result, you will build a strong and knowledgeable team that will remain loyal for years on end. If you are spending too much time and money on labor, or feel your workforce is not running on all cylinders, my advice is to start at the beginning to rectify the end result.

Source: Adam Eisen, *Hospitality News*, December 2002/January 2003, p. 13.

COMPETENCE

There are four stages of competence to be identified when assessing the knowledge and skills of workers to be trained. The four stages are listed in Figure 9.1.

TYPES OF TRAINING

Various training methods are used to deliver learning. The type of training required and the nature of the learning outcomes for the training program determine these methods. Most individuals are familiar with mechanical/ technical skills training, which are commonly called skills training programs. The most

> **Conscious-Competence:** The stage in which the skills are new to the worker, and the worker performs the skills slowly and deliberately.
> **Unconscious-Competence:** The stage in which the worker knows the skills well and can perform them quickly, without deliberate concentration.
> **Unconscious-Incompetence:** The stage that exists when the worker does not possess required knowledge and skills and does not know what knowledge and skills are required.
> **Conscious-Incompetence:** The stage in which the worker knows what learning is needed to perform the job and realizes the lack of knowledge and skills.

Figure 9.1. The Four Stages of Competence.

on-the-job training (OJT)—Training that takes place at the worksite during hours of operation.

commonly known method of implementing these programs is through training methods that occur at the actual worksite during the hours of operation. This method of training is **on the job training (OJT)**. Professional managers have a tendency to look unfavorably upon this method of imparting technical skills. This is not because the method is inappropriate, but instead because the implementation of the method is known to be haphazard in many organizations. For instance, if a manager says, "Just follow Mary and do what she does," this is an example of haphazard OJT. Appropriate OJT training involves all of the steps applied to other formats for training individuals in the mechanical skills of the job. If one were to step into a department and witness a trainer working alongside a trainee at the worksite, while using a checklist and providing methodical explanations of the standards being employed with each step of service, that witness would be observing a methodical approach to an OJT training process. Figure 9.2 provides categories of training content.

The next point of consideration is for the training manager to consider the delivery technique to be employed in the training facilitation. We already discussed one delivery method called OJT training. Others include classroom methods, which occur in an actual classroom setting, which is appropriate for most knowledge training program and certain types of skills training programs. Vestibule training takes place in an area away from where the actual skills will be practiced, such as a flight simulator, or the use of a new piece of

> **Orientation:** Provides information to new employees for the purpose of assimilating them into the culture of the organization. Classroom settings and tours are commonly used for this purpose.
> **Product knowledge:** Provides an overview of products and services provided by the organization. Classroom settings and tours are commonly used techniques.
> **Mechanical/technical skills:** Involves the use of hand-eye coordination to perform technical tasks. On the job training (OJT) methods combined with classroom and vestibule training are commonly used.
> **Administrative/technical skills:** Involves forms, paperwork, and computerized procedures for processing tasks within departments of the organization. Classroom settings are commonly used for this type of training.
> **Management/professional skills:** Includes abstract concepts associated with analysis and professional practices. Classroom settings are commonly used.

Figure 9.2. Categories of Training Content.

equipment. Geographic product knowledge training is often provided by tours or site visitations to the actual areas in which various functions are carried out. For instance, it is important for front-line hotel workers to be familiar with the layout of the resort property to advise guests on locations of certain recreational or amenity areas. Hence, as part of a new employee orientation, the facilitator will take the group of newly hired employees on a tour of the hotel facilities as part of their training. Figure 9.3 provides a listing of training delivery techniques.

DEVELOPMENT AND EVALUATION OF TRAINING

The learning objectives drive the development and implementation of the training program. The objectives state the intended outcomes of the training. The objectives should be specific, measurable, challenging, and attainable. It is equally important that the trainer and the learners clearly understand the objectives for every training program. It is also imperative for the trainer to convince the learners of the personal benefits that will be experienced as a result of the training program. This is called **WIFM**: What's In It for Me? This is an aspect crucial to delivering training to adult learners.

WIFM—What's In It For Me; the motivation for individuals to learn.

Classroom setting: The use of a meeting room away from the work area for knowledge and skills training.
On the job training (OJT): Training that occurs in the work area during "live" operations.
Vestibule training: A type of simulation training that occurs away from the work area for the practice of new skills.
Tours: Visits to areas of the organization to gain familiarity with operations in other departments as part of product knowledge training.
Combinations: Use two or more of the training techniques listed.

Figure 9.3. Training Delivery Techniques.

EVALUATION OF TRAINING PROGRAMS

All things are measurable; training outcomes are no exception. The criteria for measuring training include cost/benefit to the organization, accomplishment of objectives, and personal improvement in the behavior and morale of workers. All of these things can be measured in quantifiable and qualitative terms.

Repetition is the mother of learning. A trainer cannot be too repetitive. The golden rule of training is listed in Figure 9.4.

feedback—Evaluative information in response to a process.

Feedback is the breakfast of champions. Plenty of positive feedback should be provided throughout the training program. When in training mode, the supervisor is acting as a coach to the trainees.

PROVIDING EFFECTIVE TRAINING PROGRAMS

All training may be placed into three categories: knowledge training, skills training, and a combination of knowledge and skills training. There are two recommended formats for delivering knowledge training. The formats are listed in Figure 9.5.

Knowledge training is usually conducted in a classroom setting. Trainers should realize that most individuals have had a negative training or educational experience. For this reason, it is important for trainers to overcome initial resistance on the part of learners. The underlying objective of the trainer is to make every training session an enjoyable experience for the learners.

An understanding of adult learning theory developed by researcher Malcolm Knowles and others will enhance the ability of the trainer to provide programs and formats that appeal to learners.[1] The researchers contend that adults learn what they need to know and prefer experiential training techniques. One factor for consideration in training implementation is the element of participation. Trainers should try to get some form of participation early in the session. One rule states that the trainer should seek some form of audience response within the first five minutes of a presentation, even if the response is as simple as asking people to raise their hands. Trainers are cautioned to avoid training designs that force the audience into passive roles.

There are three keys to providing effective skills training: tell, show, and do. Tell the learners how to perform the task. Show the learners how to perform the task. Let the learners do the task for practice. The steps for effective skills training are listed in Figure 9.6.

EMPLOYEE ORIENTATIONS

New employee orientations fall within the category of knowledge training. For this reason the sessions are conducted in a classroom setting with a training facilitator, who is often the training manager herself. This process is an

```
Tell Them What You Are Going to Tell Them.
Tell Them What You Are Telling Them.
Then . . .
Tell Them What You Told Them.
```

Figure 9.4. Golden Rule of Training.

1. Introduction/overview. Preview activities, WIFM, learning objectives, announce test.
2. Content of the Program. Three to five main points, sub-points for each main point, facilitate questions and conversation, encourage participation.
3. Test Knowledge. Test for success. Provide positive feedback. If the test is an oral test, choose people who are likely to answer successfully.
4. Summary/conclusion. Review discussions, congratulate participants and provide preview of next session.

Figure 9.5. Knowledge Training (Four Steps).

exchange of the custody of the new employees from the domain of the employment manager over to the training manager. Most organizations benefit from two types of new employee orientation. The first may be referred to as a **general orientation** session(s), with the second phase referred to as the **department orientation** session(s). In many cases the department manager will act as the facilitator for department orientation programs.

general orientation—
An orientation for all newly hired employees.

department orientation—An orientation for all newly hired employees within a specific department.

assimilate—Adapt to an environment and its people.

The primary objective of orientation programs is to **assimilate** new employees into the organization. This means that the new employee should be made to feel comfortable with the new position by learning a little about the organization and the people who work there. The reason for assimilating new employees into the organization is to familiarize them with a strange new work environment. Think about the first day you spent in a new job or at a new school. The experience is almost hostile—you are entering an unknown environment that is full of people who are strangers to you. The first immediate response for most people in this situation is to refrain from returning to the uncomfortable environment. If they are persistent, however, the environment becomes comfortable to them in a short period of time. The purpose of the new employee orientation is to ease this transition into the organizational environment, by sharing information that explains the whats, whys, and wheres in an effort to make the new workers comfortable in their new positions within the organization.

Many individuals have experienced poorly run orientation programs. For instance, you arrive on your first day at a new job and someone places you in a room to watch boring old video programs, then sends you off to work. This type of orientation, although well intentioned, is a waste of training

1. Introduction/overview. Preview activities, WIFM, learning objectives, announce test.
2. Content of the Program. Three to five main points, sub-points for each main point, permit questions and conversation, encourage participation.
3. Demonstration. Show learners how to perform the skill, demonstrate a small segment of the skill application, work slowly and explain each step, repeat the demonstration if necessary.
4. Practice. Choose someone to demonstrate the task, test for success. Provide positive feedback. Choose people who are likely to perform the task properly. Facilitate self, peer, and trainer positive critique.
5. Summary/conclusion. Review discussions, congratulate participants, provide preview of next session.

Figure 9.6. Skills Training (Five Steps).

resource dollars: It fails to accomplish its main objective of assimilating the new worker into the organization. Proactive organizations will provide an entertaining orientation program for new workers that will be conducted by a dynamic and enthusiastic training professional. This is why in many cases the training manager will personally conduct the sessions. Figure 9.7 provides an orientation checklist for trainers to follow.

Pre-orientation reception for new workers to meet and greet	30 minutes
Welcome, not everyone who applied is here today—you are special	10 minutes
About our organization	15 minutes
Our history and traditions	15 minutes
Where we are today and where we will be tomorrow—mission and vision	15 minutes
How we do it and how you can help	10 minutes
What's in it for you—oh the places you can go with us, if you want to . . .	10 minutes
Refreshment break	15 minutes
Your compensation	10 minutes
Your benefit package	10 minutes
Our objectives	10 minutes
Our strategies and tactics	10 minutes
Our policies	10 minutes
Our standards and procedures	10 minutes
Our rules	10 minutes
Refreshment break	15 minutes
Meet our leaders	30 minutes
Our divisions and departments	30 minutes
Lunch with the leaders	45 minutes
A few learning activities	30 minutes
The tour	90 minutes
Meet your department/division staff members	As needed
Reconvene, conclusions, and the next steps in the process for everyone	20 minutes

Figure 9.7. Staff Member Orientation Checklist.

Notice that the session begins with a small reception that should be attended by executive leaders, department managers and the entire human resource office staff. It is important to note that at this point, the HR people have been working with the newly hired workers through the employment process, so they are familiar with the new employees. This is an ideal opportunity for individuals who are known to the staff members to introduce them to others who work within the organization. Remember that every activity that occurs during a new employee orientation is designed to make the new workers comfortable with the people and environment of the organization. This is a powerful first step.

At the conclusion of the reception, the new employees are invited into a meeting room to begin the session. The room should be comfortably arranged to provide facilitative interaction. The trainer will begin the session with an **icebreaker** activity to facilitate participation among attendees. The orientation session then moves toward items that are of benefit to the new employees. These items are at the top of the training agenda to reinforce the WIFM associated with employment in the organization.

icebreaker—A training technique used to set the "stage" as part of a training program.

The amount of time spent on each agenda item will vary by organizations. Figure 9.7 allocates times that are typically allocated to each item. There is a tendency for orientation programs to hit participants with **information overload**, sharing everything there is to know about the employment relationship. The facilitator will address this issue at the beginning of the session, explaining that it is not necessary for participants to know the information, but to gain a feel for the issues of employment. The facilitator might use the employee handbook to walk the participants through visual representations of the topics, noting that when the time is appropriate, staff members may find the information in the locations noted in the handbook.

information overload—Large amounts of information that cannot be absorbed in the prescribed time period.

At a point in the orientation presentation just before the luncheon, executive leaders of the organization may be invited to address the group. Afterward, these leaders may attend the luncheon, strategically placed at tables to provide interaction with the new workers during the meal. This is a nice way to create familiarity with organizational leaders, especially in our business, which is a "people" business.

The orientation should conclude with the next steps for employee assimilation into the organization. One way to do this is to have the department managers take the new workers to the department to begin an orientation on that level. You may notice that this employee orientation scenario requires a healthy budget allocation from the training resources. However, as we say in the business, "You never get a second chance to make a first impression." Since these new workers represent "human capital" to the organization, they are worthy of an initial investment in their comfort with the organizational environment.

DEVELOPMENT PROGRAMS

In keeping with the human capital aspect of the employment relationship, proactive organizations take steps to identify talented workers for potential career advancement with the organization. The identification process occurs through performance appraisals, which are discussed in Chapter 11. Performance appraisals are just one aspect of performance management systems, which combine strategic planning initiatives with performance evaluation criteria. One aspect of this process is to identify individuals within the workplace

HOSPITALITY NEWS *You've Got a New Hire*

Hiring and keeping good employees is one of the greatest challenges facing operators today. To ensure a good transition into your business, managers can do a number of things to help motivate the new employee.

First, personally introduce each new hire to your staff. Explain the person's qualifications and how you see him or her as a real asset to your organization.

During the training phase, always allow enough time for directions on how to complete a job. Ask the new employee to repeat your instructions or demonstrate the duty so that you are sure the employee understands precisely what is expected.

Allow your employee to make mistakes. The two best teachers are trial and error. Let the employee know that making mistakes is just part of the learning curve and that we all make mistakes before we're fully trained.

When making the initial assignments, don't give employees all their duties at once. This gives you the power to reward excellent performance with the assigning of new tasks.

Encourage feedback. Make sure new employees understand where they should turn if they are having trouble with an assignment or don't remember how to perform a task.

Watch for ways to reward your new employees. When they have mastered a skill, make sure that you congratulate them and thank them for being such fast learners. It has been reported that an average employee needs positive feedback at least once every seven work days. For new employees, it is much more frequent than that.

Be very careful about whom you choose to work closely with the newcomer. Assign certain people from various levels to spend orientation time with your new hire. Make it clear that everyone wants this new employee to succeed.

Meet frequently with your new hire. Probe for signs of rough spots. Listen to any frustrations or concerns that the individual may have and then develop a plan immediately to resolve the problem.

When criticism must be given, make sure that you don't talk down to your employee. Depersonalize the issue. Say something like, "Let me show you a way that might work."

Source: Hospitality News, May 2003, p. 30.

---

succession-planning—Career development planning that combines forecasted promotional opportunities and development activities required to prepare a person to work at a more advanced level.

development—Training to prepare individuals for career advancement opportunities.

management development—Training for advancement in management positions.

who possess the desire and potential to pursue career advancement with the organization.

The process of combining career advancement potential with organizational advancement opportunities is referred to as a **succession-planning** program. Succession planning activities use statistical forecasts to estimate timelines for potential employee advancement, which provides windows of opportunity to prepare workers for future advancement. The process of imparting knowledge, skills and abilities for future career advancement opportunities is known as employee **development**. Since most of the advancement opportunities in our industry exist within the realm of hospitality and tourism management, most of these programs fall within the realm of **management development** programs.

Proactive organizations provide continuous training to individuals with the potential for advancement through management development programs aimed at preparing line personnel, supervisors, and managers for next-level positions. Succession plans articulate the specific competencies required for each promotional opportunity, with the attrition forecast providing timelines for anticipated promotional vacancies. Workers who are on an advancement track

HOSPITALITY NEWS *Reasons New Managers and Executives Fail*

A recent study of 1,000 executives shows that in the first 18 months in a new position, four out of every ten managers and executives are terminated, resign, or get poor performance reviews. The survey findings reveal the top six reasons they fail:

1. Performance expectations are unclear.
2. They can't make tough decisions.
3. The learning curve to perfect their new job responsibilities is longer than expected.
4. They haven't built relationships with other personnel and the team they manage.
5. They simply don't understand the politics of the company.
6. The balance between personal and work lives is not in order.

Source: Hospitality News, August 2003, p. 24.

seek to demonstrate the attainment of promotional competencies to place themselves as prepared candidates for anticipated promotional opportunities.

Development programs may be conducted within in the organization (in house) or through external training activities. Most organizations provide for a combination of internal and external training development programs. There are other aspects to development training in addition to management development programs. In keeping with the human capital approach to worker development, any set of competencies that enhances the worker as a holistic being may be considered to be a form of development. Some organizations refer to these types of programs as **human development** programs. For instance, certain quick service restaurants that hire very young workers will help those workers to earn college degrees. While those college degrees may not be in the field of restaurant management, these programs are offered as employee retention strategies, with the organization benefiting from the human development aspects attributed to the workers as they progress through their academic training.

human development— Holistic training that adds to the person as a being.

SUMMARY

This chapter has presented information for human resource practitioners to use in developing training programs. The steps for conducting training sessions have been outlined in the chapter. While needs assessment is vital to identifying a training problem, there is one more important element for supervisors to practice.

Human resource practitioners are not the sole source of training within the organization. Training is the primary responsibility of every manager in that organization. The training manager is a professional who facilitates training needs assessment, training program design and development, training evaluation and **reinforcement**, and cost/benefit analyses to justify the investment of organizational resources into training activities. The training manager also oversees the new employee orientation process, which assimilates new workers into the organization. Finally, the training manager administers succession planning, management development, and human development

reinforcement— Method to habituate new knowledge and skills to reach a state of unconscious competence.

programs to enhance the potential of existing human capital within the organization.

The training isn't over at the completion of a program. One reason that operating managers have the primary responsibility for training is that the training must be continuously reinforced in daily operations. Reinforcement involves transfer of learning into habitual behaviors. Operations managers ensure that the skills learned in the training programs are transferred to the daily performance of tasks and activities. This is known as the follow-up or reinforcement process for the training program. The goal of reinforcement is

---

In the Real World . . . (Continued)

As soon as the HR director leaves the training manager's office, you say to Tom, "Were you really getting angry at her?"

Tom replies, "Naw, this is a trick that she taught me, actually. Sometimes you challenge your leader's support to make sure she will back you up. I know if she could have talked sense into the GM, she would have. Sometimes it takes a few days for the GM to come to his senses. This plan just buys us a little time," Tom smirks.

"Let me show you a few tricks," he continues "First, always have a "plan in the pocket."

"What does that mean?" you ask.

"Well," since our most vulnerable measurement in this business is guest service, you always have to have a new way to teach it on the drawing board. I have been developing my next program for a while now. But, you don't tell anyone that you have this program "in your pocket"; that way they will give you a reasonable period of time to come up with one from scratch." He continues, "The second trick for a training manager is to be keenly aware of what is going on in the operating departments." He says, "I walk around the property every day and talk with the staff. I know exactly where the source of this guest service problem lies."

"Where is the problem?"

"It's at the front desk during check-in and check-out." He continues, "The controller ordered a new software package that forces the desk agents to use nine screens for this process, compared with three screens used with the old system. This is causing the guests to wait three times longer for each check-in and check-out process."

"Why didn't you just tell the director that?" you ask.

"Because," Tom says, "I have to be able to prove it. Otherwise, I am pitting our director against the controller, and she wouldn't win the argument without proof."

You ask the obvious question, "How are we going to prove it?"

Tom replies, "I have two words for you: needs analysis. That is always the training manager's proof of problematic causes."

After working through the needs analysis process for a few days, you and Tom complete a report that offers two solutions to the GSI problem. The first proposal identifies Tom's "new" training program and the second proposal suggests taking a "systems approach" to fixing the glitch in the new software. The human resource director presents the proposals at the next executive committee meeting and immediately visits the training office at the conclusion of that meeting.

You and Tom are sitting there as she walks in with a broad smile on her face. "Tom" she says, "You did it again! The AGM confirmed your findings and the focus is totally on the systems problems." She continues, "The GM will stop by to visit you later today to apologize for putting you on this project and to thank you for your analysis." She concludes with that knowing smile, "Now I am going to lunch with the controller to commiserate with him for being the focus of the GM's wrath this morning."

to habituate the news skills. Once a skill becomes a habit, the worker performs it in a state of unconscious competence.

DISCUSSION QUESTIONS

1. Usually the training department in an organization is the first to go when financial times get tough. Is this a wise decision? Why or why not?

2. Sometimes a general manager will respond to poor scores on a guest service index (GSI) with a mandate for new training. Would you do this, or would you want more information first? If so, what would you want to know?

3. It is no secret that there is a labor crisis in the hospitality industry as well as certain other service sectors. Could training play a role in lessening the crisis? How?

4. Most operations managers think that training is a waste of money. How might you convince them otherwise?

KEY TERMS

administrative/
  technical skills
assimilate
classroom setting
conscious-
  competence
conscious-
  incompetence
department
  orientation
development

feedback
general
  orientation
human
  development
icebreaker
information
  overload
learning gap
management
  development

mechanical/tech-
  nical skills
needs analysis
on-the-job
  training (OJT)
orientation
problem
product
  knowledge
reinforcement

succession-
  planning
tours
unconscious-
  competence
unconscious-
  incompetence
vestibule training
WIFM

CHAPTER TEN

Employee Retention Strategies

OBJECTIVES

By the end of this chapter, the reader will be able to:

1. Understand the strategic nature of retention practices.
2. Comprehend the basics of compensation practices.
3. Recognize the different types of benefits offered in most organizations.
4. Understand the basic provisions of the FLSA.

In the Real World . . .

You are working as a clerical assistant in the human resource office for a large resort. You have just finished a three-month assignment with the employment manager to assist with their recruiting and selection process. You arrive for work this morning to find the director of human resources in a meeting with the compensation manager and the director of housekeeping. They invite you to join them.

It turns out that they are discussing alternative compensation plans for guestroom attendants. Currently, the attendants are paid an hourly wage. The housekeeping director believes that wages just encourage workers to put in "time." She wants to restructure the compensation format to encourage productivity. She starts by saying, "Look, our standard is 16 good rooms per attendant per day. This is an allocation of 30 minutes per room. I have mostly good people, and I know they can clean a room in less time. But why should they? If they produced clean rooms at a faster rate, their hours would be cut and they would be penalized by lower wages." She finishes by saying, "There has to be another way to reward good workers."

The HR director has been listening closely, and matter-of-factly says, "This sounds interesting. Give us a few days to come up with something for you."

The housekeeping director leaves and it is just you, the compensation manager and the HR director in the office. When the housekeeper is out of earshot, the HR director says, "This is exciting! I have been waiting for someone to get creative in one of these departments." She looks at you both. "We have a golden opportunity to do an experiment here."

You say, "I guess this will be my new project."

The director smiles, as she replies. "What a wonderful opportunity for you to be creative."

INTRODUCTION

Considering the topics addressed in prior chapters, the organization spends a good deal of financial resources to recruit, select, train and develop its employees. Some organizations throw these investments away by failing to realize that simple management activities are required to maintain a staff of satisfied employees. When employees become dissatisfied, they find jobs in other organizations. They sometimes realize later that they had better work lives with the former employer, but by that time it is too late. The particularly sad fact is that the best employees will be the first to leave. In such a case, the organization has spent large dollars in staffing and training activities, only to realize later that they are retaining mediocre workers at best.

When this happens, the shareholders put pressure on the organization to limit its allocation of recruiting and training budgets, since it becomes evident that the managers are wasting money on selecting and developing the skills of employees who then go to work for the competition. How many times have general managers been heard to say, "Why should we spend money on employees to prepare them to go work somewhere else?" This is dangerous thinking that serves as an incentive for talented human resource practitioners to seek positions with more proactive organizations. This spiral continues as the HR personnel are replaced with cut-rate semitrained practitioners. In such a case, the company controller proudly notifies the shareholders that expenses in the human resource office have been cut in half and that the training budget has been eliminated altogether.

The shortsighted shareholders applaud the reductions of these expenses and look forward to handsome financial returns at the end of the fiscal year. The general manager and company controller earn attractive bonuses for their cost-cutting activities that year. While all appears to be well in the executive offices, there is trouble brewing down by the employee entrance. Fewer individuals are applying for positions than before, and those who do apply seem to be the least talented people in town. Personnel requisitions for position placement remain open for months and operating managers are becoming frustrated with chronic shortages of staff. Since there is no training, many of the new hires quit their jobs within a few days. Those who are left are not well versed in steps of service. At the same time these managers feel like they are being held hostage by the remaining staff and become lax in the enforcement of standards for fear of not being able to find replacements for underperforming employees. Guest complaints continue to rise, and guest satisfaction scores start to fall to all-time lows. The marketing staff responds to this by discounting rates charged to customers. The upscale guests start to realize that the organization is catering to the riffraff and take their business somewhere else, where they may enjoy the levels of service that they are willing to pay for.

One year later the general manager and controller are fired for poor performance. Replacements are brought in. Maybe they know how to fix the operation, or maybe they don't. If they don't, they are gone in the following year, and the spiral continues until the value of the business asset is so low that it is sold to a new corporate entity for half of its original value.

All of this can happen when managers do not understand the simple steps in retaining the best and brightest workers. And it only takes a couple of years for an excellent hospitality organization to become another acquisition statistic.

RETENTION

Employee retention—Retaining valuable workers in the organization.

Employee turnover—Combined voluntary and involuntary separation from an organization.

Employee retention is an outcome associated with solid management practices and proactive decision-making activities. The flip side of retention is **employee turnover**, which is the total number of voluntary and involuntary separations from the organization divided by the total numbers of employees. Turnover rates are reported in percentages of the total employee population for a specific organization. The hospitality industry is notorious for high levels of employee turnover relative to other industries. Numerous studies report broad arrays of turnover statistics with very little numerical corroboration among studies. Suffice it to say that most hospitality organizations have annual turnover rates that are between 50 percent and 100 percent of the total employee population. An organization with an annual turnover rate of 100 percent is theoretically replacing the equivalent of every position in the organization once. Again, studies on the cost of turnover vary drastically, so for our purposes, let's say the cost of turnover for a position is about equal to one year of salary and benefits for that position. Most studies arrive at these figures by calculating direct costs along with hidden costs that begin once an employee decides to leave a position within an organization. Another way of viewing the cost of turnover is to place a flat dollar rate of about $18,000 for a

HOSPITALITY NEWS *Employee Retention*

The food service industry in general has a higher turnover rate than most other industries. There are, however, a number of questions that you might need to ask if you are having trouble keeping your employees.

Do problems go unresolved? Do your employees have fun on the job? Compared to similar operations, how do your compensation and benefits compare? Is there a lack of management direction? Do employees get praised enough for the food work they do? Are employees treated fairly? Are there future opportunities for those who stay on the job? Is the training adequate?

Many successful operators believe that, "You may not stay with us forever, but while you are here, we want it to be a good experience for both of us." What are you and your managers doing to help employees have a good experience? When employees quit, do you try to find out why they're leaving?

Source: Hospitality News, October 2002, p. 17

service position and about $35,000 for a management position. Hence, an organization with 1000 employees and a turnover rate of 50 percent is spending quite a bit of money to replace workers each year.

There are three management areas that may contribute to the retention of good workers. First are management policies concerning compensation and benefits afforded to workers within the organization. Second are professional management practices, which have been discussed in prior chapters, but are worthy of discussion once again. Third are management policies and practices concerning employee incentives to perform above the standards set by the organization. These three strategic approaches to management contribute to employee satisfaction, which produces the outcome of employee retention.

It is important to note that we use the term *satisfaction*, not happiness. The goal is not necessarily to make employees happy, just satisfied. There are numerous scenarios in which customers witness very happy employees who are very unproductive. Visit certain government agencies intended to provide services to the public and it will sound like there is a party going on behind the partition that separates the staff area from the public area. While the employees in the back sound very happy, the one or two at the counter take forever to process your mail, or renew your vehicle registration, while they make sure you get a dose of "attitude" before you are permitted to leave the premises.

COMPENSATION

Compensation may be defined as consideration (money paid) for services rendered through the employment relationship. Thus, the company pays employees to provide work that is aimed at the accomplishment of the objectives of the organization. Compensation may be broken down into two categories; **direct compensation** and **indirect compensation**. Direct compensation includes pay and financial incentives as consideration for work that is performed through the employment relationship. Indirect compensation may be

Compensation—Pay and benefits afforded to workers in an organization.

Direct compensation—Wages, salaries, piece rate, or commissions paid to employees on a regular basis.

Indirect compensation—Benefits and perquisites.

Wages—Pay for time worked, usually by the hour.

Salary—Standard rate of pay from period to period.

Piece rate—Pay per units produced.

modified piece rate—Stratified payment for varying levels of production. Also referred to as differential or stratified piece rate.

incentive pay—Pay for performance.

commissions—Percentage of production revenues, usually sales.

bonuses—Lump sum payments for performance.

benefits—Rewards for organizational membership.

perquisites—Rewards beyond benefits for organizational membership, usually for executive personnel.

considered to be those aspects of compensation that are not paid directly through dollars, but provide something of value to the worker in return for being employed by the company.

There are a few ways to provide compensation in the form of pay to employees. One is to provide **wages**, which are calculated based on time worked, usually by the hour. Another form of pay is called **salary**, which is calculated at a consistent rate from pay period to pay period. **Piece rate** is payment based on units of production. Stratified unit production payment is referred to as **modified piece rate**. This is also referred to as stratified or differential piece rate. **Incentive pay** includes **commissions** and **bonuses** based on levels of performance.

The most common form of indirect compensations involves employee **benefits** and **perquisites**, commonly referred to as perks. Benefits reward employees for membership in the organization and include items such as insurance, and time off benefits. Perquisites are luxury items intended to reward employees for organizational membership, such as company cars, country club memberships and access to recreational facilities.

The two major external factors that influence compensation strategies are labor market conditions involving the supply and demand of KSAAs, and the compensation practices of competitors in the industry and geographic locations. Internally, there are three potential factors influencing compensation strategies. These are the commitment to be a wage and salary leader, laggard, or follower. A wage leader strategy involves being the best paying organization relative to the competitors, while the laggard intentionally pays below the competitive rate. The wage follower will match the average rate of pay among the competition for each employment position. There is no right or wrong strategy, as the mission of the organization should drive compensation practices. If the mission for an organization is to be the best in its field, a wage leadership strategy would be appropriate. If the mission articulates the purpose of providing the lowest prices in town, then a laggard strategy may be appropriate. Of course, other internal factors will influence the ability of an organization to adopt a compensation strategy. For instance, a startup or-

ganization may lack the financing to adopt a wage leadership strategy. The combination of payment and benefits constitute labor dollars as an expense item for the organization. The hospitality industry is noted for being labor intensive, as the single highest expense in all sectors of the industry is **labor dollars**. For instance, the labor dollars for a luxury hotel could easily be in the range of 50 percent of revenues, vs. a retail establishment in which less than 10 percent of revenues will be labor expenses.

labor dollars—Payroll and benefit dollars spent on workers.

Legal Factors

The major federal statute that affects compensation practices is called the **Fair Labor Standards Act (FLSA)** (1938). This law applies to private and public sector organizations with two or more employees and gross revenues of $500,000 or more. Agricultural workers are exempt from the law, as are organizations doing business in states with more stringent requirements than the provisions of the FLSA. This law provides for the federal **minimum wage**, overtime payment provisions and the protection of child labor (those under the age of 18) in the workplace.

Fair Labor Standards Act (FLSA)—Federal law that provides minimum wage, overtime payment provisions, and child labor restrictions.

 In states that do not provide more stringent standards, the federal minimum wage is the lowest hourly wage permitted by law to be paid to workers. Over recent years, Congress has passed increases to the federal minimum wage, which is currently at $5.15 per hour. In the case of tipped employees, the minimum wage provisions provide for reductions in the actual amount paid per hour to workers in the form of a **tip credit**, based on rules of the state in which the organization is doing business. If an employer chooses to take a tip credit against a minimum wage of $5.15 per hour, the actual amount paid to servers and bartenders would be $2.13 per hour. When the minimum wage is increased, the tip credit amount will increase. For instance, Florida uses a 40 percent tip credit amount. Hence, when the minimum wage was $3.80, the tip credit amount was $2.09. Prior to that, the minimum wage was $3.35, and the tip credit amount was $2.01 per hour.

minimum wage—The lowest hourly wage permitted by law.

tip credit—The difference between actual pay and minimum wage permitted for tipped personnel within a given state.

 The FLSA provides for overtime wages paid to workers who exceed 40 hours of work in a given week. The overtime rate is 1.5 times the hourly rate. So, a worker who earns $5.15 per hour would begin to earn $7.73 per hour during the 41st hour of work in a given week. Workers who are eligible for overtime payment are classified as **nonexempt** employees. Some managers wrongly believe that any person who is paid a salary does not have to be paid overtime at a rate of time and a half. The truth is there are salaried-exempt positions and salaried-nonexempt positions. In order to preclude an individual worker from overtime payment, that person must meet the exemption standards established by the FLSA. Table 10.1 shows a listing of **exempt** status provisions.

nonexempt—Not exempt from overtime payment.

exempt—Exempt from overtime payment.

 The majority of management and supervisory overtime payment exemptions fall within the **executive exemption** category. The applications of this exempt status in organizations have been challenged by the Department of Labor (DOL), which oversees the enforcement of the FLSA. Burger King and Marriott are examples of organizations that have been involved in precedent-setting cases resulting in stricter corporate policies to substantiate executive exemption status.

executive exemption—Exempt status for management workers.

 The **professional exemption** is reserved for individuals who perform work that requires professional level diagnosis and decision-making that is

professional exemption—Exempt status for professional workers.

Table 10.1 Exempt Status Provisions

Exempt Status	Coverage
Executive exemption	Supervises at least two individuals, at least 40 percent of the total work time. Does not perform the work of subordinates during subordinates at least 40 percent of the work time. Salary is equal to at least 1.5 times the wages of those supervised.
Professional exemption	Work is of a nature that is autonomous and beyond the scope of supervision. Makes decisions requiring high-level expertise.
Administrative exemption	Works in an unsupervised capacity performing duties that are administrative in nature.

comp time—
Compensatory time off in lieu of overtime payment.

not supervised by other professional individuals. An information technology manager may fall within this description, since she performs high-level work on an autonomous level, even though she may not supervise other individuals. The administrative exemption is reserved for those individuals who do not meet the professional designation, but do perform duties that are beyond perfunctory functions and are not supervised. Some organizations claim this status for top-level executive administrative assistants.

A common practice in organizations is to offer **comp time** in lieu of time and a half payment for overtime hours worked. From a legal perspective, the use of comp time in the private sector is not permitted unless the paid time off is at a rate of 1.5 the wage and is awarded in the same week as the overtime work was performed.

Administration

compensation man-ager—Specialist who administers compensation and benefit programs.

The **compensation manager** is the specialist who oversees compensation and benefits administration in the human resource department for an organization. This person is responsible for the strategic direction of compensation practices, as well as the administrator for all plans that fall within that jurisdiction. The compensation manager monitors the labor market supply/demand and competitive practices of other organizations representing local hospitality organiza-

---

HOSPITALITY NEWS *Attention Managers: Here's What Most Employees Want*

Most employees want their employer to:

1. Treat them as a partner, respect and involve them, and share information.
2. Provide them with important challenges in their careers.
3. Value their contributions.
4. Let them know what they do is appreciated.
5. Use their suggestions and ideas, and give them credit.

6. Demonstrate a caring attitude. Be fair and stand by them when something happens, such as a personal crisis.
7. Hold people accountable for what they commit to and let them know that they are a necessary part of a team.
8. Pay them fairly and appropriately.

Source: Hospitality News, November 2002, p. 7.

tions and geographic location. From an internal perspective, the compensation manager evaluates the relative worth of position functions in organizations for various benchmark jobs, which are those performed by large numbers of workers. The compensation manager establishes pay grades for management and non-management workers based on job analysis criteria. For instance, the compensation manager may categorize management positions based on levels of supervision, scope of responsibility, decision-making impacts, confidentiality requirements, and other factors that demonstrate contributions to the organization. By performing this process the compensation manager is able to stratify positions from the executive level to the supervisory level.

The same process would occur for every other position category within the organization. For each position category, there would be a worksheet that calculates the value of positions within the category to the performance of the organization. Next, the compensation manager will establish pay grades for each position category that include low, middle, and maximum ranges. The compensation manager will measure the pay practices of the competition through annual participation in a number of wage and salary surveys, administered by professional organizations or local universities. Participation in these surveys is anonymous, as to not disclose the information for specific competitors, while providing statistics of low, middle, and high compensation levels. This is the criterion that would be used for a compensation strategy aimed at leader, follower, or laggard policies within an organization.

Table 10.2 provides a sample of a pay grade chart for hourly administrative personnel within a hospitality organization. The job category in this case is that of an administrator, who could be any position from a clerical worker up to an executive level administrator. All of these positions would be nonexempt, as they do not meet any of the criteria for **administrative exemption** status. The grade numbers for each position determine the administrator level assigned to workers in this category, ranging from smallest to largest. So, as administrator I could be an input clerk, housekeeping or security dispatcher, or a reception worker. The administrator II would require slightly more responsibility than the grade below to include functions such as guest services agent, front desk agent, or payroll clerk. A person at the administrator II level would perform higher level administrative functions such as administrative assistant, general cashier, or concierge. The top level would be reserved for the highest level of administrative work, while remaining in a nonexempt category such as supervisors, purchasing agents, storeroom supervisors, or executive assistants.

Note that Table 10.2 provides minimum, mid-range and maximum pay rates for each category. If a person worked at a job within the administrator I category for a number of years and achieved an hourly rate of $8.50, it is

administrative exemption—Exempt status for high-level administrators.

Table 10.2   Sample Pay Grade Chart

Position Category	Minimum	Mid-range	Maximum
Administrator IV	$13.50	$14.50	$18.00
Administrator III	$11.00	$12.00	$13.00
Administrator II	$8.75	$9.75	$10.75
Administrator I	$6.50	$7.50	$8.50

maturity curve—The curve of experience in which proficiency exceeds the value of the position to the organization.

feasible that the person would perform at levels that exceed the expectation for the position based on experience. In this case the **maturity curve** of the worker exceeds the maximum pay rate for the position, which means that person's ability is beyond the value of the position to the organization. While this seems inappropriate, there have been scenarios in hotels, for instance, where housekeeping personnel who received annual seniority pay increases ended up earning in excess of $15.00 per hour. At some point, the value of the work being provided to the organization will reach a cap, even though the maturity curve of the worker will be beyond the level of those coworkers receiving the same rate of pay. The only alternative for such a worker is to move up to a function that possesses higher value to the organization. This is the premise behind pay grade analysis.

Suppose the organization decides to increase the starting wage for the administrator I category, due to heavy competition in the labor market to attract qualified applicants for positions in that category. Let's say the starting wage goes up to $7.00 per hour. The organization hires new individuals at this rate and they find themselves working alongside others who have been in the position for over one year making only $7.50 per hour. The workers with more seniority would be likely to find this situation to be unfair. This would be an example of **wage compression**, in which an increase to the minimum creates a smaller gap between the start rate and the mid-range rate for the same job. The next question may be, "How does the mid-range worker know what the new worker is making?" There are two policies regarding compensation systems. One approach is to have an **open pay system** in which pay grades are openly communicated to the employees. Or an organization may choose to have a **closed pay system**, in which wages and salaries are classified information available only to those with a need to know. Most HR practitioners will jokingly tell you that regardless of the system, people will know what the others are earning.

wage compression—Shrinking gap between newly increased start wage rates and pre-existing middle rates.

open pay system—An open communication policy regarding pay and benefits in an organization.

closed pay system—Guarded communication of wages and salaries restricted to those with a need to know the information.

There is a number of justifications for pay increases that may vary by company policies. One method of awarding pay increases would be to base them on **seniority**, or length of employment with the organization. In this case, the organization is rewarding longevity. This is a common scenario in companies that have employee union representation.

seniority—Amount of continuous service in a position or an organization.

Another strategy would be to award increases based on **merit**. This is a pay-for-performance strategy that requires a great deal of administrative work to ensure equity and avoid claims of discrimination. Some organizations look at economic indicators such as the consumer price index (CPI) to be used as a barometer to award **cost of living allowances (COLA)**, which are increases in pay to keep pace with the buying power in the economy.

merit—Wage and salary increases based on performance measures.

cost of living allowances (COLA)—Increases in wages and salaries based on economic indicators.

From a motivational perspective, it is important to note that compensation means different things to different people. The obvious meaning of pay systems is the economic ability to obtain the necessities, and perhaps a few luxuries, in life. Beyond that, there is a psychosocial aspect of compensation that equates to social status, a means of keeping up with the Joneses, or feelings of psychological self-worth. For those individuals who value personal achievement, growth may be a motivational factor associated with compensation levels. When the scholars tell us that money is not a motivator, what they are really saying is that the meaning of money motivates people beyond the money in and of itself.

EMPLOYEE BENEFITS

Employee benefits are forms of indirect compensation usually made to full-time workers as rewards for membership in the organization. There are two types of benefits: those that are voluntary on the part of the employer to provide to employees, and those that are mandatory as determined by law. Table 10.3 provides a comparison of **mandatory** and **voluntary benefits** in the workplace.

Mandatory Benefits

It is clear from Table 10.3 that most benefits provided to employees are voluntary on the part of employers. However, the mandatory benefits serve an appropriate purpose in safeguarding the individuals in the workplace. **Workers'**

voluntary benefits—Those benefits that the organization chooses to provide for employees.

mandatory benefits—Those benefits that the government requires organizations to provide for employees.

workers' compensation—Medical, disability, and death benefit insurance for work-related injuries or illnesses.

Table 10.3 Comparison of Benefits

Mandatory Benefits	Voluntary Benefits
Workers' compensation	Health insurance
Unemployment compensation	Life insurance
Social Security	Disability insurance
COBRA benefits	IRA, 401k, Keogh plans
FMLA	Leaves of absence
	Paid holidays
	Paid vacations
	Paid sick and personal time
	Education assistance
	Child care assistance
	ESOP, stock options, and profit sharing
	Social and recreational benefits

compensation is a benefit that provides medical care, disability payments and death benefits resulting from a work-related accident or illness. The employer hires a workers' compensation insurance carrier to provide these benefits. Workers' compensation laws vary by state; however, in most states the premium paid to the insurance carrier is based on four years of claim experience. For this reason, it is in the interests of organizations to take proactive approaches for workplace safety. Workers' compensation premiums are often in the 100s of thousands of dollars range for medium-size hospitality organizations. Another factor influencing workers' comp premiums is the risk assigned by industry. Most areas of the hospitality industry are considered to be high-risk workplaces, according to workers' compensation actuaries.

unemployment compensation—A portion of wages or salaries paid from a state insurance funds to individuals who have lost their jobs due to layoffs or company closures.

Unemployment compensation is also a state-enforced mandatory benefit that provides compensation payments to individuals who are unemployed due to layoffs or other downsizing situations. Again, the rate paid to most states is based on claims experience; hence, human resource managers enforce strict policies concerning involuntary separations from the organization, and zealously defend the company in compensation claims disputes.

Social Security benefits—Federal government fund that provides supplemental benefits to retired, disabled, or family dependents of deceased workers.

Social Security benefits exist as a result of the Social Security Act and are administered by the Social Security Administration, a federal agency. The employer matches payments into Social Security retirement accounts for each employee on the payroll. It is important to note that Social Security was never intended to provide total retirement to individuals in their later years the intent of the benefit is to supplement other retirement income for retirees.

COBRA—Consolidated Omnibus Budget Reconciliation Act; requires employers to provide health insurance continuation based on qualifying events.

COBRA stands for the Consolidated Omnibus Budget Reconciliation Act, a federal law that provides for extension of health insurance coverage to employees who are eligible for "qualifying events." Qualifying events are defined as circumstances surrounding an employee's situation after leaving an employer. Those former employees who are eligible for extended insurance coverage for a period of 90 days must pay the full premium plus a 2 percent administrative cost to the former employer.

As we discussed in a prior chapter, the FMLA stands for the Family & Medical Leave Act, which provides for mandatory leaves of absence to employees with a qualifying family or health care need. The usual extent of a mandatory leave is 60 days and the employee must be returned to the same type of position with equivalent pay levels.

Voluntary Employee Benefits

The reason employers offer benefits to employees is to compete with other organizations in the industry and geographic location in terms of creating employee loyalty to the organization. The importance of benefits seems to vary with age groups. For instance, younger workers seem to place less emphasis on retirement benefits than older workers. Workers with families place more of an emphasis on family benefits, as opposed to individual benefits, and so on.

HMO—Health maintenance organization health insurance.

Most individuals are familiar with insurance benefits. Insurance benefits provide coverage for individuals in need, given certain circumstances. Health care coverage is very important to most people, as the costs of medical care continues to spiral upward. Most organizations offer two types of health care coverage: HMO and PPO plans. **HMO** stands for health maintenance organization. The original intent of HMOs was to provide preventative care to individuals before they became ill. However, over time, the original intent has turned into managed health care, in which plan administrators seek the most inexpensive means to provide medical care. **PPO** stands for preferred provider option, which is a hybrid of what was once referred to as indemnity insurance. While HMO plans provide for flat rate co-pays on the part of a patient, PPOs usually involve deductibles that are paid by the patient up to certain limits. Also, most health care plans are contributory. That means the employer pays only a portion of the insurance premium and the employee pays the balance through payroll deductions. The employer-to-employee payment ratio is usually 60/40 in terms of percentages of premium payments.

PPO—Preferred provider option health insurance.

Other types of insurance include life insurance, which pays a benefit to named beneficiaries in the event of the death of a worker. These payments are intended to provide final expenses and provide a small portion of income for remaining family members. Disability insurance provides income to individuals who are unable to work due to illness or accidents. This is different from workers' compensation, which applies to workplace accidents and illnesses only. There are two types of disability insurance: long-term and short-term. Short-term disability provides incomes for shorter ranges of time, after which a long-term policy would start to contribute if an individual has such coverage. The employee usually pays nothing for the life insurance premium and 100 percent of the discounted rate for any disability coverage. Again, any contributions from the employee are deducted from the paychecks. The one advantage to this is that at the current time, benefit contributions are pre-tax deductions, meaning employees do not pay Social Security and FICA tax on that portion of their income.

Retirement benefits are designed to provide a stream of income during the years after a person retires from working full time. As we said before, Social Security is a supplemental retirement fund, with the majority of retirement benefits derived from individual retirement accounts (IRAs), 401k plans and for independent contractors and certain executives, Keogh retirement plans. The law that ensures proper administration of qualified retirement plans is referred to as the Employment Retirement Income Security Act (ERISA). This law mandates conservative plan administration and prohibits discrimination in employee retirement plan benefits.

Another category of benefits is referred to as time off benefits. With these, the employee is paid for time that is not actually worked. These include paid holidays, vacations, and sick or personal pay. Most hospitality organizations provide full-time employees with six holidays and four to six sick days per year. Vacation policies usually call for one week after one year, and two weeks after two years. Some organizations provide for three or four weeks of vacation for long tenure, such as five or ten years of service to the organization.

Assistance benefits help employees with uninsured expenses, such as education. An education assistance or reimbursement program will pay portions of tuition and other training dollars to encourage employees to pursue self-development interests. Most organizations require job relatedness as a condition of education assistance, since they feel that they should only pay for those development activities that will enhance the employee's performance in the organization. Due to the very high costs associated with child care, only a few hospitality organizations provide this benefit; those that do certainly earn the loyalty of parents with young children.

Another category of benefits is known as financial incentive benefits. These provide buy-in to the performance of the organization. Employee stock ownership plans (ESOP) and regular stock options (the option to purchase company stock at a discounted rate) are directly related to the public valuation of the corporation. Profit sharing permits employees to benefit from the short-term profitability of the organization. Also, a number of hospitality organizations have social and recreational facilities and offer the use of these areas to the staff as employee benefits.

PERFORMANCE MANAGEMENT

Direct pay provides consideration to employees for rendering services and employee benefits reward organizational membership. These are two basic factors that, when absent, could create dissatisfaction with the organization. However, employee satisfaction is just the basic premise. The value-added manager enhances productivity levels every day. The goal of every manager is to have value-added workers. This requires more than good pay and benefits; it requires good management practices. Let's revisit our discussion from Chapter 7 by considering the model presented in Figure 10.1.

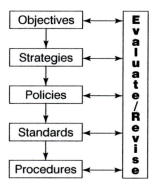

Figure 10.1. Objectives and Strategies.

When the right environmental factors such as pay and benefits are in place, smart managers take advantage of this to generate performance levels that exceed the standards, resulting in peak performance. Managers know that their job is to accomplish the objectives of the organization through the activities of others. They develop objectives and design strategies to achieve those objectives. The strategies become key drivers for policies, which provide general performance guidelines for the organization. Once the policies are in place, the managers create standards for performance that serve as benchmarks for what good performance looks like. For each standard, the managers walk the employee through each step in sequence, called procedures, that facilitate the accomplishment of the standards. The procedures reach the standards, which satisfy the policies that meet the strategies that attain the objectives for each operating department in the organization. Once this is in place, the human resource office provides an opportunity for managers to exceed the performance standards by establishing worker incentives.

EMPLOYEE INCENTIVES

Incentives may be described as additional compensation that is tied directly to performance standards. Incentives may be established on three levels. One level is the individual incentive, in which particular workers strive to earn their own incentive rewards. Group incentives are shared among members of a work unit, such as an operating department. Finally, incentives may be offered on an organization-wide basis, in which all workers will share in the accomplishment of a goal that exceeds normal operating standards. The correct design of incentives depends on the organizational culture and climate, as well as the objective that is intended.

incentives—
Additional compensation based on performance.

For instance, in scenarios in which individuals provide services to guests of a resort, it may be appropriate to provide a financial incentive for those workers who demonstrate service excellence. As for those who support the line workers (internal customers) they could participate in programs providing financial incentives for excellent levels of assistance to the service workers. In both examples, people are attempting to earn individual incentives.

A department manager may come up with a goal to achieve incremental revenues in a specific work area. In this case, individual incentives will not encourage teamwork that may be necessary to reach the incremental goal. Hence, the manager could establish a group incentive for all participants in the department to share a substantial financial reward if the goal is met. A bystander may say, "This sounds unfair, because some will do most of the work and the others will cruise and still receive the reward." "Not likely," the experienced manager would say. If the reward is substantial, a phenomenon called "peer pressure" will emerge. The coworkers will ostracize those individuals who behave like slackers, which will force them to perform or seek a position elsewhere.

A truly proactive organization would consider putting together a form of organization-wide incentives called "gain share" if it really had a great mission in mind. For instance, let's say the corporate office has approved the annual budget. Now, the management team puts together a plan to reduce costs below those in the budget and exceed budgeted revenues. The result, if the

---

HOSPITALITY NEWS   *Why Good Managers Leave*

Good managers are hard to find. Management turnover is costly and time consuming. Here are four reasons good managers leave their jobs.

1. *Employers stop asking for their advice.* A person worthy of being hired as a manager probably held an important position elsewhere. That means he or she has brought along valuable skills and information that should help the restaurant or company to improve and grow. And, in the end, a manager's perspective is often unique and usually insightful.
   Solution: In meetings and conversations, reserve your comments until everyone else has had the opportunity to express their opinions. This allows you to gather more information and to show your managers that their outlook is important to your decision making.

2. *Employers often direct when they should lead.* Managers want to know their precise parameters and exercise their best judgment. When employers stifle their abilities by continually telling them what and how to do their job and by throwing up barriers to their creativity and ingenuity, employers drive a wedge between owners and managers that is difficult to dislodge.
   Solution: Encourage managers to be risk takers. Let them know that some situations call for unorthodox moves and that as long as a decision does not cause irreversible harm to the company, employees, and customers, you will back their call.

3. *Employers are entirely too overbearing.* Good managers are often driven away by owners and upper management who refuse to give them breathing room. When we say things like, "No, don't do it that way"; "Before you take another step, come see me first"; or if we make managers feel inferior for having made a little mistake, three things happen: we get frustrated; managers get frustrated; and the managers the leaves, disillusioned and unhappy.
   Solution: Empowering people frees you to oversee the business and not be tied down by the details of the operation. Make sure everyone in the organization has a written job description, including yourself. Then let go of some of the everyday duties others are paid to handle. Instead, concentrate on your own job description. When your people experience freedom and empowerment, they will exceed your expectations and you will find yourself getting more things accomplished as well.

4. *Employers try to solve all the problems.* Problem solving is one of the fun and most rewarding parts of management. When employers walk in and assume control over every situation, managers are left with a feeling of inadequacy. Soon they stop growing. This action on the employer's part is contradictory to almost any philosophy of development.
   Solution: Challenge managers to explore all the possibilities available to them, to get their people involved, and to make brave decisions.

Source: Hospitality News, March 2002, p. 27.

---

workers were successful, would be incremental profit (profit beyond what is budgeted). Let's further say that the managers arrange for a percentage of those profits to be allocated to the employees that could result in a lump sum bonus of at least $1,000 to be paid to each worker just before the winter holidays. All the employees have to do is take good care of the resources and upsell products and services to achieve the bonus. Do you think these employees

would be interested in a little teamwork to put at least $1,000 dollars in their pockets just before the holidays?

EMPLOYEE RECOGNITION

Most people are familiar with the standard employee recognition programs that include employee of the month, the quarter, the year and others. In some organizations these programs don't really "wow" any of the workers, who often don't even know why someone was designated for recognition. In other organizations, the recognition programs lack credibility because of the perception by the staff that award winners are chosen for political reasons. Any experienced human resource manager will expound on the many failed attempts to provide really motivating recognition programs over the years. Some human resource practitioners consider recognition programs to be categorized as nonfinancial incentives. Other practitioners believe in the cash is king philosophy.

One ideal scenario is to combine a challenging and legitimate financial incentive program with individual and team recognition rewards. This appeals to both intrinsic and extrinsic needs of most achievement-oriented individuals. The key to this is credibility, which is based on employee trust. Whatever the incentive or recognition program, it must be perceived to have value in the minds of the staff members. In order to make this happen, HR practitioners must become guardians of legitimacy for each program. This means programs that truly recognize teams and individuals that everyone knows are deserving of the particular award.

safety programs— Systematic programs aimed at accident and illness prevention through audits and safety campaigns.

risk managers— Professional trained in reducing organizational liability through prevention and relations with insurance companies.

Occupational Safety and Health Act (OSHA)—The main federal statute providing for workplace safety requirements. Administered by the Occupational Safety and Health Administration, which has the powers of enforcement, investigation, and adjudication.

safety committee— An organized decision-making body consisting of representatives from various departments and levels within the organization that takes primary responsibility for safety audits and prevention programs/campaigns.

wellness programs— Programs offered to employees to assist with physical, mental, and emotional health.

employee assistance programs (EAP)— Programs that provide special needs to employees concerning issues of physical, mental, and emotional health and wellbeing.

Once an organization produces a program of combined financial incentives with recognition status, the implementation phase is all about reinforcement. Reinforcement takes the form of rites and rituals, which are formal or informal practices in work areas and departments. Rites and rituals also include symbols such as award pins, plaques, trophies, ribbons, or certificates. Human resource managers may arrange for the entire organization to come together for an annual celebration of excellent performance in one grand awards ceremony. If incentive and recognition programs are truly credible in the eyes of the employees, these ceremonies will create enormous levels of celebratory energy.

Human resource practitioners will tell you that there is nothing that creates more enthusiasm than credible programs that facilitate opportunities for employees at all levels of the organization to celebrate each other. These same HR people will also describe the embarrassment associated with being responsible for dull and lackluster programs that are supposed to motivate workers to seek recognition. It is all about employee credibility, when it comes to developing and implementing such programs.

SAFETY AND WELLNESS PROGRAMS

It falls within the domain of the human resource manager to ensure that the work environment is safe and comfortable for the workers. Also, many organizations have programs in place to assist with the physical, mental and emotional welfare of the staff.

Safety programs and campaigns are usually joint ventures between the HR office and the security department. In large organizations, fulltime **risk managers** are employed to ensure that the workplace provides for accident and illness prevention. As mentioned earlier, the high costs associated with workers' compensation premiums provide motivation to proactively prevent workplace injuries. Additionally, the **Occupational Safety and Health Act (OSHA)** provides for safety regulations for worksites. Many organizations adopt **safety committees** that oversee accident and illness prevention programs. As is the case with any proactive project, there must be support from the senior managers in the organization to make a safety campaign successful. There are two approaches to worker safety. The first is psychological, with focus on the behaviors of the employees. The second is an engineering issue dealing with the physical plant. There really are only two aspects that cause accidents or illnesses in the workplace—unsafe actions (behavior) and hazardous environments (engineering).

In addition to safety programs, human resource practitioners usually provide other programs to assist the workers with personal issues. These programs are collectively referred to as **wellness programs**. Wellness programs may include physical fitness programs, health and nutrition programs, financial counseling, and other activities aimed at the welfare of the employees. The philosophy behind wellness programs is that healthy and focused people are productive workers. Most human resource offices offer **employee assistance programs (EAP)**. EAPs usually involve outsource referrals to a variety of health care and legal professionals such as mental health counselors, substance abuse and other addiction programs, financial debt counseling, legal assistance, marriage counseling and other services. Individuals within the

In the Real World . . . (Continued)

You start working alongside the compensation manager on the new compensation project for the housekeeping department. He lays out the objectives for the project by saying, "Okay, we have to come up with an incentive-based regular pay system that is in compliance with the FLSA regulations and doesn't increase payroll expenses."

You joke, "Sounds easy enough to me."

He chuckles. "Well, it looks like one way to approach this is to structure a piece rate method."

"Hmmm." you say, "Instead of paying by the hour, we pay by the cleaned guestroom. But, if they clean 16 rooms in 8 hours, wouldn't they be breaking even with the hourly rate, all things being equal?"

"That's true, the manager says, "But the housekeeping director is telling us they can clean rooms faster if there is an incentive to do so." You reply, "So we pay them X per room and if they clean the rooms in less than 8 hours, they go home early." You think for a minute and continue, "But, if they demonstrate that they can clean 16 rooms in less than 8 hours, why wouldn't we just raise the standard to 18 rooms in a shift?"

"Now you are thinking like a GM," the manager jokes, then continues, "Actually, anyone who has cleaned guestrooms knows that it becomes harder to clean each room as the day goes on. It's kind of like doing bench-press repetitions in the gym; the first few are easy, then as you get tired, it gets harder to push up the bar."

"That's true," you say. "The few times I have cleaned guestrooms my back was aching after just four hours. So we have to build in the assumption that each room gets progressively harder to clean due to fatigue and if that is true, the 17th or 18th room is worth more than the first few rooms."

"The manager quips, "Now you are thinking like Albert Einstein or something." He continues, "You have something here though; it looks like we should consider a modified piece rate per guestroom."

"Is that the same as a stratified piece rate?"

"Yup." "Stratified, modified, differential . . . they all mean the same thing."

You both stop talking as each of you starts to picture what it is you are trying to create. After a long pause, the manager starts to sketch out the plan on a notepad. You watch as he draws a diagram.

"I've got it!" you exclaim, "Let's pay the same amount of piece rate per room, but let the housekeepers bid on how many rooms they want to clean above 16 rooms. We'll do it like an amateur golf tournament, with A, B and C flights. C flight will be those who can do 16 rooms; B flight will be 18 rooms; and A flight will be 20 rooms."

The compensation manager mulls this idea over, then says, "From a psychological standpoint, the A and B workers would become the elite and the C workers would be viewed by their peers as slackers." He continues as if in deep thought, "So the C flight workers would strive to be in the B flight and the B flight workers would try to get into the A flight. The C flight workers who can't advance would probably become turnover statistics. But when the word gets out on the street that we pay premiums for people who can clean 20 guestrooms, good housekeepers will leave our competitors and apply for the positions vacated by our slackers."

"I like it," the manager says.

"Me too," you reply.

"Let's go show this to the director."

human resource office (a male and female) are appointed to handle EAP is-sues on a highly confidential basis taking every precaution to safeguard the anonymity of individuals seeking assistance through the EAP. Wellness pro-grams may include proactive programs such as fitness classes, as well as reac-tive programs like those provided through an EAP.

SUMMARY

In order for incentives to be effective, the basics of operating the organization must be in place. This includes solid compensation and management prac-tices. We have discussed the importance of retention of quality workers in or-ganizations. Retention requires attention to the extrinsic and intrinsic needs of individual workers. Compensation practices are designed to provide con-sideration for services rendered by workers, as well as reward organizational membership. The goal of these practices is to retain those workers who meet or exceed performance standards. In order to do this, managers must develop objectives, set strategies, create policies, site standards and provide proce-dures used to meet those standards. This is the only way to accomplish the objectives for an organization. It is also the only way to measure perfor-mance. With these practices in place, the organization is positioned to de-velop peak performance through individual, group, and organizational incentives. A word of caution: Incentives without solid management practices and other retention strategies will not work. We start with the basics, and then move toward excellence.

DISCUSSION QUESTIONS

1. The In the Real World . . . vignette poses a dramatic shift in thinking for traditional hotel managers. Are there flaws in this thinking? Would you be willing to tweak it to make it work? Why and how?
2. If you had a choice to become a wage and salary leader in your local area, would you select that option? How would you justify that from a cost/benefit perspective?
3. How important are benefits to you? Which are most important? Could this be different for other people? How so?

KEY TERMS

administrative exemption
benefits
bonuses
closed pay system
COBRA
commissions
comp time

compensation
compensation manager
cost of living allowances (COLA)
direct compensation

employee assistance programs (EAPs)
employee retention
employee turnover
executive exemption

exempt
Fair Labor Standards Act (FLSA)
HMO
incentive pay
incentives

indirect
 compensation
labor dollars
mandatory
maturity curve
merit
minimum wage
modified piece
 rate
nonexempt

Occupational
 Health and
 Safety Act
open pay system
piece rate
perquisites
PPO
professional
 exemption
risk managers

safety committees
safety programs
salary
seniority
Social Security
 benefits
tip credit
unemployment
 compensation

voluntary benefits
wages
wellness programs
wage
 compression
workers'
 compensation

CHAPTER ELEVEN

Performance Management Systems

OBJECTIVES

By the end of this chapter, the reader will be able to:

1. Understand the role of employee appraisal as one part of a holistic performance management system.
2. Identify performance standards as the benchmark for measuring performance.
3. Recognize commonly used formal appraisal formats.
4. Understand the role of the supervisor as providing daily informal appraisals.

> ### *In the Real World . . .*
>
> You are working in the human resource office for large resort hotel. A worker from the front desk comes into the office complaining that she didn't get her annual wage increase. You ask her if she had talked with the front office manager about it and she tells you she has mentioned it twice and was tired of asking him for the raise. You ask when her raise was due and she said it was supposed to start last month. Next, you ask her how she rated on her performance appraisal and she tells you that she doesn't know what her rating was. Surprised, you ask if she had a performance appraisal interview. She tells you that she was called into the office, told to sign a form, and that she would be getting a raise.
>
> Now, you are becoming concerned about this situation. You tell her that you will discuss this matter with the human resource director and get back to her before the end of her shift. She agrees and returns to work at the front desk.

INTRODUCTION

This chapter presents a systems approach to performance management. The preceding chapters in this book have identified all the management subsystems that result in the performance management system. A performance management system provides planning, identification, encouragement through the communication of standards, as well as evaluations of actual performance, as compared with established performance standards. The purpose of performance measurement is to provide feedback to employees about their performance and to take actions to facilitate improvement, as well as provide recognition of successful performance levels by giving rewards. Actually, this is not a stand-alone process, as some managers would have us believe. Instead, it is a multi-disciplinary approach to people management that requires daily observation and communication through coaching, mentoring and disciplinary warnings on the part of the supervisor. The effectiveness of these practices is related to levels of awareness on the part of the supervisor concerning the service perspective, leadership practice, worker motivation, and work life development.

THE PERFORMANCE MANAGEMENT PROCESS

The performance management process starts with performance standards, which are simply behavioral goals. Then job criteria (referred to as job lists) are established, which prioritize the importance of each job function by listing the procedures to meet each standard. The worker exceeds, meets, or does not meet each category of performance. Since some aspects of performance are more important than others, we attach mathematical weights (10 percent, 50 percent, etc.) to each performance category. Next, we multiply the weights (percentages) times each category. The averaged total will provide an indication of the overall performance levels. For instance, if the worker exceeds standards for a criterion that is 60 percent of the job and meets the rest, that worker is above the standards (or an excellent performer, as most managers like to say). The process just described is called a performance appraisal.

Performance Standards

What is the basis of performance standards? You have learned this: the productivity model, which measures effectiveness and efficiency. Customer relationship issues such as service levels and product quality/quantity are measures of effectiveness. Reducing resource expenses is an efficiency measurement. For example, a server in a full-service restaurant provides excellent guest service in a station consisting of 12 covers (seats). That server is being effective. Another server provides the same level of service in a station with 20 covers. That server is both efficient and effective because she is meeting the quality standards for 8 more guests than the other server. If every server had this ability, there would be fewer servers required to staff the restaurant, which will result in lower payroll costs without compromising service quality. If the manager were to staff the restaurant in stations of 20 covers with the servers providing mediocre service, the restaurant would be efficient, but not effective. The manager would be meeting only part of her performance responsibility.

The holistic approach to management performance responsibility is presented in Figure 11.1.

A performance management system includes every management activity from strategic planning through performance appraisal. The system includes the management functions of planning, organizing, influencing and control. The performance appraisal activity is a control process, in that it compares actual performance with standards for performance, which is what management control is all about.

informal appraisal— Informal feedback on performance.

formal appraisal— Systematic written performance evaluation and feedback.

Performance Appraisals

There are two types of performance appraisals. One is done daily and is mostly verbal; this is an **informal appraisal**. The **formal appraisal** is written (usually on a performance appraisal form) and occurs on a periodic basis

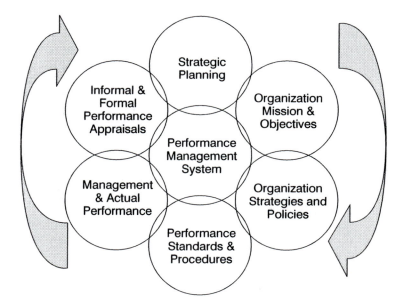

Figure 11.1. Performance Management System.

(usually annually). Who appraises whom? Well, managers always appraise their workers, but workers could appraise their supervisors as well; this is called the **180 degrees model**. In some cases, subordinates, supervisors, and peers participate in the appraisal process. This is the **360 degrees model**. Peer ratings are becoming popular with the push toward **self-managed teams (SMT)**. Almost all ratings are multi-source, as they usually include one extra step up in the chain of command. Self-evaluations are good introspection tools; however, most people lack the level of self-awareness to do this function effectively. If you use customer feedback, plus all the other ratings mentioned here, you are truly doing a multi-source rating.

180 degrees model— A review system that includes subordinates review of the supervisor.

360 degrees model— Holistic appraisal feedback from subordinates, supervisors, and peers.

self-managed teams (SMT)— Team that require little or no supervision.

HOSPITALITY NEWS *Determining Who Should Get a Raise*

Every staff member would like a raise in pay. But deciding how much additional compensation to give an employee is often confusing. Try this method from the late George Odiorne, who has been called America's premier expert regarding management by objectives.

1. If an employee is below par in performing routine responsibilities, he or she should not be kept in that position or should be given training and time to improve. No raise is warranted.

2. If the person is performing routine duties but doing nothing more, he or she is fulfilling the job description and is entitled to the same job (at the same pay) for another year.

3. Raises and bonuses should go to the individual who contributes to the progress of the business and does not simply fulfill routine duties. Staff members who actively participate in solving problems by offering helpful ideas are worth more to your company and should be awarded a raise or additional compensation.

Source: Hospitality News, August 2002, p. 23.

Graphic Rating Scale	Rating	Checklist Method	Check
(5–Excellent; 4–Above Avg.; 3–Average; 2–Below, 1–Poor)		(Check the appropriate column)	
Attendance	5	Attends every scheduled shift	X
		Attends most scheduled shifts	
		Attendance is not consistent	

Figure 11.2. Category Rating Method.

category rating method—An appraisal model listing items by categories.

graphic rating scales—Numerically scored appraisals.

checklist methods—An appraisal method in which the reviewer checks appropriate categories.

comparative methods—An appraisal method that compares individuals with their peers.

ranking method—An appraisal method in which all employees in a work unit are rated from first through last.

critical incident method—A method of recording important observations for later formal appraisal recollection.

essay appraisal—A written narrative describing strengths and areas for improvement regarding performance.

behavioral approaches—Appraisal method that focuses on specific observable behaviors.

behaviorally anchored rating scale (BARS)—Behavioral approach using standardized practices.

Management by objectives (MBO)—Top-down, bottom-up shared goal setting at every level of the organization.

There are various formal appraisal methods. The most popular is the **category rating method**, which includes **graphic rating scales** (1–5) and **checklist methods** (check off the statement that applies). Figure 11.2 shows examples of graphic rating and checklist methods.

Comparative methods rate employees against each other. **Ranking methods** rank them from best to worst. Forced distribution puts most in the middle and a few at each end (kind of like college courses). Narrative methods involve writing reports based on performance observations.

A powerful tool is the **critical incident method** that combines informal with formal reviews. You as a manager take notes on your observations of important (critical) activities (incidents) for each employee. You take five minutes to place the notes in a file marked for each worker. At the end of the year, voilà! You have a year's worth of notes on each worker's performance (a powerful tool).

Another written method of performance appraisals is the **essay appraisal**. This used for senior-level management positions in most cases and includes a thorough written essay on the performance of the executive.

Behavioral approaches focus on specific job behaviors that are predefined by some document. One approach is the **behaviorally anchored rating scale (BARS)** method that uses concrete descriptions of expected behaviors in a checklist format similar to the one presented in Figure 11.2. The BARS method adheres to the *Dictionary of Occupational Titles* in identifying position descriptions. This document is not conducive to most hospitality and tourism positions, as it is geared more toward manufacturing and administrative positions. **Management by objectives (MBO)** is both a goal-setting activity and a performance appraisal method. It involves top-down, bottom-up goals to be set for every level of the organization based on the mission. Supervisors then review the accomplishment of objectives at some later date. A few organizations have implemented a performance management system known as the **balanced scorecard**, which is a method to include quantitative measurements on one axis and qualitative metrics on the other axis. The purpose of the balanced scorecard is to provide weights for measuring service to all of the stakeholder groups, as opposed to other methods that focus solely on the contributions to the customers and shareholders.

VALIDITY ERRORS

In actual practice, the performance appraisal system will be a hybrid of many methods that have been mentioned in this chapter. There is a factor known as **rater error** that will invalidate the performance appraisal. **Recency effect** occurs when you don't use the critical incident method and can only remember the last few weeks of performance for each worker. **Central tendency** error is when you try to make everyone average. **Rater bias** occurs when personal issues cloud the objective criteria of the review. **Halo effect** is rating all categories on a single attribute. **Contrast error** occurs when comparisons are made to other workers instead of objective criteria.

The most important part of a formal review is the interview. It should be done in private, by a dialogue, and only occur after the person being reviewed has had sufficient time to read the completed appraisal document. The worst thing for a supervisor to do is to avoid issues that may be less than positive. People have a tendency to this because we don't like to deliver bad news. This practice is dishonest on the part of the supervisor and will ultimately result in negative consequences for both parties. However, in the process of delivering negative information, supervisors are cautioned to always be kind and compassionate with their interactive style.

As far as legal aspects of performance appraisals are concerned, supervisors should remember to be sure the methods used are valid, reliable, fair, uniform, and consistent. This rule is true for any supervisory practice.

THE FORMAL APPRAISAL PROCESS

The human resource office is responsible for communicating the policy and procedures for formal performance appraisal activities within the organization. The HR practitioners also handle the administrative aspect of appraisal development, distribution, and documentation. To ensure fairness, uniformity and consistency, formal appraisals usually require multi-level review and approval and include the approval of the human resource director. Figure 11.3 provides a listing of the formal performance appraisal process.

It is evident from the steps outlined in Figure 11.3 that the formal appraisal process is time consuming. However, the opportunity to provide feedback for an employee's performance is worth the time, effort and expense. Experienced managers recognize the leadership opportunity involved with taking sufficient time to provide feedback to the workers. Other managers consider the appraisal process to be a perfunctory process. If those managers were to place themselves in the shoes of the workers, they would realize that performance feedback is vital to good employee relations.

SUMMARY

What makes a performance management system a "system"? The mission for the organization, which is used to develop objective performance standards, drives a performance management system. The standards are broken down into policies and procedures for each task that is driven by these standards.

---

balanced scorecard— An x and y axis representing qualitative and quantitative performance criteria.

rater error— Statistical error on the part of a rater causing an appraisal instrument to lose its validity and/or reliability.

recency effect— Recalling a small portion of the appraisal time frame.

central tendency— Forcing individuals into a normative grouping.

rater bias—Personal attributes influencing the rater.

halo effect—A focus on a single issue that influences an entire rating.

contrast error— Comparisons to subjective criteria.

> 1. Human resource office tracks the time period of performance appraisals
> 2. Human resource office distributes appraisal instruments 30 days prior to due date.
> 3. Operating managers complete the appraisal instruments.
> 4. Operating managers attain approval of the rating from executive and human resource managers.
> 5. Operating manager establishes a scheduled interview time with the employee.
> 6. Operating manager gives the employee sufficient time to review the appraisal document.
> 7. Operating manager conducts the appraisal interview by engaging in dialogue with the employee.
> 8. Employee provides written commentary and signature on the appraisal document.
> 9. Executive and human resource director signatures indicate approval.
> 10. The appraisal document is admitted to the employee's personnel file.
> 11. Human resource office schedules the next periodic appraisal date for trace.
> 12. Human resource office processes payroll change document in the event of a pay increase.
> 13. The accounting office processes the payroll change document.

Figure 11.3.   Formal Performance Appraisal Process.

Managers and supervisors symbolize the service perspective in their daily interactions. They are aware of human motivational factors and take a personal interest in the work life development of the staff members. They engage in sound leadership practices, through which they employ effective communication skills used to coach, recognize, evaluate, counsel, and use progressive discipline with the staff members in appropriate situations. Managers and supervisors employ the use of the critical incident method to account for all-important aspects of performance. Finally, they provide constructive feedback to the workers through performance appraisal methods, which are used to redirect behaviors below the standards and to develop the careers of workers who meet or exceed the standards. Thus we began the system with the first chapter of the book and complete the system with this conclusive chapter on supervision in the service industry.

HOSPITALITY NEWS   *What to Do When Employees Complain about Wages*

As long as there are employees, there will be complaints. Certainly one of the most common complaints is dissatisfaction with compensation. According to a report in the Star Ledger, six out of ten employees think their pay is too low.

The only solution is to pay a competitive wage. Do a salary survey of peers in the same industry and share the results. That way, even if you're already paying a competitive wage (or better), workers know it. Use industry standards as a barometer. If talent warrants top compensation, remember that if you don't pay it, someone else probably will.

Contact your state or national restaurant or lodging association for a reference on wage studies being conducted within the industry. There are a number of companies that collect this type of data and make their research available to employers.

Source: Hospitality News, December 2002/January 2003, p. 25.

> ## *In the Real World. . . (Continued)*
>
> After the front desk agent leaves the human resource office, you report your conversation to the director. Upon hearing what you have to say, the director sighs, "I thought this was the case with the front office manager. This will be an opportunity for you to witness the type of conversation you have with a manager who is not living up to his responsibility."
>
> The director immediately calls the front office manager and asks for him to meet with her and you. He comes to the office about 30 minutes after the call. She begins the conversation, "Brad, we have been through this before. You know what our standard is for performance appraisals here. Whether you think it is important or not, you have to follow the process," she says. "I have been more than fair with you on this matter. If you don't want to get with the program, I am going to have to discuss this with your boss."
>
> Brad replies. "Look, I know I shouldn't have blown off the last batch of appraisals, but it has been really hectic up there. I just haven't had time . . . ."
>
> The HR director cuts him off. "Brad if this were the first time you had used this excuse, I would hear you out. But it's not. And you are being irresponsible to your staff, to me and to this organization. The worst part is, your employee should have gotten a raise over a month ago, and you never even turned in the form."
>
> Frustrated with this conversation, Brad asks, "So, what do you want me to do?"
>
> The director replies. "I want you to process the payroll change form, go to the accounting office and get a manual check cut for this young lady, sit down with her and tell her what she does well and what she can do better, and apologize for the payroll mistake by the end of her shift."
>
> Brad retorts, "I will need the AGM's approval for a manual check! That will make me look bad."
>
> "You already look bad to your employees, which are more important than your boss. Would you rather have me call the AGM to discuss your mismanagement practices?"
>
> "No" he replies, "I'll handle it." "Good." And when you finish with the employee, send her to see me, so I can check up on the way you handled it. And finally, Brad" she warned, "You either get with the program or I am going to come after you. Do you understand me?"
>
> He replies, "I got it," and leaves the office in a huff.
>
> After Brad's departure, the director says to you, "Go on up to the front desk and let the young lady know that things will be taken care of by her manager and ask her to see me when she is finished meeting with him."
>
> You salute and say, "Yes, Ma'am!"
>
> She laughs, "Well," she says, "Sometimes you gotta get tough with these guys. Now you know how to handle one of these situations."

DISCUSSION QUESTIONS

1. Some people believe that managers fill out performance appraisal forms without giving them much thought. Do you think this is true? How would you feel if someone did that to you?

2. Sometimes a manager runs a department and everyone in it is above average. She leaves and a new manager takes over. When the new manager does appraisals, she rates everyone as average. How can this be, if there has been no change in performance?

3. You sit down with a manager for your performance appraisal interview. The manager starts citing dates and times of specific behaviors performed by you over the past year. Do you think that manager has a photographic memory, or is he using some other technique? Would you use such a technique? Why or why not?

4. At the end of the In the Real World . . . vignette, what should the human director have done after she sent you to visit the front desk?

KEY TERMS

180 degrees model
360 degrees model
balanced
  scorecard
behavioral
  approaches
behaviorally
  anchored rating
  scale (BARS)

category rating
  method
central tendency
checklist methods
comparative
  methods
contrast error
critical incident
  method

essay appraisal
formal appraisal
graphic rating
  scales
halo effect
informal appraisal
management by
  objectives (MBO)

ranking method
rater error
recency effect
self-managed
  teams (SMT)
rater bias

CHAPTER TWELVE
Communication Strategies

OBJECTIVES

By the end of this chapter, the reader will be able to:

1. Understand and use the communication model.
2. Understand the importance of effective listening.
3. Recognize effective feedback techniques.
4. Identify formal and informal communication networks.
5. Understand the importance of multi-directional communication flows.
6. Comprehend the basics of written and oral communication presentation skills.

> ### *In the Real World...*
>
> You are working alongside the employee relations manager in the human resource department for the cruise line division of an internationally known theme park and attraction organization. As is the case with most cruise operations, there are individuals from many diverse ethnic backgrounds on the shipboard aspect of the operation. Most of the captains and deck and engine crew are European, as are the food and beverage personnel. Onboard hotel managers are mostly from the United States and England, and the crew is from Caribbean and Asian nations.
>
> You notice that the employee relations manager works on board for at least four days per month. After watching the employee relations manager handle a number of complaints from shore-side personnel, you notice that most of these boil down to communications breakdowns. One day you ask the employee relations manager how he handles communications with the diverse onboard personnel. He says, "Come on board with me next week and I'll show you."

INTRODUCTION

Since human resource managers are manager's managers, which places them in the role of management educators, it is necessary for the human resource practitioner to become an organizational communications expert. One reason for this is the responsibility of the human resource manager to act as an internal marketing representative to all of the workers and candidates for positions within an organization. A second reason is that the communication of objectives, strategies, policies, standards, procedures, and rules that collectively comprise the expectations for worker performance in an organization fall squarely within the domain of the human resource manager. A third reason is that human resource practitioners must teach effective communications skills to all of the managers within the organization.

The most important tool for a manager or supervisor is the ability to engage effectively in communication activities with other individuals. A person may know all there is to know about supervision and still be unable to be an effective supervisor if he does not possess a solid base of communication skills. Hence, managers who do not possess effective communication skills will not possess the ability to act as effective managers. As we already know, the success of human resource practitioners works in tandem with a team of successful operations managers.

communication—The sharing and understanding of ideas.

There are many definitions of communication in organizations. This chapter presents a simplified definition for the reader. **Communication** may be defined as the sharing and understanding of information among individuals.[1] While this sounds simple, the process of engaging in effective communication is really quite complex. This is due to the individuality of people. Individuality affects personal perception: Each person perceives information in different ways. Therefore, while everyone in a group of people may hear the same message, that message will mean different things to different people. A perfect example of this is the old game of passing a message along a line of people. Each person whispers a message in the ear of the next person in line. At the end, the message repeated by the last person in line is usually very different than the original message. Take this phenomenon and multiply it times the numerous incidents of communication that take place among people in an organization. It becomes evident that organizational communication is a very complicated topic. Consultants tell us that lack of effective communication is the most prominent problem in organizations.[2] A model for organizational communication is presented in Figure 12.1.

THE COMMUNICATION MODEL

Notice that the model starts with the **sender**. The sender thinks of an idea, a thought in the sender's mind. The sender must **encode** the thought into a message. This means the sender is using words to symbolize the concepts within the thought. After the sender identifies the words or symbols to be used to represent the thought, the sender chooses a **medium** for the message. A medium may be written a format such as a memo or letter. A medium could also be electronic, such as a telephone, intercom, or email. A medium could be verbal, such as an interview, a meeting, or informal discussion. All of these examples represent means though which a sender packages and sends a message. Since the message is packaged for the **receiver** of the message, the package is known as the medium. The medium carries the message to the receiver, who then must **decode** the message. The process of encoding into a medium and decoding by the receiver comprises the **channel** of the message. After the receiver decodes the message a **feedback** loop is used for the receiver to respond to the message. The feedback loop closes the cycle. This permits the process of sender, medium, and receiver to begin again.

Consider an example to demonstrate the communication model. A manager has decided to enact a change in staff scheduling practices. The manager notices that individuals sometimes prefer specific days off for various

sender—An individual with an idea to be communicated to a receiver.

encode—Placing an idea into communication symbols, such as words to be sent to the receiver.

medium—The communication vehicle for a message.

receiver—The intended target of a message.

decode—Making personal sense from a message on the part of a receiver.

channel—The directional flow of a message from sender to receiver.

feedback—The loop moves from the receiver back to the sender to confirm understanding of the message.

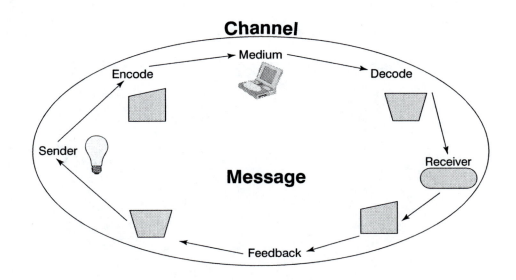

Figure 12.1.   Communication Model.

reasons. In the interest of fairness, the manager develops an idea that will enable members of the staff to request days off before the schedule is made for the following week. So far, this is just a concept in the mind of the manager. Now the manager must put the idea into words (encoding). The manager jots down a few notes concerning the idea. Next the manager must decide how the message will be sent to the staff. The manager decides to announce the new practice in an upcoming shift meeting and to follow up with a printed notice concerning staff requests. In this case, there are two **mediums**; one is the meeting (verbal), and the other is a notice (written).

A shift meeting is scheduled for Wednesday. At the meeting, the manager presents the new procedure for requesting days off prior to each week's posting of the schedule. The manager looks at the facial expressions and body language of the participants to ensure that all understand the new procedure (feedback). Finally, the manager asks if anyone has any questions about the procedure (feedback). A member of the staff indicates that she has a question. At this point, the feedback loop is closed and a new communication process is about to begin. The person with the question becomes the sender. She thinks about what she wants to ask, finds words to encode her message, verbalizes the words in the form of a question (medium), and watches the manager (receiver) for a response (feedback). As the manager decodes the question, the manager prepares a response; thus, the manager is starting a new communication process as the sender.

This is the communication model at work. We communicate so quickly that we don't recognize the steps involved in our communications. We develop ideas, encode them, place them in a medium, send them for decoding, watch or listen for feedback, and await a response in fractions of seconds.

WHY ARE COMMUNICATION SKILLS IMPORTANT FOR MANAGERS?

If the practice of management involves accomplishing the objectives of the organization through the activities of others, then it seems that the ability to communicate effectively is crucial to the success of the manager. Imagine

knowing all there is to know about the field of management. Also imagine how effective you would be with that knowledge if you could not talk, write, or otherwise communicate with the workers. No matter how much knowledge a person has in the field of management, if that person is unable to communicate with other people, tasks and goals will not be accomplished. Therefore, that person will not be a successful manager.

LISTENING SKILLS

How well do most people listen? According to some experts, the majority of individuals listen at an effectiveness rate of 25 percent.[3] Experts indicate that individuals who work in senior management positions spend as much as 85 percent of their communication time listening to other people.[4] It is a fact that listening skills top the list of effective managerial communication skills. While effective listening is the most important communications skill, it is perhaps the least taught skill.

One reason for possessing effective listening skills is that, as the human resource manager, you will teach other managers to make decisions based on

---

HOSPITALITY NEWS *Tips for Becoming an Effective Communicator*

One of the most valuable skills a manager can acquire is to become an effective communicator.

Ineffective communication often results in poor cooperation and coordination, lower productivity, undercurrents of tension, gossip and rumors and increased turnover and absenteeism.

Experience shows there are many ways managers can improve internal communications. Here are eight things to try:

1. Understand that communication is a two-way street. It involves giving information and getting feedback from employees. It isn't finished when information is given.
2. Put more emphasis on face-to-face communication with employees. Don't rely mainly on bulletin boards, memos, and other written communication.
3. Each time you give an instruction, ask yourself if the message is clear. Be specific. Don't just tell an employee to "show more interest" in his or her work. If an employee spends too much time chatting with others, be more specific about it.

4. View information as service to employees and not power over them.
5. Take time to listen to your employees; show respect for them when they speak. They'll feel like part of the team and will tend to be more dedicated and productive. Ask questions to show interest and clarify points.
6. Don't just talk open-door policy. Show it by walking around and talking to your employees. Allow people to disagree and to come up with new ideas.
7. Conduct one-on-one meetings. Ask each employee to tell you how you can help him or her do a better job, then how the employee can help you do a better job.
8. Concentrate on building credibility with employees. Managers who lack credibility and fail to create a climate of trust and openness aren't believed, no matter how hard they try to communicate.

Source: Hospitality News, "A Little Help for Managers," February 2002, p. 23.

information presented to them. Your managers will be involved in the following types of listening scenarios:

Problem-solving	Scheduling
Conflict resolution	Assigning duties
Performance evaluations	Hiring personnel
Resource allocation	Coaching and discipline
Brainstorming	Policies and rules
Strategic planning	Practices and procedures
Organizing departments	Other activities to support your staff members
Customer satisfaction indicators	

Each of the activities listed in the box requires effective listening skills for maximum decision-making. Therefore, the smart manager is in the listening business. As managers assume higher levels of responsibility, their listening skills become more important.

Barriers to Effective Listening

Effective listening requires time, energy, concentration, technique, and objectivity. Listening actively actually requires more effort than talking or writing. Many managers think they are actively listening to people, when they are, in fact, creating barriers to effective listening. Some barriers to effective listening are:

Diverted attention

Mood and experience

Judgmental attitudes

Noise (distractions)

Planning responses

Lack of interest

Failure to ask probing questions

Here are examples of a few typical scenarios.

An individual arranges to meet with the manager. As the individual approaches the manager's office at the appointed time, the manager is on the phone. The manager waves the person into the office without missing any of the phone conversation. The person sits down and waits for the phone conversation to end. Finally, the manager hangs up and addresses the person sitting in the office. As the person begins to speak, the manager shuffles through papers on the desk. This is an example of diverted attention. The manager is not fully listening to that person, who is likely to feel uncomfortable with the lack of attention.

In another situation, a person may enter the manager's office only to find that the manager is under severe stress. The manager is obviously fatigued and distracted. This is an example of mood as a barrier to effective listening. Perhaps the person wants to talk to the manager about a problem that has been recently addressed by many other workers. Upon hearing the topic of discussion, the manager indicates disinterest in what the person has to say; the manager has already "heard it all." This is an example of experience as a barrier to effective listening.

In yet another scenario, a person is attempting to explain to the manager the reason that some action was taken. The manager appears to be closed minded. This is an example of judgmental attitude as a barrier to effective listening. In another instance, there is a small meeting with four participants. One participant stands up and gazes out the window. Another person is doodling. Another is tapping a pencil. These are examples of noise as a barrier to effective listening. In this case, noise does not necessarily have to mean noise in the audible sense. Any distraction, even silent distractions, creates a form of distraction called noise.

Planning the Response

One expert describes the two-person conversation as a multiple-party monologue. In this scenario, both parties are concentrating on what it is they want to say. Both start talking, and the first person to draw a breath is declared the listener.[5] However, this person is not really listening. Instead, the person is mentally rehearsing a response to interject when the speaker stops talking.

This is often the case in organizational discussions. Planning the response is a common barrier to effective listening. When this occurs, the speaker should reiterate the message until the listener indicates that it has been heard, by responding appropriately. Another technique for overcoming

---

HOSPITALITY NEWS *Understanding Your Employees*

To succeed, you must constantly talk and listen to employees. It's just good business. The following are some questions you might want to ask your employees:

- How fairly are you and your colleagues treated by management?
- Is there enough effective communication between management and the workforce?
- Do the instructions and training you're receiving seem sufficient for you to perform your duties?
- How do you see your future here?
- What do you think of your workload? Is work generally distributed fairly?

- Does your supervisor tell you what you need to know?
- How do employees get along with each other?
- Is the equipment you use adequate?
- Do you feel your work is important? Why or why not?
- What do you want management to continue doing? What do you want management to stop doing? What do you want management to start doing?

Source: Hospitality News, February 2001, p. 28.

this barrier is to permit the intended listener to talk first. After all has been said, the barrier of mental rehearsal should be overcome.

Mood and Experience

Most individuals have high and low spans of attention throughout the workday. Some individuals are morning people; others are afternoon people. Peak times are those during which the individual is energized and focused. Since effective listening requires focused energy, it may be appropriate for managers and supervisors to schedule discussions during peak periods. Often, workers will approach the manager during an inconvenient time. The manager now has a dilemma. If the manager takes the time to talk with the worker, it is possible that the manager may be distracted and not listen effectively. On the other hand, if the manager does not talk with the worker, the worker may feel that the manager does not value the worker's existence. Perhaps an appropriate response on the part of the manager would be to reinforce that the worker's feedback is important. However, due to the current level of activities, it may be an inappropriate time for the discussion. The manager might further state that the discussion should take place when both parties are able to concentrate effectively on the topic. The manager would then proceed to schedule an appointment for the discussion.

Lack of Attention

In every department there seem to be one or two workers who spend large amounts of time discussing seemingly unimportant issues with the manager. The manager eventually comes to believe that these people will waste time. The manager must work to overcome this judgmental barrier. In order to do this, the manager must assume the optimistic view that, one of these times, this person is going to focus on an issue of substance. The manager thus expends effort to listen effectively, just in case this becomes that opportunity. A word of caution to the inexperienced manager: Some individuals prefer talking to working. The manager must determine if the worker's visit is a work-avoidance tactic. If it is suspected that this is true, the manager should suggest that the worker schedule another time for the discussion.

FORMAL AND INFORMAL COMMUNICATION

Formal communication takes place when people are representing the interests of the organization as part of their appointed duties. A manager who conducts a performance appraisal is communicating formally because the manager is acting in an appointed capacity, and is engaging in a form of communication that will be documented for the record. Other types of formal communications include, but are not limited to, memos, letters, meetings, bulletin board postings, announcements, policies, procedures, standards, and newsletters.

grapevine—An informal channel of communication that carries social information and gossip among workers.

Informal communication exists outside the mainstream of the organization's communications channels. A commonly cited example of informal communications is called the **grapevine**.[6] Practically all members of an organization (minus a few senior managers) participate in the grapevine. It is the informal communication process that takes place among people within the organization or industry. Usually, the grapevine consists of rumor, innuendo, speculation, and hearsay information. Topics of communication may extend beyond organizational issues into people's personal lives. The grapevine is often labeled as the rumor mill or the word on the street. At times, the grapevine may be a source of accurate information that travels faster than the flow of information in the formal communications process. Regardless of the accuracy of information traveling through the grapevine, managers are advised to pay close attention to what is being communicated. The grapevine is an important source of information concerning the attitudes and morale of workers in an organization. Some studies indicate that the speed and accuracy of information within the grapevine increases significantly in organizations with poor formal communications flow.[7] The opposite seems to be true for organizations with open, honest, and free-flowing channels of communication.

Managers also possess opportunities to engage in constructive informal communications with workers. As a matter of fact, experienced managers often report that they get much more done while acting informally than they do through formal communication modes.

Nonverbal Communication

A good deal of information gained during face-to-face interactions comes from nonverbal cues. These include body language, facial expressions, eye contact, posture, and gestures. Some research indicates that as much as 75 percent of information is gained through observing nonverbal cues.[8] Interpreting nonverbal behavior is often subjective. Cultural differences provide varied interpretations associated with nonverbal cues. For instance, for people of western European cultures, lack of eye contact may indicate dishonesty. For individuals from other cultures, the same action may symbolize respect for authority.[9]

Choosing Message Media

Recall from the communication model that the sender encodes a message into a medium for transmission to the receiver(s). Media may take the form of informal conversations, email, meetings, notes, memos, letters, and other forms of transmission. Most forms of media may be classified in one of two categories: written media and verbal interaction.

Like most people, managers have a tendency to avoid confrontation. For this reason, some managers seem to prefer placing messages in a written format as opposed to engaging in verbal interaction. In many instances, putting messages into writing may be less constructive than face-to-face interaction. Face-to-face interaction provides both parties with opportunities to extract information through nonverbal cues discussed in a previous chapter. Personal interaction often adds to the perception of importance of the topic of communication. Also, people feel important when they are invited to interact with a manager or supervisor. Finally, familiarity often develops as a result of personal interaction. As long as professional distinctions are maintained, familiarity makes the work environment comfortable. Therefore, it is suggested that managers take every appropriate opportunity to communicate verbally with members of the staff.

There are occasions that call for written communication media. Written messages have posterity; that is, they last for long periods of time and provide future reference materials. Also, written communications provide documentation of an event for future reference or as a matter of record. More formal occasions call for written media. For example, a worker who has demonstrated superior performance may appreciate a formal letter of congratulations from the manager. One recommended technique is to use hand-written thank you notes sent to staff members for appropriate reasons. Of course, any issue that requires documentation requires the use of written communications. Finally, conversations or meetings may be clarified through written follow-up documents.

Managers must decide on the appropriate communication media for each set of circumstances. Whenever possible, it is suggested that personal interaction be chosen as a medium for communication. Some circumstances may warrant verbal interaction with written follow-up correspondence. The problem with over-reliance on written communications is the perceived lack of importance of memos and other correspondence in most organizations. This is due to the paper avalanche and information overload associated with written messages in organizations.

DIRECTIONAL FLOWS OF ORGANIZATIONAL COMMUNICATIONS

Recall the communication channels cited in the communication model. The medium is the means of message transmission. The channel is the direction of transmission throughout the organization's hierarchy (organization chart). Many managers are familiar with the traditional downward direction of communication. The managers send directives downward through the organizational chart, and workers adhere to the directions. Managers should be aware that effective communications require flows of information in multiple directions. Figure 12.2 illustrates the directional flow of communications.

HOSPITALITY NEWS *Defusing an Angry Employee*

When an angry employee confronts you, you must respond—but not in kind. You need to carefully control your response and work to disarm this person who is attempting to intimidate you. Here are some suggestions:

- *Don't respond impulsively.* This is a natural reaction: to lash out or defend yourself or your position. Doing so rarely contributes to a positive outcome. Instead, think carefully and respond deliberately. Ask yourself, "Will what I'm about to say help or hurt the situation?"
- *Don't take it personally.* This is harder to do, but rarely are people attacking you personally. There is usually some more complicated reason behind their harsh words, and your task is to find out what their motivation is all about.

- *Put yourself in the other person's place.* This will help you avoid taking his words personally and responding impulsively. Hostility often arises out of anxiety, exhaustion, frustration, or overwork. Don't make excuses for bad behavior, but understanding the circumstances might enable you to respond more positively.
- *Most important of all, control your voice, tone, and language.* Often our voices rise to a higher pitch when we are excited or angry. That's a sure sign you are losing control and when you realize that, it will help you control your voice and your emotions. Never respond by using foul or harsh language.

Source: Hospitality News, April 2002, p. 46.

Notice that communications flow in many directions in a healthy organization. Directions include upward, downward, lateral, and diagonal flows. Upward flows should include open feedback to managers who support those working on the line. Lateral flows provide organization of tasks among operating departments. Diagonal flows provide support information from higher levels in the organization to line workers. Upward diagonal flows provide feedback to diagonal support networks.

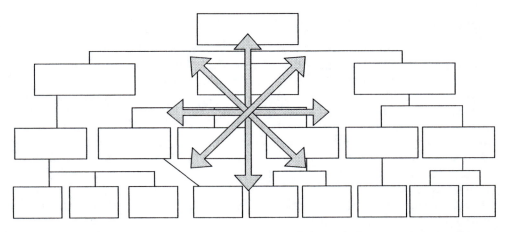

Figure 12.2.   Directional Flows of Communication through the Organization Chart.

COMMUNICATION SKILLS FOR HUMAN RESOURCE PRACTITIONERS

The human resource practitioner engages in verbal and written communications processes on a daily basis. In addition to employee relations counseling, employment interviewing, dispute resolution, incident investigations, and other daily interactive processes, the HR manager is the author of many written documents that are matters of official communication within the organization. As we learned in earlier chapters, the written communications skills of human resource managers commonly fall within the scrutiny of third party investigators that include administrative agents, attorneys, adjudicators, as well as other external reviewers. Hence, the HR manager must develop impeccable written communications abilities in order to represent the organization as an effective practitioner.

The human resource manager must also communicate internally within the organization by compiling documents such as policies, procedures, rules, and manuals. In addition to these skills, the HR practitioner must be effective in authoring less complicated written materials such as letters, memoranda, notices, incident reports and disciplinary warning documents.

Further, the human resource manager is placed in a position where she must influence large numbers of individuals through formal presentations to collective groups of people. This requires solid presentation skills on the part of the practitioner. Formal presentations might include executive proposals, third party testimonies, recognition ceremonies, and seminar presentations.

Finally, it is the place of the human resource practitioner to be an excellent interviewer in cases of employment, complaints, grievances, personality conflicts and other stressful verbal interactions. HR managers must possess more than the verbal aspects of these types of communications, by possessing the ability to read nonverbal cues including eye contact, proxemics, facial expressions, gestures, and other subtle cues. It is the expectation for HR managers to know these aspects of human communication to a degree that permits them to teach these skills to other managers. Hence, part of being a manager's manager, includes being a communicator's communicator, as effective communication abilities are the essence of effective managerial interactions.

HUMAN RESOURCE INFORMATION SYSTEMS (HRIS)

MIS—Management information system; converts data into useable information.
HRIS—An MIS for human resource practices.

One form of communications in practically all organizations is provided by a digitized system of interfaces that convert data (facts) into useable information called a Management Information System (**MIS**). A management information system that is used for human resource management applications is referred to as a Human Resource Information System (**HRIS**). You may recall from our discussions on productivity that resources include people, materials, equipment, and finances. In the world of MIS, the input side of the productivity model consists of data resources. Data must be managed for efficient and effective allocation and utilization as inputs to the transformation process, which yields outputs in the form of products and services. In the case of MIS, the outcome (product/service) is information that is usable for managing organizational processes. As is the case with most organizational functions, human resource management has specific informational processing needs. Hence, an MIS for HR is referred to as an HRIS. Why is an HRIS a form of communication? The HRIS process converts data into useful information that is used to produce reports and other outputs that are shared with multiple parties. So, the HRIS will use data to create information (sender/encode), and then transmit that information (channel, media) to individuals with a need to know that information (decode/receivers) with a conclusive mechanism for responses to that information (feedback loop). It is safe to say that all management information systems include HRIS systems.

Just as material resources are housed in storage areas, data resources reside in **databases**. There is a hierarchy of structure in databases, ranging from the smallest to largest entities. The most basic data element is called a character, consisting of a single alphanumeric or other symbol. A grouping of characters would exist in a field or data item. Related fields are grouped into records and a group of related records comprise a file. Files may be classified by the application of the data such as a payroll file or inventory file. Some files are classified by the data contained within them, such as a document file or graphical image file. Other files may be classified by permanence, such as history files or transaction files.

databases—An integrated collection of logically related records (objects) that are sorted into files.

A database is an integrated collection of logically related records (objects) that are sorted into files. A human resource database would consist of records located in employment (personnel actions and applicant flow data), compensation (payroll and benefits), job analysis (job descriptions and job specifications), and training/development files. Figure 12.3 shows the relationships of data items located within an HRIS.

Notice in Figure 12.3 that data is input into the HRIS, which requires the completion of fields that comprise sorted records, with the information

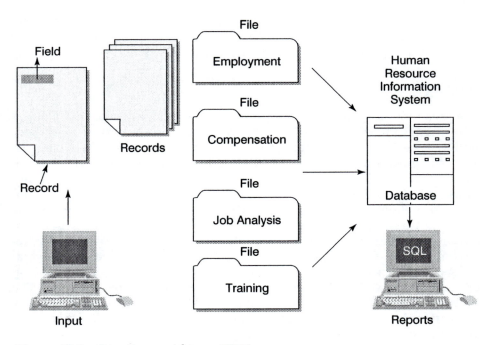

Figure 12.3. Data Items within an HRIS.

from the records divided into files. For instance, the name of a new employee would be placed into the "name" field of a "personnel action form" and that name would be replicated as a field on a record for each of the four files. Entering the new employee's name, creates an employment, compensation, job analysis, and training record in each of the respective files. If the employee is later promoted, that personnel action form would trigger just the employment, compensation and job analysis file, since a promotion would result in a higher pay grade (compensation file) with a new job description (job analysis file) and a change in title (employment file).

In another scenario, let's say the employee completes first aid and CPR training. The input in this case would trigger the training file (list of completed training) and the employment file (additional credential for an employee). The job analysis file and the compensation file would not be updated unless this training resulted in a change of duties or pay levels.

All of this information is stored in the HRIS database. When human resource practitioners need to manipulate the data to generate reports, for instance an EEOC report, they would select certain fields on a report generator screen to sort and format the data into a conceptual report. Standard Query Language (SQL) is one commonly used software application that permits this manipulation process.[10]

In addition to traditional administrative functions facilitated by an HRIS, there are many newly developed communication processes that permit direct access to certain database areas by employees. The process that facilitates this form of interaction is called a corporate intranet, which replicates the Internet by providing search engine capability to help users to find and enter information. Additionally, the Internet itself is commonly used for employment purposes to include job postings, applications and other recruitment and selection processes. Newly developed intranet applications for employees within an organization fall within the domain of Business-to-Employee (B-2-E) applications. This aspect of employee relations is a new and exciting component of human resource interactions.

SUMMARY

Communication skills are vital to a manager's ability to accomplish the objectives of the organization through the actions of others. Therefore, the responsibility for communicating effectively in all directions lies squarely with the immediate supervisor. Messages must be honest, and appeal to the perceptions of others to be effective. While written communications are sometimes appropriate, they are often less effective than verbal interactions. The communications model demonstrates the development of the message by the sender, the transmission of the message through a medium, the sending of the message through the channel, the decoding of the message by the receiver(s), and the feedback loop. The feedback loop closes one communications sequence and starts another sequence. Therefore, the feedback loop goes beyond clarifying the receiver's interpretation of the message. The grapevine is an example of an informal communication system. In a healthy organization, it is recognized that complaints and grievances are useful and important parts of the communication process.

> ## *In the Real World . . . (Continued)*
>
> After boarding the ship, your only task is to follow the employment manager as he makes his rounds. You notice a small office with a title on the door, "Ombudsman." The employee relations manager explains that he places one person on each ship to handle complaints and disputes. This person is called the ombudsman, which is an old term used to describe a neutral party to hear complaints. He goes on to tell you that the ship's captain is the supreme decision-maker while the ship is at sea. The ombudsman listens to complaints and grievances of shipboard personnel to help the captain in handling such matters. The ombudsman also relays the information so the employee relations manager may advise the captain in certain important matters.
>
> While looking around this tiny office on board the ship, you notice printed materials that replicate all of the items in the shore-side HR office. These are printed in many languages, to accommodate the diverse workers on the ship. After spending four days at sea, you have observed that the only activity performed by the employee relations manager has been to walk the decks and talk with the staff (who all seem to know and like the manager).
>
> At the conclusion of the trip, you ask the employee relations manager, "Why do you go to sea every month? It seems that the ombudsman handles all of the disputes and complaints and all you do is walk around shaking hands."
>
> The employee relations manager says to you with a smile, "Communication is not always about writing and speaking. The most important form of communication is showing that you care, just like we say we do in the handbooks. When these people see me on board once a month, it reinforces the fact that I care enough to be out there with them, which makes them feel like I am keeping tabs on their fair treatment while they are at sea. Between that and the presence of my onboard ombudsman, the staff feels secure in knowing we are safeguarding their fair treatment, no matter what country they are from. This," the manager concludes, "is called proactive employee relations."

DISCUSSION QUESTIONS

1. Human resource managers are managers' managers. What does this really mean? How could this concept be applied to organizational communications?

2. Which communications skills are most important for a human resource practitioner: listening, writing, talking, presentations? Consider scenarios in which an HR practitioner would be likely to use each of these skills.

3. Since most schools do not teach effective listening skills, how would you go about learning and practicing these skills?

4. If you were a human resource practitioner, what types of training programs would you develop to teach managers how to communicate in organizations?

KEY TERMS

channel	decode	grapevine	HRIS
communication	encode	MIS	receiver
databases	feedback	medium	senders

CHAPTER THIRTEEN
Leadership Strategies

OBJECTIVES

By the end of this chapter, the reader will be able to:

1. Understand the relationships of leaders, followers, and the environment (situation).
2. Identify the characteristics associated with leadership traits.
3. Recognize types of interactions that are associated with transactional leadership.
4. Understand the concepts of transformational and transcendental leadership.

> ## *In the Real World . . .*
>
> You are working in the human resource office of a large brand
> level. The director of human resources invites you to attend th
> source Association chapter meeting after work. You realize thi
> work with other HR practitioners. You arrive at the meeting a
> attendees, who include directors as well as HR specialist (com
> training, labor relations) managers.
>
> The topic of the meeting is leadership strategies. A guest s
> on leadership development programs. After the presentation,
> sion session. Since you want to learn as much as you can ab
> attention to the interactions of the discussion session. You start to notice after a w....
> these HR managers, while somewhat knowledgeable, seem to be lacking some quality that
> your director has.
>
> At the office the next morning you are having coffee with the training manager. You start to
> tell him about your experience at the association meeting. You then mention, "Is it me, or is
> there some quality that our HR director has that the other practitioners don't have?" He just
> smiles at you.

178

INTRODUCTION

Leadership is one area of human resource management that has not received a great amount of attention. One simple description of leadership is the power of influence to generate the authentic desire on the part of others to act in a certain way. Leadership is all about the power of influence over others. While the body of research has attempted to describe this power in terms that are consistent with the **scientific method** of analysis, to this date there is really very little agreement about the definitions of the terms **leadership**, **leaders**, and **leading**.[1] Leadership in the field of management seems to be the power of influence that creates a willingness to accomplish the objectives of the organization. Most HR practitioners are familiar with this description of leadership; but why do HR managers spend so little time trying to understand the phenomena associated with leadership power?

One reason that many HR managers are not well versed in the practice and theory of leadership is that such a practice is contrary to the traditional functions of human resource management. HR managers are trained in the law and organizational management. The nature of HR practice is focused on management activities, which are contrary to the activities of leadership to a certain extent. This is not to say that HR practitioners disregard leadership concepts; in fact, the opposite is true. Many organizations have replaced the job title of *manager* with the word *leader*. In some organizations the term *department* or *work unit* has been replaced by the title *team*. The use of these titles is certainly a step in the right direction to create general awareness of leadership and teamwork within organizations. However, most anecdotal reports indicate that units and managers within these organizations are doing nothing more than traditional management practices. There isn't anything wrong with traditional management practices, as many individuals in possession of the title manager have yet to learn these concepts and it is certainly

scientific method—A method used in management science based on hypotheses, data collection, and analysis to prove original assumptions.

leadership—The power to influence others to take action willingly: In management, it is the willingness of individuals to accomplish the objectives of the organization.

leaders—Individuals who possess the power to influence others.

leading—Leaders in the practice of exercising power to influence others.

one major task of HR practitioners to train these managers in these practices. Leadership, however, goes beyond management practices. Many case studies concerning great moments in management are centered on individuals who demonstrate both leadership and management skills in the process of achieving greatness. Leadership is one area of research that is still in its infancy, so there is much to be learned about it.

Proactive human resource managers take every opportunity to train themselves in the comprehension of the leadership phenomenon. They seek to become leaders in their own management practice. Finally, they pursue the grand strategy of imparting leadership development training to every manager in the organization. It is possible for a person who is not a manager to teach management. For some reason, however, it seems impossible for a person who is not a leader to teach leadership practices.

THE PRACTICE OF LEADERSHIP

Leadership is a common topic of discussion in organizational and institutional settings. Curricula in schools of business administration, and hospitality/tourism management, include courses, seminars, or cross-curriculum infusion of topical areas that are related to leadership concepts. The word leadership is commonly used in the course of daily conversations in professional and administrative settings. Printed literature includes articles and advertisements for professional development workshops on the topic of leadership. Employers rank leadership skills near the top of desired abilities of candidates for supervisory employment. Finally, a good deal of academic research has been conducted to develop leadership paradigms.

While the concept of leadership is much discussed, it still remains difficult to describe. Individuals seem hard pressed to provide agreeable descriptions of what leadership really is. This factor may contribute to the many definitions that have been provided to describe the many aspects of leadership.

WHAT THE RESEARCHERS SAY ABOUT LEADERSHIP

Machiavellian theory—The belief that leaders are born and not made.

The **Machiavellian theory** that leaders are born, not made, remains present in some modern-day thought. Others contend that leadership may be learned by anyone with a desire to lead others. If this is true, the question for trainers and educators seems to be, "How do we teach people to become leaders?"

One study provides comparisons between leadership and management in organizations to determine differences between the activities of leaders versus managers.[2] Another investigation discusses characteristics and qualities of leaders as means to provide case study examples of leadership situations.[3] One researcher provides a developmental model as a means for teaching leadership relations.[4] Some studies identify leadership credibility factors as determined by the perceptions of others to describe leadership qualities.[5] Other academic investigators take research-based model approaches to present paradigms to develop an understanding of leadership phenomena.[6] Finally, recent research provides focus on the transformational leadership paradigm to describe leadership dimensions,[7] as well as universal systems models.[8]

It would seem that regardless of the approach taken to understand and teach leadership, three **interdependent** factors must be considered. First, we must observe the behaviors and attempt to identify the characteristics of leaders. Second, we should gain an understanding of the perspectives of followers. Third, we must analyze contributions of the environment or **situation** to leader/follower interactions. This view may seem simplistic; however, when attempting to understand complex concepts, simplification may be the means through which we clarify our understanding.

It is apparent that those who have been mentored or exposed to dealing with great leaders possess a clear snapshot of leadership in action. Therefore, it may be possible that an experiential approach to learning is appropriate in the study of leadership topics.

interdependent—The highest level of relationship with subsystems that is achievable by an individual or other subsystem. It is beyond the levels of dependence and independence.

situation—The environmental factors influencing a leadership style at a given moment.

LEADERSHIP AND MANAGEMENT

People often confuse leadership and management, when in fact they are two different things. One illustration of this is the advice for supervisors to manage "things" and lead "people." This suggests that leadership is an influencing activity, while other aspects of management refer to planning, organizing and controlling functions.[9] It is important to note that not all managers are leaders and not all leaders are managers. Think for a moment about people with supervisor titles that just don't come across to you as leaders. Now, consider those with no formal authority who seem to influence co-workers to follow their lead.

Some experts speak of leadership from the standpoint of the support role owed to the followers, which are referred to as **stewardship** qualities of leaders.[10] The philosopher Lao Tzu proclaimed that leaders must learn to follow, which is one of the signs of stewardship.[11] One tendency of effective leaders is their willingness to share the role of leader and follower in appropriate situations. Leaders also demonstrate the capacity to provide simplified interpretations of complex issues.[12]

stewardship—Self-sacrificing service by a leader to the followership.

HOSPITALITY NEWS *Are You a Manager or a Leader?*

There are many managers and only a few true leaders. Here are the skills that define the elite group of men and women we call leaders. Effective leaders have the ability to:

Build or use a compelling vision of what's achievable and then communicate that vision to others.

Encourage people, sharing authority and responsibility in order to make others feel significant and needed.

Establish objectives that make the most of opportunities and resources, and make plans to reach those objectives.

Think creatively. Find untapped opportunities, look for additional options, locate new needs, and solve problems.

Source: Hospitality News, August 2002, p. 30.

TRADITIONAL MODELS AND THEORIES

There are sufficient amounts of traditional models and theories concerning the topic of leadership. Consideration of traditional models reviewed by the experts seems to provide evidence that research is not the key to developing a practical understanding of leadership. A number of research articles are available for review. Yet the data seem to provide ineffective knowledge for the purpose of imparting leadership skills. This, once again, seems to provide evidence that the concept of leadership is phenomenal in nature.

Organizational theory frames provide us with categories of leadership strengths. However, no single frame provides a holistic picture of an actual leader. Instead, leaders are categorized as having conceptual strengths in structure, relations, political skills, or facilitative skills. Most widely acclaimed leaders possess strengths in all these categories.

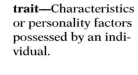

trait—Characteristics or personality factors possessed by an individual.

A number of studies have been conducted to identify characteristic and response theories to explain leadership.[13] **Trait** theories cite personal characteristics which help us determine to what extent leaders will gravitate toward transactional vs. transformational leadership styles. Behavioral theories focus on internally motivating factors of task and relations, while contingency theory considers the same tendencies from external motivating aspects. These traditional theories assume an objective viewpoint of interactions between leaders and followers. Other research departs from this tradition by identifying means used by leaders to elicit follower participation. These are basically focused on communications skills. The underlying inference is that leaders manipulate followers through symbolic gestures such as rites and rituals, or that leaders create mythical perceptions in the minds of the followers.

Regardless of the focus, the technique seems to involve the construct of perceived realities consistent with the beliefs, attitudes, and values of the followers.

In practice, it may be true that leaders possess and employ the ability to communicate in terms identifiable with followers' cultural systems. This activity might be viewed as the ability of the leader to communicate **empathetically** with followers through an innate understanding of the internal value systems of individuals and groups. While this may be labeled as a form of manipulation, it may be more accurately described as effective managerial communication to achieve common and constructive outcomes.

empathy—The ability to communicate with the same emotional sensibility of the individual who is the recipient of the communication.

ETHICS AND LEADERSHIP

Is there a moral component in the leadership paradigm? An interesting departure from the traditional viewpoint associated with the achievement of transformational leadership through power and influence is the diminished moral connotation within the model. Some of the research indicates that the moral aspect has evolved into a code word for innovative and motivational leadership. It would be hard to imagine a true leader who did not create an image of personal morality in the minds of followers. Even leaders in illicit environments portray a code of personal values in their behaviors and communications.

Regardless of the semantics, most researchers and practitioners agree that credibility is the key to a leader's ability to influence people. This credibility evolves from perceptions of the leader by peers, followers and other leaders. Credibility is attained by peoples' perceptions of a person's behavior and expression of thoughts. The leader, by the nature of her or his relationship to others, is highly scrutinized in this regard. Therefore, it seems likely that the credibility factor is greatly influenced by the moral and ethical value systems of the person occupying a leadership position.

HOSPITALITY NEWS *Trust: The Competitive Advantage*

It's been scientifically proven that managers who have the trust of their employees are at a competitive advantage in this day of the ebbing worker pool. A team of investigators asked more than 370 restaurant employees to rate how much they trust their general manager, and to rate the degree to which they had confidence in the manager's ability, integrity, and respect for employees.

They balanced those ratings against the operatives of the restaurants. Their finding: Restaurants where employees trusted their managers achieved high levels of sales and profitability during the following quarter—and trusted managers were those with strong reputations for ability, integrity and employee respect.

Courtesy of *Food Industry News. Source: Hospitality News,* April 2002, p. 22.

Finally, discussions concerning leadership diversity provide a departure from traditional views, different than those presented by other authors. In this case the word traditional refers to the white male leader, as opposed to the nontraditional leader of different gender or color (to include national origin). While it is certainly true that cultures have provided limitations to the achievement of legitimate power possessed by repressed classes of people, it is unlikely that differences exist as to the inherent ability of these individuals to lead. It appears that these writings are concerned more with cultural challenges than actual leadership concerns.

EMERGING THEORIES AND MODELS

change agentry—The process of enacting systematic change.

Emerging theories in leadership seem to reflect the dynamic environment in which organizations and institutions currently function. Less focus seems to be placed on narrow models of leadership. Holistic leadership paradigms are now emerging. Visionary aspects of leadership are becoming a dominant consideration in discussions of leadership effectiveness. **Change agentry** is also a prominent concern. It stands to reason that today's leaders need to be skilled visionaries capable of enacting change. Organizations are rethinking, restructuring, and revitalizing the types of work that are done and processes aimed at the achievement of outcomes. Therefore, it is appropriate for effective leaders to possess skills in supporting the followership in these environments.

The leader of today deals with such diversity as to require much more advanced levels of sophistication than possessed by former leaders. Emphasis in emerging leadership models provides focus on the dynamics of the followership. Individuals in today's organizations possess stronger values of individualism and sophisticated convictions with regard to quality of lifestyle issues. Also, today's workforce comprises individuals who are knowledgeable, and adamant about the preservation of individual rights in the workplace. This affects the ability of leaders to provide effective influence over others, and further enhances the moral component of leadership influence.

PURPOSE, MISSION AND VISION

Certain environments provide what one might call motivating missions.[14] In such cases, people seem to be naturally motivated to perform at peak levels. Usually, these scenarios are project based. Common examples are special events that occur in organizations that challenge and energize workers to work toward a common purpose, and to achieve a common set of goals. During these events, the job of leadership is somewhat simplified. Also, during these times, unsuspecting leaders tend to emerge temporarily. The unfortunate aspect of this scenario is that it seems to be unsustainable; when the inspiring mission is fulfilled, the performance levels and enthusiasm seem to drop to normal (sometimes mediocre) levels.

The challenge for leaders is to provide sustainable purpose and mission that motivate the workforce. Most institutions and organizations do not serve a naturally glamorous or exciting purpose; it becomes the challenge of the leader to embrace and communicate the mission and purpose in ways that impassion others.

The current trend in organizations and institutions goes beyond purpose and mission to include vision statements. Unfortunately, when the word statement is added, bureaucrats become licensed to turn visioning into an exercise. One expert draws contrasts and comparisons to approaches taken by managers vs. leaders to develop and communicate visions.[15] The managers have a tendency to formulate administrative representations, similar to what is taught in strategic planning sessions. The leaders bring the vision to life. They depict the vision in terms that are consistent with the value systems and description preferences of the people in the organization.

BUILDING AND SHARING POWER

According to some researchers, leaders possess the ability to use informal means to align people.[16] They do this by developing informal networks within various areas of the organization. Bureaucratic managers tend to rely on formal lines of communications, such as written reports and job descriptions. While formal documents have their place in an organization or institution, bureaucrats rely more on these tools than their leader counterparts.

Leaders seem to be highly skilled communicators. Whether these skills are acquired or inherent, leaders recognize the power behind effective communications. They seem to use all means of communication available to them. Their mannerisms, body language, appearance, posture, and examples seem to be orchestrated to drive home the message being sent to people. Leaders also seem to possess the ability to convert complex concepts into simplified strings of messages. This probably is attributable to a thorough understanding of and rapport with people in the organization. Finally, leaders seem to recognize the importance of active listening. They realize that by listening effectively, they can better understand the people with whom they are dealing. Leaders seem to be keenly aware of the importance of information gained through informal interactions.

SELF-ANALYSIS AND CONTEXTUAL RELATIONS

Just as before leading, one must learn to follow, before one can know others, one must know oneself. This may be the basis for the understanding of human behavior that many leaders seem to possess. Leaders seem to take time for introspection and creative thinking (popular terms are meditation or focused reflection). Leaders may spend a good deal of time in contemplative silence (daydreaming might be another label). This quiet time may permit an individual to analyze the self and interactions with others. This activity may help to create a certain type of wisdom within an individual.

One expert reminds us that leaders see individuals as holistic beings.[17] People are more than their positions, accomplishments, and status. They are fully developed human entities with all of the experience, knowledge, and emotions possessed by our beings. Leaders take the time to consider the human factors of people. They are also capable of identifying individual talents, preferences, motivational factors, and feelings. The researchers also remind organizations to be on the lookout for corporate entropy,[18] signs that indicate the settling-in of bureaucratic thought processes. As these processes take hold, the organization begins to decline. One sign is when individuals begin to lose sight of the purpose, mission, and vision for the organization. These symptoms, if left unaddressed, may lead to cultural shifts in organizations in which leadership values may ultimately decline, only to be replaced by bureaucratic values which may be detrimental to the survival of those corporations.

DEVELOPING AND IMPROVING LEADER RELATIONS

Leaders seem to be self-developing people. Since leaders are people who self-analyze, they are usually aware of their strengths and weaknesses. Someone once said that great leaders have great weaknesses.[19] Yet leaders appear to be aware of those areas in which they need assistance. For this reason, a leader would tend to enlist the support of individuals in specific areas. The leader might also have a tendency to empower or align appropriately with others to facilitate accomplishment of the overall mission. In this sense, leaders are sensible. They seem to recognize that none of us is as good or smart as all of us.

In addition to possessing an awareness of how to select human capital to increase overall strengths, leaders seem to have the ability to energize individuals toward achievement. It is likely that they do this in a manner that provides personal satisfaction to people as well as benefit to the organization or institution. Leaders seem to maximize relations with others for the common welfare.

TRANSACTIONS AND TRANSFORMATIONS

transactional leadership—Leadership that focuses on the moment of leading only.

Transactional leaders seem to be those who possess the ability to influence others through highly developed interpersonal relations skills. The power of influence is certainly a key skill shared among all leaders. In some organiza-

tions, leaders may rely more heavily on this set of skills, depending on organizational structure. Often in these organizations, individuals are provided legitimate power through the attainment of positions, such as division or department director. In some settings, workers tend to resist people who have been given titles. One factor which may contribute to these attitudes may be the tendency by senior managers to promote individuals who do not possess credibility with the workers; lack of credibility may usurp acceptance of formal authority. People who possess appropriate levels of credibility with the workers in these organizations seem unaffected by the overall lack of respect for people with formal job titles.

THE NATURE OF CHANGE

For years now, students of management have been told about the impact of external environmental factors on organizations. Models are provided to assist managers with identifying and predicting external events, for the purpose of making decisions to limit threats and opportunities looming outside the organization. Being good students of management, they have learned to perform auditing, scanning, forecasting, and analytical activities. A factor that seems to be overlooked is the importance of making decisions to modify how the organization operates to remain congruent with its environment. We are entering an era in which those external factors of influence are becoming exponentially more dynamic. As the world around us changes, people must also change. For this to happen, people must accept responsibility and accountability for changing their lives; evolutionary change involves personal growth. Leaders who pursue paths of personal growth for themselves and their followers are practicing the highest level of interaction, called **transformational leadership**. In today's business environment both transactional and transformational leaders are considered to be change agents.

Transformational leadership— Leadership that focuses on the intrinsic desires of all involved parties that is applied to leading those parties.

Change Agentry

Most of us have met individuals who are natural troubleshooters, always seeking challenges that require implementing change. Some personality tests identify people who prefer to work in troubleshooting capacities. Troubleshooters who possess training and skills in effective change implementation may be referred to as change agents.

This is not to say that all change agents are troubleshooters; in the same way, not all troubleshooters are effective change agents—some are muck stirrers. While they mean well, they lack the ability systematically to implement change that is accepted by others. One organizational aspect that change agents and troubleshooters face is conflict. Most of us deal with conflict on a regular basis. We have a tendency to consider conflict to be negative; however, there are forms of conflict in organizations that are constructive. This type of conflict may be called managed conflict. A leader who recognizes the synergistic outcomes of creative idea generation might welcome this form of conflict. When constructive conflict is present, the threat of the groupthink phenomenon is reduced. This type of conflict fosters multiple viewpoints to generate outcomes greater than those that may be established by an individual working alone.

In the Real World . . . (Continued)

Finally, you say to the training manager, "Are you just going to smile at me? Or are you going to explain why I am sensing a difference between our leader and the other members of the association?"

He laughs. "You just answered your own question."

"What are you talking about?"

"The difference is leadership. Our director is a leader." He continues, "I have worked with her for some time now. When I started with her, she used to drive me crazy by never giving me direct answers to my questions. She seemed to take almost sadistic pleasure in watching me try things and fail. Some days, she would be very nurturing and on other days, she would be a hard-driving task manager. I thought she was "schizo" in the beginning." The training manager pauses in his reflection about the past. "Then it dawned on me—she was a leader who was teaching me (in her own twisted way) to become a leader just like her." He smirks a little, and then continues, "As soon as I achieved that awareness, she told me that I was now "getting it." It was like she was reading my mind." He concludes, "We have been leadership partners ever since."

"Wow" you, say to him. "How do you get that way?"

He replies, "I don't know, but if she takes you under her wing, you will know you have reached leader status when she no longer appears to you to be the director from hell." He laughs.

SUMMARY

In this chapter, we have identified the characteristics of leaders. Interactions among leaders, followers and a given situation (environment) are the basis of transactional leadership. Transformational leadership considers these same factors in addition to the evolutionary growth of all participants in the interactions. This type of influence among individuals requires perceived credibility on the part of leaders; thus leaders are viewed as possessing qualities associated with personal and professional integrity. Transformation is preceded by the enactment of change. Leaders are change agents who systematically develop individuals to grow with the dynamic external environment. While the topic of leadership has been widely considered in research settings, the best way for practitioners to become skilled leaders is to model and engage in mentorship relationships with those established leaders in the workplace.

DISCUSSION QUESTIONS

1. Some people say that leadership is a natural ability and others say that these skills may be learned by anyone who wants to be a leader. What do you think?

2. If you were to analyze your leadership style and come to the conclusion that you are mostly task oriented (focused on what needs to be accomplished), what style would you look for in your assistant? Would she be just like you or different than you? Why?

3. Think about great leaders in history or in your personal experience. What qualities do you think made them great?

4. Now consider those individuals who may not be classified as good leaders at all. Where were they deficient? Is there anything to be learned from their examples?

KEY TERMS

change agentry
empathy
interdependent
leading
leaders

leadership
Machiavellian
scientific method
situation

stewardship
trait
transactional
  leadership

transformational
  leadership

CHAPTER FOURTEEN
Employee Motivation

OBJECTIVES

By the end of this chapter, the reader will be able to:

1. Identify a few theories of employee motivation.
2. Apply motivational strategies to managing workers.
3. Recognize differences in individual motivators.
4. Apply techniques to motivate groups.

In the Real World . . .

You have been working in a human resource office for a large exclusive resort and vacation ownership organization, nestled in a high-end private community. A new human resource director has been hired to head the department. You aren't sure why the last director left; he just disappeared one day.

The last HR director had developed an employee recognition program that called for guests of the resort to vote for an employee who provided excellent service. Guests were asked to drop a guest service ballot in a large locked box located next to a shiny new two-seater sports car located in the center of the lobby. The estimated value of the car was $35,000 and a large sign was on display that said, "One of our staff associates will win this car based on your ballot demonstrating excellent service." Needless to say, guests were impressed by this gesture. They thought the management team at the resort must be wonderful to award such a prize to an employee.

After one week of observation and individual meetings with each HR practitioner, the new director called a meeting with all of the HR staff. After some preliminary items of discussion, the director asked, "Whose idea was it to do this car recognition thing?" One of the staff members said, "I think it was the last director and the executive committee." The director responded, "Bad idea, don't you think?" After a long silence, one of the staff members voiced an opinion; "I think we could have come with something that would give a lot more motivational bang for $35k." Another staff member chimed in with, "This program means nothing to the staff; they think it is a joke." She continued, "This is just a PR thing to make the guests think we are generous employers."

After many more opinions along this line, the new director said, "I'm glad to hear you share the honest truth." She continued, "Did you share this information with the past director?" Most of the staff looked down and smirked. Seeing this the director said, "Let me guess . . . you were never asked for an opinion." Everyone started laughing at the obvious truth. "Well" said the director, "There is nothing for us to do now but watch this whole program blow up in the executive committee's faces. It is apparent that whoever designed this scheme knew nothing about the human needs of our staff." Everyone at the table nodded in agreement.

INTRODUCTION

Any experienced human resource practitioner will tell us that as managers of people we must learn as much as we can about applied human behavior. Certainly our discussion from Chapter 13 would be worthless if we did not move into an understanding of the underlying factors that influence individuals to behave in certain ways. That is the purpose of this chapter.

As a manager's manager, or "management educator," as we established in the last chapter, the human resource practitioner must know as much as can be known about human motivation. No management development program is complete without motivational training seminars. While it is true that many managers in organizations studied motivation as part of their curriculum at school, it is apparent from watching them in the real world that many don't know how to apply it to the management of people. Hence, the human resource manager is the teacher, reinforcement agent and guardian of motivation applications on the part of all the managers within the organization.

MOTIVATION

Motivation may be defined as a willingness to do something. Managers are interested in motivation applications because they want workers to be willing to perform tasks and activities aimed at the accomplishment of the objectives of the organization.[1] Workers who are willing to do the work do better jobs. Willing workers also permit the manager to act as leader instead of manager. Motivated people do not need to be managed; they simply require leadership to remain focused on the collective attainment of objectives.[2]

Factors motivate individuals in different ways. This is because motivation is based on the perception of unfulfilled wants, needs, and desires.[3] These perceptions vary among individuals. For instance, most people agree that money is a motivator. The experts indicate that, for most people, it isn't money that motivates, but the unfulfilled material needs associated with having money.[4] Some are definitely motivated by the opportunity to earn unlimited income. These people have a tendency to work in commissioned sales positions. Others value earning the most income in the shortest period of time spent working. These people may have a tendency to work for gratuities or large bonuses. Another group may prefer to work in pleasant surroundings with specifically scheduled work hours and standard work routines. These people may prefer administrative positions. Managers are often motivated by challenging work, achievement, recognition, and a personal sense of accomplishment as an important member of an organization. Managers usually perceive the need to make a decent income but often choose management positions over more lucrative positions such as commissioned sales jobs. For many managers, a performance bonus is primarily a measurement of accomplishment, with the actual dollar amount representing the reward for achievement.

Individuals have varying needs and priorities of need. For this reason, there is no general rule concerning motivators for different people. The manager does not possess the ability to motivate another person. This is because motivation comes from within a person, not from external sources. Therefore, the best a manager can do is to get others to motivate themselves. Managers accomplish this by identifying unfulfilled perceived needs and wants for each individual. Once needs and wants are identified, the manager makes every attempt to combine need fulfillment with performance outcomes. This combination results in motivated workers.

MONEY

For most workers, money (in the form of salaries and hourly wages) is not an effective motivator. Instead, it is a potential dis-satisfier.[5] This may be partially due to compensation structures in organizations; most people are paid for time worked. Organizations have limited resources concerning the amount of money that can be paid to workers. When a worker receives a pay raise, that person is content for a few weeks. After that time, the amount of the paycheck becomes the expectation, and the worker feels that more money is deserved. However, there are ways to structure compensation practices to attach financial rewards to performance achievements. In these cases, money (or at least its intrinsic meaning to the worker) can serve as a strong motivator.

HOSPITALITY NEWS *Motivated Employees Are Essential for Customer Service*

Keeping your employees motivated to provide consistently high quality customer service is a task just short of monumental for many companies. But it can be done, as long as you focus on one customer at a time. Here are a few tips:

Practice what you preach. If you want a motivated staff, you need to be motivated first. In all you do, are you continually assessing the customer service that you personally are giving to your customers? Unless you are "walking the walk," you won't be able to motivate your employees.

Hire the right people. The rule is either to hire smart or manage tough. Hiring smart also requires that you are motivated yourself. You can only attract people who are excited about what you do by being excited yourself. Make customer service and your expectations a part of the hiring interview. When training, make sure your employees understand your expectations for customer service.

Keep score. If you don't measure performance, your employees will be in a perpetual warm-up mode. Let employees know what they are being measured for and how it is relevant to them, customers, and your organization's bottom line.

Reward. Make sure you reward. When you overhear a server offer a sincere cheerful greeting to a customer, later say, "I really like what I'm hearing from you, and I can tell our customers like it too!" Don't neglect to offer a verbal thank you to your dedicated employees. Then include a coupon for a tiny token of your appreciation in his/her next paycheck with a personal note. (A free car wash or video rental is enough.) At team meetings share success stories with your other employees. "I can't wait to tell you what I've been observing!" People appreciate being acknowledged in front of their peers.

Source: *Hospitality News*, August 2002, p. 17.

THEORIES OF MOTIVATION

Over the years, many researchers have developed theories concerning motivation of individuals and groups of people. This chapter presents a few popular concepts. The theories that describe the "whys" of human motivation are referred to as **content theories**. Those that explain "how" to motivate people are considered to be **process theories**. In this section we start with content theories and conclude with process theories of motivation.

content theories—
Theories describing what might motivate individuals.

process theories—
Theories describing how managers might motivate employees.

Hierarchy of Needs

Psychologist Abraham Maslow developed a model that depicts unfulfilled wants and needs as motivating factors.[6] Maslow contends that five categories of needs exist in a hierarchy that ranges from lower level needs to higher order needs. As one set of needs becomes mostly fulfilled, the set of needs on the next level becomes a motivator. Maslow indicates that individuals who mostly fulfill lower level and higher order needs will seek fulfillment of the highest possible need. That need is called the need of self-actualization.

Self-actualization occurs when a person seeks to be all that a person can be in a holistic sense. This person is at peace with the self, having attained a self-perceived level of spiritual, material, and personal contentment. In the past, most people pursued self-actualizing needs only in later adult years. Current generations of adults start reaching for self-actualizing goals in their early 20s, due to higher levels of evolution among newer generations.[7] According to Maslow, less than 2 percent of the world's population attains the level of being completely self actualized. The hierarchy of needs is presented in Figure 14.1.

Two-Factor Theory

Researcher Frederick Herzberg agrees with Maslow that there is a hierarchy of lower to higher order needs. Herzberg suggests that lower order needs are extrinsically (external) based, while higher order needs are intrinsic (internal).[8] According to Herzberg, lower order needs are not motivators; rather, they are hygiene factors. By this, Herzberg implies that lower level needs do need to be satisfied for individuals to pursue higher order needs. The potential satisfaction of lower level needs does not motivate people to perform work. Instead, the absence of needs fulfillment, such as pay, working conditions, and safety, will make workers dissatisfied. Dissatisfied workers will not be motivated by higher order needs. Maslow and Herzberg provide two of the most popular content theories of motivation. A comparison of Herzberg's theory to Maslow's is presented in Figure 14.2.

OTHER CONTENT THEORIES OF MOTIVATION

Some theories contend that Maslow and Herzberg provide theoretical constructs that are not conducive to empirical studies. Additionally, some motivation scholars contend that core motivators may be altered more subtly by immediate workplace experiences. Clayton Alderfer reworked Maslow's hier-

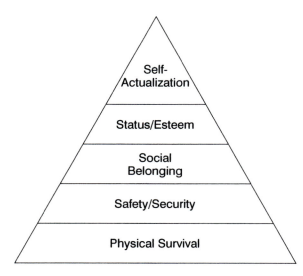

Figure 14.1. Hierarchy of Needs.

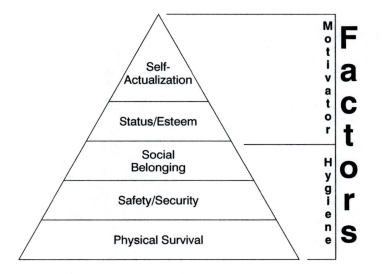

Figure 14.2. Two-Factor Theory.

archy into three core needs categories that include: E–existence; G–growth; and R–relatedness. Appropriately, he named this theory the **ERG** model.[9] Let's say that two individuals are competing for promotion to a single position. Both would be motivated at that time for the G need, or need for growth. Only one person will be promoted to the position, which means the other will not receive the promotion. The person who earns the promotion will continue to be motivated by growth. The individual who does not receive the promotion will revert to another core needs group, such as relatedness (R need) as a means to cope with the disappointment resulting from not being selected for promotion. So, while this person may have not socialized very much with coworkers, that person will return to higher socialization levels to feed the R need, which that person uses to compensate for the inability to satisfy a growth need. When another promotional opportunity occurs, that person will once again shift into growth orientation.

> **ERG**—Existence, relatedness, and growth needs.

Another focus of needs development ties motivators to personality preferences for certain individuals. David McClelland and associates developed a model called the **theory of needs**.[10] Similar to the ERG theory, the theory of needs focuses on three needs categories. These include achievement, affiliation, and power. One interesting way to identify varied dominant needs is to observe the office or work spaces for individuals. High achievement work areas will be decorated with plaques, trophies, diplomas and certificates. High affiliation work areas will be adorned with social symbols such as pictures of friends, family, and pets; favorite coffee mug, plants and home style touches and the like. The power office will be designed with dark colors that are often contrasted with red shades, a large desk with high back (throne-style) chair; decorations may include medieval weapons or other power symbols. One executive was reported to have his desk on top of a platform, with very low chairs about three feet in front of it.

> **theory of needs**—Achievement, affiliation, and power needs.

All of the content theories have some applications in organizational settings. For this reason, managers must be well versed in the substance of the

theories and work to apply them to the practice of understanding the whys of human behavior for members of the staff.

PROCESS THEORIES OF MOTIVATION

Process theories of motivation describe how people respond to motivators through behavior. While the content theories described previously discuss the whys of human behavior, process theories focus on how to motivate workers to enhance their performance levels.

Behavioral Modification

The behavioral school of thought focuses on reinforcement and punishment associated with stimulus and response to explain motivation. Behaviorist B.F. Skinner provides a model of reinforcement of desired behaviors as a form of motivation.[11] Reinforcement occurs in response to a desired behavior; for instance, praise for a job well done will reinforce future positive performance. Those who subscribe to this reinforcement philosophy believe that only positive actions should receive a response; punishment does not provide a sustainable change in a person's behavior or attitude. Therefore, some individuals contend that undesirable behavior should be ignored. This theory is called extinction. However, as discussed in former chapters, managers are responsible for addressing all incidents of performance related behavior. Therefore, managers must provide reinforcement for desired behaviors and other appropriate responses for undesired behavior. It is important to remember that workers, unlike pigeons, are cognitively and emotionally developed individuals.

Reinforcement always rewards desired behaviors. It does this in two ways. **Positive reinforcement** attaches something pleasant to the performance of desired behaviors. **Negative reinforcement** takes away something considered to be unpleasant as a reward for desired behavior. For instance, a

positive reinforcement—Giving something pleasurable in response to a desired behavior.

negative reinforcement—Removing something unpleasurable in response to a desired behavior.

worker does a particularly good job on a project and receives a nice bonus. This is positive reinforcement. Or the supervisor could remove an unpleasant task (like side work for a restaurant server) in response to the good job on a project. This is an example of negative reinforcement. Both are approaches to providing rewards for desired behaviors. Therefore, negative reinforcement is not a bad thing; it is just another way of providing a reward.

Other Process Approaches

While behavioral modification is perhaps the most widely used process motivational tool for supervisors, there are other theories that are relevant to managers above the supervisory ranks. One process theory is called **expectancy theory**, which deals with structuring rewards that hold value relative to the amount of energy expended by the worker to earn the reward; this is coupled with the expectation that the reward will actually be received by the worker upon achieving the stated goal.[12] For instance, the supervisor may be empowered to award a $50 bonus to the restaurant server with the highest amount of wine sales. If this is worth the up-selling effort to the server, and if the server trusts that the bonus will be paid at the end of the shift, this may result in additional wine sales.

Another process theory that is relevant to compensation practices is **equity theory**.[13] This concept is based on perceived fairness in pay and benefits among the workers in a department. Individuals who believe they are paid less than others performing similar work are likely to lose motivation to perform. Managers should keep this in mind when designing compensation structures.

One powerful motivational tool is shared goal setting from the top of the organization through every level of the organization. This technique is called **management by objectives (MBO)**.[14] In organizations that do not implement this strategy, supervisors may choose to provide it on the departmental level; they do this by establishing department goals and sharing those with

expectancy theory— Process theory that considers the task, the effort, the reward for performance, the value of that reward, and the likeliness of the worker receiving the reward.

equity theory— Process theory that indicates individuals will behave in various manners when there is an inequity of treatment in the workplace.

management by objectives (MBO)—Top-down, bottom-up shared goal setting at every level of the organization.

HOSPITALITY NEWS *Praise 'Em!*

It's amazing that something so simple is so often overlooked by management. We all crave praise. It's one of the simplest and least time-consuming ways to motivate your work staff. Managers should be eagerly engaged in seeing who they can praise. But watch out—some managers have a tendency to reserve praise for extraordinary effort.

It is true that there should be an abundance of praise for an employee who expends extraordinary effort. But if you only praise that kind of effort, your workers may begin to feel they have

to jump through too many hoops to garner your attention. This can lead to overwork and an overly competitive environment that undermines teamwork.

Managers can avoid this over-reaction by praising workers on a regular basis and by encouraging them to derive satisfaction from knowing they've done their jobs well rather than relying solely on your validation.

Source: Hospitality News, June/July 2003, p. 18.

the workers. Based on these goals, each worker contributes with his or her objectives for performance. Supervisors and workers agree on these goals and use them to evaluate performance. The advantage to this process is that workers feel a sense of buy-in to the objectives for the department. This generates a sense of ownership and empowerment on the part of each worker. When we own a goal, we usually strive to make it happen.

OTHER FACTORS THAT CONTRIBUTE TO MOTIVATION

Motivation concepts are certainly important for understanding the dynamics of workers' attitudes. Attitudes have to do with the willingness of workers to perform tasks and activities. A motivated workforce does not necessarily guarantee productivity. Productivity depends on psychological factors as well as engineering factors. Work area layout, division of tasks, tools to do the job, technology, and other factors are within the scope of workplace engineering. A combination of engineering design and management of behaviors is required to affect worker satisfaction and enhance productivity.

JOB DESIGN AND MOTIVATION

job rotation—Moving people among various similar jobs.

Job rotation is a management technique of providing different forms of work with equal levels of responsibility. This technique is sometimes used to break the monotony of doing a single fragmented task. While this may offer variety, it is not necessarily a motivational technique for improved performance.

job enlargement— Giving a worker added responsibilities or duties.

In these times of corporate downsizing, **job enlargement** is a popular alternative. Job enlargement involves adding more duties to an existing job. The additional duties do not usually include added responsibility and authority. Therefore, job enlargement is not a motivational technique. Sometimes

---

HOSPITALITY NEWS *No Way; You Haven't Hired a Slacker, Have You?*

Have you hired a slacker? Following are top ten rules of most slackers. It might help you to understand your employees better if you understand his/her rules.

1. If something is worth doing, let someone else do it.
2. If you can't succeed, just forget it.
3. I'm a firm believer of what's mine is mine, and what's yours is mine, too.
4. Deadlines are a waste of my time.
5. I'll continue to make excuses and not to be a team player.
6. I'll always find a reason for my failures because surely they are not my fault.

7. I don't give a darn what my family, friends, and co-workers think of me. It's their problem, not mine!
8. I'll spend many hours explaining my problems and inadequacies to anyone who will listen.
9. I receive satisfaction from being a difficult person to deal with.
10. I don't need to improve my knowledge about my job.

Source: Hospitality News, June/July 2002, p. 10.

managers inadvertently penalize good workers by adding additional responsibilities to their jobs. Managers do this because they know that the worker will be able to handle the additional assignments. However, the manager who does this actually discourages workers from becoming top performers.

Job enrichment (also known as job enhancement) is a technique of restructuring a job to provide added autonomy, responsibility, and authority.[15] Job enrichment is a motivational job design method because it provides benefits to those workers who prove they are capable of more important positions based on their performance.

job enrichment— Giving a worker more status, autonomy and authority.

SUMMARY

Managers prefer to work with motivated employees. When workers are motivated, managers may perform fewer tasks associated with people management, which provides opportunities for the supervisor to focus more on leadership tasks. It is much easier and more fulfilling to lead people than it is to manage them.

More than motivation is required to affect productivity. Workplace engineering issues must be combined with managing people to provide enhancements to productivity.

Some managers believe that demonstrating favoritism will provide motivation for others to improve performance. The opposite is true. The individuals receiving preferred treatment will feel uncomfortable interacting with peers. The other workers will resent the preferential treatment and usually become less than constructive in their behaviors. Managers who are perceived by workers as playing favorites will eventually alienate all of the staff members in a work unit.

In the Real World. . . (Continued)

Well, the big day finally arrived. It was the end-of-season employee recognition ceremony. With the help of the HR staff, the new director managed to put together some very enjoyable activities, including an employee breakfast, barbecue and dinner. Now it was time to award the sports car. The car was on a huge platform. A barrel containing all the guest ballots for the season was prepared for the drawing. The resort president drew a ballot out of the drum, and announced the name of housekeeping attendant.

It turns out that the winning housekeeping attendant was an elderly lady who had recently immigrated to the United States. She was a single head of household for five children. She had no driver's license. When her name was called, she was brought onto the stage to receive the car keys. As the executives looked on, they thought she was crying tears of joy. In reality, she was scared to death because she didn't have a clue as to what to do with this two-seater vehicle that she didn't even know how to drive. You and your colleagues from the HR staff just stood there and shook your heads, thinking about the great program you could have put together with that money.

The story does have a happy ending, however (at least for the housekeeping attendant). The new HR director convinced the executive committee to return the car to the dealer, yielding about one-third of the original value of the car. This was eventually awarded to the housekeeping attendant. She used the money for a down payment on a little house in another town, where she took a job with another resort.

DISCUSSION QUESTIONS

1. Sometimes we use job design methods and at other times we use individual and group methods of motivation. Sometimes we combine the two. Which ones work the best?

2. Some people seem to like the process theories of motivation more than the content theories. Do you think the process theories make more sense? Do you think they have anything in common with the content theories?

3. Some people say that money is definitely not a motivator. Is this true? Why or why not? Could we say that the meaning behind the money has anything to do with motivation?

KEY TERMS

content theories	job enlargement	negative	theory of needs
equity theory	job enrichment	reinforcement	two-factor theory
ERG	job rotation	positive	
expectancy theory	management by	reinforcement	
hierarchy of	objectives	process theories	
needs	(MBO)		

CHAPTER FIFTEEN
Putting It All Together

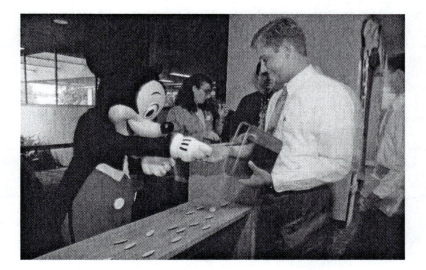

OBJECTIVES

By the end of this chapter, the reader will be able to:

1. Assess the current status of an organization from a human resource practice perspective.
2. Prioritize human resource management interventions sequentially.
3. Develop strategic direction for long-term human resource practices.
4. Evaluate and revise your strategic initiatives to ensure the accomplishment of your human resource departmental objectives.

In the Real World . . .

You have been working in the human resource office at a large resort for about two years now. You have worked along with managers in each of the specialist functions. You assisted the employment manager with recruitment and selection activities. The compensation manager worked with you to devise alternative direct pay processes to standard hourly wages. You assisted the training manager with employee orientations and have even developed a couple of training programs on your own. The employment relations manager showed you the ins and outs of handling complaints, as well as employee counseling and discipline. You even worked alongside the human resource director in handling a few legal compliance issues. So far, it has been a great experience.

The human resource director asks you into her office to discuss an "opportunity," which usually means a new problem. However, this won't be the case today . . .

She begins, "After working with all of our HR specialists, you now have an inventory of skills to qualify as a human resource generalist. You have done a great job in our department and there is an opportunity that is just right for you." She continues. "We have just acquired the small property next door. It is a good strategic move for us, as it gives us additional beach access. The property has about 90 employees. Our executive committee will direct all of the functions at the property, so I will be in charge of the human resource function there." She continues, "I am offering you the position of human resource manager for this property. It will be you and an administrative assistant." She concludes, "Are you interested?"

INTRODUCTION

The staffing rule of thumb is approximately one human resource practitioner for every 160 employees, until the organization starts to reach economies of scale (at about 2,000 employees). Economies of scale mean that the operation is large enough to have systems in place that will permit an increased ratio of employees to HR practitioners. In this chapter, you are the human resource manager for a small operation of 90 employees, which warrants a single HR generalist and no allocation for specialist positions. You will be a one-person HR operation, with assistance from your administrative assistant in handling phones, correspondence, and filing. The fortunate aspect of your situation is that you have resources available to you at the property next door, since you will be reporting to the human resource director and have access to her staff of specialists should you require special assistance. This is a great opportunity for you since, you will run your own small department and still have direction and resources available from the adjacent property.

Given your situation with this new human resource department, you have four major activities ahead of you. First you must assess your current situation by auditing various functions at the new property. Next you must prioritize your interventions to take care of those issues of primary importance. The following activity will be to establish a strategic approach to doing business as a human resource department. Finally, you continuously evaluate and revise your strategies to ensure you are meeting your objectives for the department.

ASSESSMENT

Human resource assessment involves two major activities. The first activity is to conduct a number of **audits** to identify current issues and ensure compliance within a number of HR practices. The second activity is **data collection**, to identify the existing factors within the organization, such as organizational culture and climate, management practices, planning activities, employee KSAAs (knowledge, skills, attitudes, abilities), guest satisfaction levels and other pertinent data used to appraise the current status of the organization. A good first step is to begin with a **pending claims** audit, which will indicate any third-party activities that will require your immediate attention. Figure 15.1 provides a pending claims activity checklist.

audits—Checklist method of reviewing internal practices.

data collection—Collection of factual information for use at a later time.

pending claims—Claims that are in the process of investigation for discovery.

As you know from Chapter 4, a number of allegations concerning the various discrimination statutes could result in the filing of claims with the EEOC or local agencies based on disparate treatment, disparate impact, and/or failure to accommodate based on protected class status. The existence of any such claim, in which the complaining party becomes the complainant and the organization becomes the respondent, would require immediate and focused intervention. The same would be true for those claims that may arise from wage and hour disputes as protected by the FLSA (Chapter 10); these would also require your undivided attention.

As for other claims, many of these occur as part of the regular course of business, requiring you to monitor the progress. These issues would not be highly time consuming. Workers' compensation claims usually involve communication with the insurance provider and attorneys to monitor the progress of the case and provide additional documentation in the form of incident reports or accident reports as needed. Unemployment compensation claims occur regularly and begin with a paper hearing notice in most states, in which the HR manager would respond in writing to articulate the circumstances of an employee separation matter. These cases involve separated employees challenging their eligibility to collect benefits, which only pertain to the loss of job income through no fault of that employee. Hence, an employee who is discharged for performance failure or misconduct would not be eligible to collect unemployment compensation benefits. In the event of a dispute in such a claim, a hearing date would be set with a **claims hearing officer**, which would require your appearance to contest the dispute. The objective in such matters is to only permit the payment of unemployment compensation

claims hearing officer—Administrative adjudicator who presides over disputes.

Claim	Status
EEOC complaints	
Department of Labor complaints	
Workers' Compensation claims	
Unemployment compensation claims	
COBRA insurance continuation claims	
Small claims court cases	

Figure 15.1. Claims Activity Checklist.

experience rating—
Claims history used to
determine frequency
to be applied against a
payment or premium.

nuisance—A legal set-
tlement based on the
opinion that the mat-
ter of dispute is not
worth the time and ex-
pense to present a de-
fense.

legal compliance—
Adherence to the
stated and presumed
provisions of a law.

insurance benefits for legitimate claims. You would dispute any other claims, as they would count against your **experience rating**, which results in an inflated unemployment compensation tax rate that is paid to the state by your organization. COBRA continuation claims merely involve verification of the qualifying event and the processing of coverage continuation and collection of fees. In most states, some vacation pay issues are brought to small claims court and are usually settled as a matter of **nuisance** to the organization.

Legal Compliance Audits

The next step for a newly appointed human resource director would be to conduct a **legal compliance** audit in the workplace. The practitioner would rely on the listing of state and federal statutory laws in Chapter 4 to conduct this audit. Compliance issues may be reactive (those things absolutely required by law) and proactive (those issues that are solid claim protection techniques). Figure 15.2 provides a checklist for legal compliance measures in the workplace that would be used in such an audit.

Compliance with many of the local, state and federal statutes includes prominent displays of posters and notices to be placed in conspicuous locations within the employee areas of the organization. There is usually a bulletin board near the human resource office that may be reserved for these postings, as well as other employee information postings. It may be advisable to post replications of posters and notices inside the public area of the human resource office. If the organization has an employee cafeteria or break rooms, postings would be appropriate in these areas as well. The first task of the audit

Legal Compliance Practice	Yes	No
Civil Rights Act 1964,1991 postings		
Age Discrimination in Employment Act postings		
Workers' Compensation postings		
Americans with Disabilities Act postings		
Immigration Reform and Control Act postings		
Unemployment Compensation Insurance postings		
Equal Pay Act postings		
Sexual Harassment Policy postings		
Sexual Harassment Training Notice postings		
Sexual Harassment Complaint Procedure postings		
Employment-at-Will postings (if applicable)		
Social Security Administration postings		
Fair Labor Standards Act postings		

Figure 15.2. Compliance Measures Checklist.

is to ensure that the postings are in fact displayed. The postings should be up to date and should be in good repair. If notices are yellowed, torn, tattered, or contain graffiti, they should be replaced. A good rule of thumb is to replace all notices annually. Many of the appropriate administrative agencies will provide the organization with posters and literature on a free-of-charge basis.

Notifications that reference the CRA, ADEA and IRCA are usually statements of non-discrimination on the part of the employer. This is a declaration that the organization has policies which preclude forms of discrimination that are prohibited by law. The IRCA posting may also provide notice that documentation of the right to work in the United States will be required as a condition of hire. Notices concerning the ADA also state non-discrimination and may include statements indicating the practice of reasonable accommodation for individuals with differing abilities. State government notices are usually intended to advise workers of their rights under the law, such as Workers' Compensation and Unemployment Compensation programs. On the federal level, Social Security Administration and FLSA postings relate to payroll policies, with a portion of the FLSA notification also pertaining to child labor protections.

Personnel File Audit

The next audit to take place will be a review of each personnel file. This activity may require the services of a temporary task force of human resource practitioners, as these audits are tedious and time consuming. The purpose of this audit is twofold:

1. There are documents that must be located within the file, as well as items that are appropriate for inclusion, but not necessary. For instance, an application blank must be in the file. A positive customer service letter does not have to be in the file, but could be in the file.

2. There are documents that individuals often include in those files that do not belong there. The existence of inappropriate items in a personnel file creates a potential liability for the organization.

The file audit looks for necessary items, as well as appropriate items, and purges inappropriate items from each personnel file. Table 15.1 provides a checklist that may be used for personnel file audits.

Anything that is located within a personnel file may be used in the course of an investigation by a third party. For instance, if the organization chooses to include I-9 forms in the personnel file, the Department of Justice in reviewing I-9 forms may use any personnel form in those files to charge the employer with non-compliance with the Immigration Reform and Control Act. Hence, human resource practitioners keep separate files for those items that are not related to the employment relationship or performance. Also, as part of your audit, you will want to ensure that **active files**, those of current employees, are kept separate from inactive files. The **inactive files** should be retained for a period of at least three years. In the event that a formerly separated employee returns to your organization, you would re-activate her inactive file. Another good practice is to mark the exterior of the files to differentiate different employment status of **full time**, **part time**, and **on call**. Finally, you are the custodian of records for the organization. Hence, it is your responsibility to secure the personnel files. It is recommended that they be kept within the HR office in a separate room that has a locked door. Each file cabinet should be locked individually as well.

active files—Files pertaining to currently working employees.

inactive files—Files pertaining to previous employees.

full time—An organization's definition of a regular employee (usually based on 40 hours per week of work).

part time—Those employees who regularly work fewer hours than full-time workers.

on call—Casual labor that works on an as-needed basis.

Job Description Audit

Your next task will be to audit existing job descriptions and job specifications. These documents should list the date they were written, and there should be no more than a year since the last update. With this audit you are checking

Table 15.1   Personnel File Audit Checklist

Include	Remove
Application forms	I-9 forms
Payroll change notices	Medical forms
Performance appraisals	Background investigations
Corrective interviews/commendations	Credit reports
Change of information	Motor vehicle reports
Insurance selection forms	Employee vehicle identification form
Position requisition/hire form	Security incident reports (nondisciplinary)
Relocation agreement	Schedules
Request for transfer/promotion	Insurance claims
New employee checklist	
Vacation requests	
Policy receipts	
Federal and state payroll tax withholding	
Attendance history	

for format and relevance to the jobs that are actually performed. You know that at some time in the future, you will conduct a thorough job analysis, but now is not the time; you might spot-check job description and job specification content with certain employees for relevance.

Employee Relations Documents Audit

Now you want to audit the employee relations documents that should be in place. You might begin with a review of the employee handbook. Does this document contain all of the information discussed in Chapter 10? If not, you would schedule a rewrite of the document in the future. Also, you should review the managers' manual, policy manual and SOP manual. Again, you are checking for relevancy and currency. Don't be surprised if you can't find these documents, as they do not exist in many organizations. However, you know that you will work on the development of these materials in the future.

The next place to look is the recruitment and selection practices that are in place. Do these comply with the information discussed in Chapter 8? You may want to use a checklist for this audit, similar to the one presented in Figure 15.3.

At this point you may be able to make some minor adjustments. However, you must keep the recruitment and selection process rolling. As is the case with your other audits, most of this data will be used when you shift into human resource strategic planning mode.

Recruitment Processes	Adequate	Revise
Recruitment and selection budget		
Job specifications		
Job descriptions		
External recruiting sources		
Internal recruiting sources		
Compensation levels		
Applicant inquiry processing		
Application blank information		
Selection Processes		
Preliminary review of applications and resumes		
Pre-screen interviews		
Screen interviews		
Pre-employment testing procedures		
Department interviews		
Job offers		
Employment processing		

Figure 15.3. Recruitment and Selection Checklist.

Training Audit

The next step in the auditing process would be to take a look at training processes and programs. You know from your training that there should be a number of programs in place, but you realize that many organizations neglect this aspect of employee preparation and development. What you are looking for in this audit is to find out if programs similar to those discussed in Chapter 9 exist in this new workplace, and to determine their levels of effectiveness in providing knowledge and skills to the employees. Perhaps Figure 15.4 will help you in this discovery process.

The first thing you want to use this checklist for is to determine the existence of each type of training program. It would not be surprising if many of these did not exist, especially since you have just taken over a small operation. The programs on this checklist range from most important (at the top) to preferred (at the bottom). If you are placed in the position of developing your own training programs, you might begin with orientations and work your way down the list. If any of these programs do exist, do they need revision? Obviously, it would be easier to revise training programs than to create them from scratch. On the other hand, you must remember your great resource just next door. Since you have a nice rapport with all the members of that HR department, they will be more than happy to assist you in your new assignment.

HUMAN RESOURCE STRATEGIC PLAN

Once your audits are complete, it is time for you to combine them under the overall heading of an internal audit. Next, you analyze the findings of your audits and determine the HR strengths and weaknesses for your new organization. Now you look at the competitors and the labor market to identify those threats and opportunities that may exist outside your organization. For instance, if your compensation practices are a weakness and there is limited supply of KSAAs in the labor market (a threat), you will need a strategy to overcome that scenario. You have now completed a SWOT (strengths, weaknesses, opportunities, and threats) analysis for your new HR department. You

Program	Yes	No	Create/Revise
New employee orientation			
Departmental orientation			
Codes of ethics training program			
Technical training programs			
Administrative training programs			
Supervisory training programs			
Management development programs			
Leadership programs			

Figure 15.4. Training Checklist.

want to convert any weaknesses into strengths, which means you will have to fix those things that are not done right in the human resource department. You would also like to convert threats into opportunities. For instance, if compensation is a weak point and a limited supply of willing workers from outside the organization is a threat, you may come up with a plan to be able to afford additional compensation practices through some productivity enhancement measure, which would attract more applicants from outside. By fixing the compensation weakness, you are limiting the impact of the labor market threat. This type of thinking will be included in all of your planning activities. Eventually, you will be in a position to establish objectives and strategies in all of the areas identified in Figure 15.5.

Figure 15.5. HR Strategic Planning Categories.

IMPLEMENT, EVALUATE, AND REVISE

Once the strategic direction for the organization is in place, you as the human resource manager create your own objectives, strategies, policies, standards, and procedures to accomplish the goals for the HR function within the organization. Your strategies will fall within the headings at the top of each column in Figure 15.5. Notice that the practices listed under each heading coincide with our discussions throughout the text. As a human resource manager, you will be in a position to balance a number of issues at the same time. You will identify your priorities from the lists in the figure; those will be your primary areas of concentration. However, you will want to make some progress in all the areas listed in the figure, as each is a part of the human resource functional whole.

Perhaps your one-year plan will look similar to the one listed in Figure 15.6.

Objective	Strategy	Completion Date
Legal compliance	Maintain current status.	Ongoing
Code of ethics	Set up ethics committee to establish code of ethics for all workers in the organization.	January 30
Employee rights	Revise progressive discipline procedure to include due process format.	February 10
Employee relations	Enhance current employee handbook to include all items listed in the audit checklist.	March 10
Performance appraisals	Revise performance appraisals to be standards based. Implement weighted scales for manager review.	April 1
Compensation/benefits	Participate in two wage surveys to establish bench-mark for next year's strategic plan.	December 30
Employment processing	Develop streamlined employment process.	October 30
Polices, standards, procedures	Develop managers' manual, policy manual, and SOP manual.	December 30
Orientation	Develop general and department orientation programs.	January 15
Technical training	Develop steps of service program.	May 10
Administrative training	Develop administrative forms training.	June 10
Supervisory training	Develop supervisory skills course.	July 10
Management training	Develop management effectiveness course.	August 15
Management training	Develop effective interviewing course.	September 20

Figure 15.6. Sample One-Year Plan.

From this point on, it is all about planning your work and working your plans. Every day, you try to accomplish one more step toward the way you want your HR office to operate. Over time, you find that everything will start to fall together. Take a look at your objectives and strategies listed in Figure 15.6. This looks like a hectic year. Notice, however, that your goals aren't overly energetic, because you will only be able to devote a small amount of time per day to proactive items, like those listed in the table. The rest of each day will be spent solving problems on a reactive basis. Also, notice that there are no objectives scheduled for completion in the month of November. This is to permit room to slide other projects into that time slot, should you run behind schedule. On the other hand, you may find yourself pushing projects to earlier completion dates because you are working ahead of your established completion dates. The thing to remember is that early, on time, and late completion are acceptable, as long as you have a contingency plan and communicate that to your supervisor, which in this case is the director of human resources at the property next door.

Just think of the sense of personal satisfaction you will have when you do complete this list of objectives and strategies one year from now. You will be proud. The director will be ecstatic. And you will have made a difference in a number of peoples' lives at your new little property. So what happens after that? You push it further along in year 2, and even further in year 3. By that time, you will be running a model human resource office and other practitioners will be asking you for advice. But by then, you will be ready for a bigger HR challenge. Also, by then, your director should have made it to vice president of human resources. I wonder whom she will choose to fill the vacant director's slot?

Congratulations on completing this training.

SUMMARY

This chapter has walked us through the process that practitioners use to evaluate and revise human resource functions for a hospitality organization. The process begins with a thorough assessment of all HR functions. Audits provide data collection activities that result in snapshots for each functional area within the human resource management domain for the organization. The data are then analyzed to determine strengths and weaknesses of the current HR operation. The next phase consists of generating an overall strategic direction that capitalizes on existing strengths and rectifies noted weaknesses within the existing HR functions. Objectives and strategies are then developed for each functional HR area, which becomes the one year plan for the human resource office. The plan is then implemented, evaluated and revised continually to measure and redirect the human resource activities from a strategic viewpoint. The final outcome of implementing a strategic human resource plan will be enhancements to the organization, its shareholders, guests and the staff members. Sound human resource practices result in winning outcomes for all constituencies affiliated with a proactive hospitality enterprise.

In the Real World . . . (Continued)

It has been about a year since you took over the human resource function at the little property with 90 employees. Things are running quite well. You have a very good recruitment and selection process in place; you have drafted managers' manuals, policy manuals and SOPs for all operating areas. Your retention strategies are paying off with low employee turnover and an excellent management team. The property now adheres to a proactive code of ethics. Your legal compliance is impeccable. There are training programs ranging from general orientations through management development programs. You have initiated some very nice performance-based incentive programs, which encourages all members of the staff to be value-added workers, with these behaviors rewarded through your performance management system.

The human resource director is very pleased with the way you have developed the human resource function at this property. You are proud of the job that you are doing. And you really feel like you are making a difference in the lives of the staff at your property. This alone makes your hard work all worth while.

DISCUSSION QUESTION

1. Suppose you have no intention of becoming a human resource practitioner, but you do plan on working in the field of management. Should you as a manager know the information that is presented? Would this information make you a better manager? Would it lessen your reliance on human resource practitioners? Are there any other reasons you should be familiar with this material?

KEY TERMS

active files	data collection	inactive files	on call
audits	experience rating	legal compliance	part time
claims hearing officer	full time	nuisance	pending claims

Endnotes

CHAPTER 1

1. Compensation resources. IOMA's Report on Salary Surveys, New York, Dec 2002; vol. 2, no. 12, p. 8. 2 pp.

2. Disability management—Improving employee health and the company bottom line. Steve Beigbeder, Journal of Property Management, May/Jun 1999; vol. 64, no. 3, p. 98. 3 pp.

3. Organizational learning style and competences: A comparative investigation of relationship and transactionally orientated small U.K. manufacturing firms. I. Chaston, B. Badger & E. Sadler-Smith, European Journal of Marketing, 2000; vol. 34, no. 5/6, p. 625.

4. Corporate collars climb. Barry Shanoff, Waste Age, Jul 2002; vol. 33, no. 7, p. 30. 2 pp.

5. D. Ellington & I. Mills, It Don't Mean a Thing if it Ain't Got that Swing. Columbia Records: EMI-Mills Music, Inc. ASCAP.

CHAPTER 2

1. D.V. Tesone. 2003. Management and Technology for the Hospitality Industry: Higher Tech for Higher Touch. Prentice Hall: Upper Saddle River, NJ.

2. D.V. Tesone. 2003. Tactical Strategies for Service Industry Management: How to Do It. Prentice Hall: Upper Saddle River.

3. D.V. Tesone. 2003. Management and Technology for the Hospitality Industry: Higher Tech for Higher Touch. Prentice Hall: Upper Saddle River, NJ.

4. Ibid.

CHAPTER 3

1. Shovels, trowels, and ice cream scoops: In search of the right tool to explain scientific management. Woody D. Richardson, Journal of Management Education, Apr 2002; vol. 26, no. 2, p. 194.

2. Ibid.

3. The balance of power. Professional Safety, May 2002; vol. 47, no. 5, p. 13.

4. Rights, rules, and the structure of constitutional adjudication: A response to Professor Fallon. Matthew D. Adler, Harvard Law Review, Apr 2000; vol. 113, no. 6, p. 1371.

5. Prioritizing privacy: A constitutional response to the Internet. Elbert Lin, Berkeley Technology Law Journal, Summer 2002; vol. 1, no. 3, p. 1085.

6. Comment on "generating scenario trees for multistage decision problems"; Pieter Klaassen, Management Science, Nov 2002; vol.48, no. 11, p. 1512. 5 pp.

7. The Essential Drucker in One Volume: The Best of Sixty Years of Peter Drucker's Essential Writings on Management. Susan C. Awe, Library Journal, Mar 15, 2002; vol. 127, no. 5, p. 43.

8. Behavioral integrity: The perceived alignment between managers' words and deeds as a research focus. Tony Simons, Organization Science, Jan/Feb 2002; vol. 13, no. 1, p. 18. 19 pp.

9. Human resource management strategies and practices in just-in-time environments: Australian case study evidence. Damien Power, Technovation, Jul 2000; vol. 20, no. 7, p. 373.

10. Contingent management in temporary, dynamic organizations: The comparative analysis of projects. Aaron J. Shenhar, Journal of High Technology Management Research, Autumn 2001; vol. 12, no. 2, p. 239.

11. Knowledge management in communities of practice. Joel O. Iverson, Management Communication Quarterly, Nov 2002; vol. 16, no. 2, p. 259. 8 pp.

12. Ibid.

13. Borderland visions: Maroons and outlyers in early American history. Mark A. Lause, Monthly Review, Sep 2002; vol. 54, no. 4, p. 38. 7 pp.

14. Ibid.

15. Ibid.

16. Ibid.

CHAPTER 4

1. Look who's looking for a court bailout. Bruce Fein, Special to the Washington Times, Washington, Dec 26, 2002, p. A17.

2. Miami Beach, Fla., Restaurant Wins Partial Victory in Sex Discrimination Case. Elaine Walker, Knight Ridder Tribune Business News, Washington, Jul 17, 2002, p. 1.

3. Keeping the Civil in Disobedience (Broward Metro Edition), The Washington Post; South Florida Sun-Sentinel, Fort Lauderdale, Nov 17, 2002, p. 5F.

CHAPTER 6

1. Why do managers learn best at work? Gordon Prestoungrange. International Journal of Contemporary Hospitality Management, 2002; vol. 14, no. 7, p. 328.

2. Consumer evaluations of unethical behaviors of Web sites: A cross-cultural comparison. Jen-Hung Huang, Journal of International Consumer Marketing, 2001; vol. 13, no. 4, p. 51.

3. The volitionist's Manifesto. Michael R. Hyman, Journal of Business Ethics, Feb 2000; vol. 23, no. 3, p. 323. 15 pp.

4. Theory of Devolution. Louis McKee, Library Journal, Oct 1, 2002; vol. 127, no. 16, p. 100.

5. Living the 7 Habits: Stories of Courage and Inspiration. Beth Farrell, Library Journal, Dec 1999; vol. 124, no. 20, p. 209.

6. A Kantian intuitionism. Robert Audi, Mind, Jul 2001; vol. 110, no. 439; p. 601.

7. The Legacy of Milton Friedman as Teacher. A. W. Bob Coats, Economic Record, Sep 2001; vol. 77, no. 238, p. 308. 3 pp.

8. Supreme Court: Enemy of freedom?: Constitutional law in Christian school textbooks. Frances R. A. Paterson, Journal of Law and Education, Oct 2000; vol. 29, no. 4, p. 405. 27 pp.

CHAPTER 7

1. D.V. Tesone 2003. Tactical Strategies for Service Industry Management: How to Do It. Pearson-Prentice Hall: Boston.

2. Human resources "expert" testimony in employment litigation. Amy L. Rogers, Employee Relations Law Journal, Autumn 2002; vol. 28, no. 2, p. 29. 17 pp.

CHAPTER 8

1. Assimilating New Leaders: The Key to Executive Retention. Blake E. Ashforth, Personnel Psychology, Autumn 2002; vol. 55, no. 3, p. 736. 4 pp.

CHAPTER 9

1. Preparing teachers for reflective practice: Intentions, contradictions, and possibilities. Victoria J. Risko, Language Arts, Nov 2002; vol. 80, no. 2, p. 134. 11 pp.

CHAPTER 12

1. The role of management history in the management curriculum: 1997. Jane Whitney Gibson, Journal of Management History, 1999; vol. 5, no. 5, p. 277.

2. Management history gurus of the 1990s: Their lives, their contributions. Jane Whitney Gibson; Journal of Management History, 1999; vol. 5, no. 6, p. 380.

3. Improving organizational communication and cohesion in a health care setting through employee-leadership exchange. Elisa J. Sobo, Human Organization, Fall 2002; vol. 61, no. 3, p. 277. 11 pp.

4. Ibid.

5. Ibid.

6. Language-based communication zones in international business communication. Richard D. Babcock, The Journal of Business Communication, Oct 2001; vol. 38, no. 4, p. 372. 41 pp.

7. Some U.K. and U.S.A. comparisons of executive information systems in practice and theory. Xianzhong M. Xu, Journal of End User Computing, Jan-Mar 2003; vol. 15, no. 1, p. 1. 19 pp.

8. How people really detect lies. Hee Sun Park, Communication Monographs, Jun 2002; vol. 69, no. 2, p. 144. 14 pp.

9. Authoring social responsibility. Janet K. Pilcher, Qualitative Inquiry, Dec 2002; Vol. 8, no. 6, p. 715. 23 pp.

10. D.V. Tesone. 2003. Management and Technology for the Hospitality Industry: Higher Tech for Higher Touch. Pearson Custom Publishing: Boston, pp. 46–49.

CHAPTER 13

1. Leadership and motivating missions: A model for organizations from science literature. D.V. Tesone, Journal of Leadership Studies, Winter 2000. vol. 7, no. 1, p. 60. 10 pp.

2. Management and Leadership Should Not be Confused. ENR, Dec 2, 2002; vol. 249, no. 23, p. 76.

3. A social actor conception of organizational identity and its implications for the study of organizational reputation. David A. Whetten, Business and Society, Dec 2002; vol. 41, no. 4, p. 393. 22 pp.

4. Corporate reputation: A research agenda using strategy and stakeholder literature. John F. Mahon, Business and Society, Dec 2002; vol. 41, no. 4, p. 415. 31 pp.

5. Tacit knowledge and strategic decision making. Erich N. Brockmann, Group & Organization Management, Dec 2002; vol. 27, no. 4, p. 436. 20 pp.

6. Ibid.

7. The transformational leadership questionnaire (TLQ-LGV): A convergent and discriminant validation study. Robert J. Alban-Metcalfe, Leadership & Organization Development Journal, 2000; vol. 21, no. 6; p. 280.

8. Leadership and the New Science: Discovering Order in a Chaotic World, 2nd edition. John Quay, Consulting to Management, Jun 2002; vol. 13, no. 2, p. 59. 3 pp.

9. The Challenge of Front-Line Management: Flattened Organizations in the New Economy. Littleton M. Maxwell, Personnel Psychology, Spring 2002; vol. 55, no. 1, p. 244. 4 pp.

10. Virtue as a benchmark for spirituality in business. Gerald F. Cavanagh, Journal of Business Ethics, Jun 2002; vol. 38, no. 1/2, p. 109. 9 pp.

11. Leading OD through linkage: Meet Dr. Phil Harkins. Therese F. Yaeger, Organization Development Journal, Spring 2002; vol. 20, no. 1, p. 53. 3 pp.

12. Ibid.

13. Expanding notions of leadership to capture pluralistic voices: Positionality theory in practice. Adrianna Kezar, Journal of College Student Development, Jul/Aug 2002; vol. 43, no. 4, p. 558. 21 pp.

14. Why elephants gallop: Assessing and predicting organizational performance in federal agencies. Gene A. Brewer, Journal of Public Administration Research and Theory, Oct 2000; vol. 10, no. 4, p. 685. 27 pp.

15. Ibid.

16. Ibid.

17. Ibid.

18. Ibid.

19. From process data to publication: A personal sensemaking. Anne D. Smith, Journal of Management Inquiry, Dec 2002; vol. 11, no. 4, p. 383. 24 pp.

CHAPTER 14

1. D.V. Tesone. 2003. Tactical Strategies for Service Industry Management: How to Do It. Pearson Custom Publishing: Boston.

2. Ibid.

3. Art for management's sake? Bradley G. Jackson, Management Communication Quarterly, Feb 2001; vol. 14, no. 3, p. 484. 7 pp.

4. The manager and continuing education. Charles R. McConnell, The Health Care Manager, Dec 2002; vol. 21, no. 2, p. 72. 12 pp.

5. Ibid.

6. Universal manager. Anonymous. Training & Development Methods. Bradford (2002): vol 16, Iss 5, p. 1048.

7. Ibid.

8. Ibid.

9. Challenging the status quo. Diane Susan Grimes, Management Communication Quarterly, Feb 2002; vol. 15, no. 3, p. 381. 29 pp.

10. Organizational politics: Tactics, channels, and hierarchical roles. Lyle Sussman, Journal of Business Ethics, Nov 2002; vol. 40, no. 4, p. 313. 17 pp.

11. A study of the influence of promotions on promotion satisfaction and expectations of future promotions among managers. Gita De Souza,

Human Resource Development Quarterly, Fall 2002; vol. 13, no. 3, p. 325. 16 pp.

12. A social actor conception of organizational identity and its implications for the study of organizational reputation. David A. Whetten, Business and Society, Dec 2002; vol. 41, no. 4, p. 393. 22 pp.

13. The confines of stakeholder management: Evidence from the Dutch manufacturing sector. Pursey P.M.A.R. Heugens, Journal of Business Ethics, Nov 2002; vol. 40, no. 4, p. 387. 17 pp.

14. Ibid.

Glossary

180 degrees model—A review system that includes subordinates review of the supervisor.

360 degrees model—Holistic appraisal feedback from subordinates, supervisors, and peers.

accommodations theory—A theory of discrimination that requires employers to reasonably accommodate the practices of specified protected class members under certain circumstances.

accountability—The duty to account for one's actions.

active files—Files pertaining to currently working employees.

administrative exemption—Exempt status for high-level administrators.

affirmative action—A process for righting the wrongs of past discrimination through goals aimed at balanced representation of those protected classes that are underrepresented due to past discriminatory practices.

application blank—A form completed by an applicant for a position with an organization.

appreciation—An increase in financial value; a way of showing thanks for a job well done.

asset—Something that adds value to an organization.

assimilate—Adapt to an environment and its people.

audits—Checklist method of reviewing internal practices.

balanced scorecard—An x and y axis representing qualitative and quantitative performance criteria.

bargain in good faith—Demonstration of continuous efforts to come to an agreement to establish a union contract.

bargaining agent—The role of a labor union in the negotiation of a collective bargaining agreement.

behavioral approaches—Appraisal method that focuses on specific observable behaviors.

behavioral science—A management model that considers the "whys" of human behavior in the workplace.

behaviorally anchored rating scale (BARS)—Behavioral approach using standardized practices.

benefits—Rewards for organizational membership.

binding past practice—A practice that establishes a precedent to be applied to future practices of the same or similar circumstances.

blue-collar—Trades and labor positions in organizations.

bona fide occupational qualification (BFOQ)—A characteristic providing a legitimate reason for excluding certain individuals in a protected class from consideration for a position.

bonuses—Lump sum payments for performance.

bottom line—Net profit or loss.

breach of contract—Failure by a party to adhere to terms and conditions of an agreement.

burden of proof—The duty of a party in a claim or charge to provide evidence of legal standing.

business agents—Full-time employees of labor unions who act as liaisons with organizations and shop stewards.

business necessity—Job-related reason to discriminate based on the safe and efficient operation of an organization.

category rating method—An appraisal model listing items by categories.

central tendency—Forcing individuals into a normative grouping.

CEO—Chief executive officer, usually the top-level manager in an organization.

chain of custody—The chain of responsibility that leads to the source of liability for a breach in the exercise of due care.

change agentry—The process of enacting systematic change.

channel—The directional flow of a message from sender to receiver.

civil assault and battery—Any form of uninvited physical contact or the indication of the intent to make such contact.

civil law—A body of law that governs actions between and among the members of a society.

claims hearing officer—Administrative adjudicator who presides over disputes.

closed pay system—Guarded communication of wages and salaries restricted to those with a need to know the information.

closed shops—Organizations that require union membership prior to hiring.

COBRA—Consolidated Omnibus Budget Reconciliation Act; requires employers to provide health insurance continuation based on qualifying events.

codes of ethics—Guidelines for conduct created by a group of professional peers.

collective bargaining agreements—Union employment contracts.

commissions—Percentage of production revenues, usually sales.

common law—Unwritten laws resulting from precedent-setting court decisions which are applied to future cases. Known as judge-made law.

communication—The sharing and understanding of ideas.

community—Outside stakeholders who are not within other stakeholder groups.

comp time—Compensatory time off in lieu of overtime payment.

comparative methods—An appraisal method that compares individuals with their peers.

compensation manager—Specialist who administers compensation and benefit programs.

compensation—Pay and benefits afforded to workers in an organization.

compensatory damages—Court awards to compensate those who have been wrongfully harmed in the opinions of a jury or a judge.

complainant—Designation of an individual who has filed a claim of discrimination with an agency.

consequences—The results of an action.

constructive discharge—Creating an uncomfortable work environment with the intent to encourage a person to resign from a position.

content theories—Theories describing what might motivate individuals.

contingency model—A management philosophy that suggests management decisions should be tailored to the situation at hand.

contraband—The possession of materials that are in violation of a company policy.

contract—A legally binding agreement between at least two parties.

contrast error—Comparisons to subjective criteria.

corporatization—The practice of establishing business regulations that place the burden of curing social problems upon corporate enterprises.

cost of living allowances (COLA)—Increases in wages and salaries based on economic indicators.

covenant of good faith and fair dealing—A promise to treat others fairly, uniformly, and consistently.

critical incident method—A method of recording important observations for later formal appraisal recollection.

cultural relevance—Adapting to the norms of behavior in a culture.

culture—Shared values, attitudes, and beliefs.

custodian of records—An individual charged with the responsibility for maintenance and security of official matters of record.

customers—A stakeholder group consisting of those who purchase products and services.

data collection—Collection of factual information for use at a later time.

databases—An integrated collection of logically related records (objects) that are sorted into files.

declaration of rights—A declaration of the rights of an employer relative to relationships with employees in the workplace.

decode—Making personal sense from a message on the part of a receiver.

defamation—False information communicated to a third party with the intent to cast poor light on the character of an individual.

defendant—The party against which a civil claim is filed in a court of law.

department orientation—An orientation for all newly hired employees within a specific department.

development—Training to prepare individuals for career advancement opportunities.

direct compensation—Wages, salaries, piece rate, or commissions paid to employees on a regular basis.

discipline—A form of training to achieve desired behaviors.

disparate impact—A theory of discrimination in which members of a specific protected class are treated adversely, as demonstrated by a statistical imbalance that may occur unintentionally.

due care—The duty to exercise reason consistent with the level of responsibility of the actor.

due process—The opportunity for an accused individual to provide a self-defense.

effectiveness—Doing the right thing. Measured in quantity and quality of products and services. Also measured in revenues.

efficiency—Doing things right. Minimizing costs for quality resources.

empathy—The ability to communicate with the same emotional sensibility of the individual who is the recipient of the communication.

employee assistance programs (EAP)—Programs that provide special needs to employees concerning issues of physical, mental, and emotional health and wellbeing.

employee handbook—A document that provides information about the company, its history, mission, structure, benefits, objectives, strategies, policies, standards, procedures, and rules.

employee relations—Every aspect of the relationship between workers and managers from the time of hire through the time of separation from the organization; maintaining rapport with workers by satisfying their needs.

employee retention—Retaining valuable workers in the organization.

employee turnover—Combined voluntary and involuntary separation from an organization.

employees—A stakeholder group consisting of the workers for an organization.

employment-at-will (EAW)—A common law doctrine that prescribes the freedom of employers and employees to engage in employment relationships.

encode—Placing an idea into communication symbols, such as words to be sent to the receiver.

Equal Employment Opportunity Commission (EEOC)—The federal agency that enforces, administers, and adjudicates for most discrimination statutes.

equity theory—Process theory that indicates individuals will behave in various manners when there is an inequity of treatment in the workplace.

ERG—Existence, relatedness, and growth needs.

essay appraisal—A written narrative describing strengths and areas for improvement regarding performance.

ethical relativism—Convenient or situational ethics used to justify unethical behaviors.

ethics committee—A cross-section of individuals from various organizational levels who administer codes of ethics.

executive exemption—Exempt status for management workers.

exempt—Exempt from overtime payment.

expectancy theory—Process theory that considers the task, the effort, the reward for performance, the value of that reward, and the likeliness of the worker receiving the reward.

experience rating—Claims history used to determine frequency to be applied against a payment or premium.

express contract—A contract that expressly identifies the terms of an agreement.

external customer—A customer or guest who purchases products or services.

external environment—Factors from outside the organization that influence the organization and its people.

external scan—The process of identifying opportunities and threats to the organization that exist in the external environment.

Fair Labor Standards Act (FLSA)—This law was enacted in 1938 and has provisions for overtime payment and child labor protection. It is the law that provides exempt and non-exempt status and is also responsible for the federal minimum wage.

false imprisonment—Prevention or the threat of prevention from permitting a person to move freely.

Federal District Court (FDC)—Area courts with jurisdiction over federal statutes to include discrimination cases.

feedback—Evaluative information in response to a process; the loop moves from the receiver back to the sender to confirm understanding of the message.

formal appraisal—Systematic written performance evaluation and feedback.

formalist—A form-oriented approach to testing the ethics and morality of an action that focuses on the form of the action with no consideration of the results of that action.

four-fifths rule—A 20% margin of leeway resulting in a requirement of 80% of statistical representation within categories used to establish a legal defense against allegations of disparate impact.

frivolous—A non-meritorious grievance.

full time—An organization's definition of a regular employee (usually based on 40 hours per week of work).

general orientation—An orientation for all newly hired employees.

givebacks—Concessions made by labor unions to return previously negotiated benefits or work rules.

grapevine—An informal channel of communication that carries social information and gossip among workers.

graphic rating scales—Numerically scored appraisals.

grievances—Perceived unfair treatment in the workplace that may include union contract violations.

gross misconduct—A severe infraction of the rules that warrants dismissal for the first incident.

halo effect—A focus on a single issue that influences an entire rating.

heterogeneous—A group consisting of multiple ethnicities.

HMO—Health maintenance organization health insurance.

homogeneous—A group that is represented by a single ethnicity.

hostile environment—Anything deemed by a person to be offensive in nature by any person of a protected class.

HRD—Human resource development.

HR—Human resources.

HRIS—An MIS for human resource practices.

HRM—Human resource management.

human capital—The philosophy that investments in the development of people result in increased value to an organization.

human development—Holistic training that adds to the person as a being.

human relations—A management philosophy that considers the emotional needs of workers.

human resource philosophy—The philosophy that workers are human capital.

icebreaker—A training technique used to set the "stage" as part of a training program.

impasse—A breakdown in the progress of bargaining in good faith.

implied contract—A contract that may be construed to exist through implications associated with the content of communication.

implied-in-fact contracts—Contracts that are not of an express nature, but have wording from which an individual may construe an intended agreement.

inactive files—Files pertaining to previous employees.

incentive pay—Pay for performance.

incentives—Additional compensation based on performance.

independent contractor—A third party who is contracted to perform a function that is not part of the regular employment relationship.

indirect compensation—Benefits and perquisites.

informal appraisal—Informal feedback on performance.

information overload—Large amounts of information that cannot be absorbed in the prescribed time period.

inputs—Resources required to generate products or services.

integrity—Actions and statements made by the organization are consistent.

intent—A knowing and willful action of illegal discrimination.

intentional infliction of emotional distress—The tort of outrage, treating an individual in a hostile manner with the intent to cause mental or physical distress.

interdependent—The highest level of relationship with subsystems that is achievable by an individual or other subsystem. It is beyond the levels of dependence and independence.

internal—Factors inside the organization.

internal audit—Data collection and analysis of practices within an organization for the purpose of determining strengths and weaknesses.

internal customer—Workers who serve the customers/guests who are customers of support workers.

internal environment—Factors that comprise the internal infrastructure of an organization.

invasion of privacy—Accessing information concerning an individual in the absence of a need to know that information.

involuntary separation—Employees who are discharged from positions in organizations.

job—Tasks, duties, and responsibilities of a worker.

job analysis—A method of collecting and analyzing data resulting in job descriptions and job specifications.

job description—A listing of tasks, duties, responsibilities and reporting relationships for an individual who is placed in a position.

job enlargement—Giving a worker added responsibilities or duties.

job enrichment—Giving a worker more status, autonomy and authority.

job specification—A listing of knowledge, skills, attitudes, and abilities that collectively comprise the qualifications for a position.

just cause—A justifiable reason to take an action that is not a breach of any term or condition contained within a contract.

labor force population—The population of individuals who are available for work.

labor intensive—Requiring large amounts of labor dollars due to many worker positions.

labor market—The external variables that influence the labor pool.

labor pool—Individuals within the labor force population who possess KSAAs for positions within organizations.

labor relations—The specialty involved with establishing and managing collective bargaining agreements.

labor strikes—Work stoppage action in which union workers refuse to report for work shifts.

labor unions—Formal associations that are engaged to negotiate collective bargaining agreements on behalf of employees.

leadership—The power to influence others to take action willingly: In management, it is the willingness of individuals to accomplish the objectives of the organization.

leaders—Individuals who possess the power to influence others.

leading—Leaders in the practice of exercising power to influence others.

learning gap—A negative gap between what the worker can do vs. what needs to be done in the job.

learning system—A feedback loop in which members of the organization gain knowledge about productivity.

legal compliance—Adherence to the stated and presumed provisions of a law.

legal creation view—An interpretation of legal law that views a corporation as an entity created by the state, which is created by society. As such, there is a legal duty for the corporation to act in accordance with the welfare of society, with a breach of that duty establishing grounds for the abolishment of a corporation.

legal recognition view—An interpretation of legal law that views corporations as free entities that merely register with the state, not an entity that is created by the state. Hence, there is no duty for a corporation to contribute to the welfare of society.

legitimate—A grievance that possesses merit.

liability—The obligation to make reparations to others who are harmed from a breach of duty.

libel—Written defamatory comments.

line employee—An employee who produces products or services or generates revenue.

liquidated damages—Punitive awards that are double the amount of regular punitive damages.

Machiavellian theory—The belief that leaders are born and not made.

management by objectives (MBO)—Top/down, bottom/up shared goal setting at every level of the organization.

management development—Training for advancement in management positions.

management science—A management model that applies the scientific method to decision-making activities in organizations.

management—The accomplishment of organizational objectives through the actitivies of others; also used to refer to supervisory agents of an organization in labor relations discussions.

manager's manual—A document of objectives, strategies and policies for managers to follow when acting as agents of the organization.

mandatory benefits—Those benefits that the government requires organizations to provide for employees.

manpower planning—A process of forecasting required position placement over a period of time.

maturity curve—The curve of experience in which proficiency exceeds the value of the position to the organization.

meaning system—A driver loop that reinforces values and purpose throughout the organization.

medium—The communication vehicle for a message.

merit—Wage and salary increases based on performance measures.

minimum wage—The lowest hourly wage permitted by law.

minority—A label attributed to individuals who fall within a protected class as defined by civil rights statutes.

misconduct—Failure to adhere to the rules.

MIS—Management information system; converts data into useable information.

mission—The purpose of an organization that includes its values and beliefs.

mission-driven organization—An organization that retains the purpose and values of its mission in all decision-making activities.

modified piece rate—Stratified payment for varying levels of production. Also referred to as differential or stratified piece rate.

moral audit—Internal audit of management decisions within an organization.

myth of amoral business—A philosophy that limits the responsibilities of a business entity to the payment of taxes and obedience of the law. This doctrine contends that when society views a business practice as harmful to society, the legislature should enact laws to regulate the practices of the business entity.

National Labor Relations Act (NLRA)—Federal law that protects workers rights to organize with unions.

National Labor Relations Board (NLRB)—An administrative agency established by the NLRA to enforce and administer the provisions of that act.

needs analysis—A process of assessing the existence of a training problem as defined by a learning gap through data collection and analysis. Also referred to as needs assessment.

negative reinforcement—Removing something unpleasurable in response to a desired behavior.

negligence—A breach of duty.

negligent disclosure—Information that is disclosed to third parties arising from access to records that should have been secured with due care by a custodian.

negligent hire—The employment of an individual that facilitates that person's ability to harm others, when the employer knew or should have known there was a propensity for that employee to inflict harm as part of the course of employment.

negligent maintenance—Failure to exercise due care in the security of items or information by a custodian.

negligent retention—Failure to remove an individual with a propensity to incur harm to others from an employment position when the employer knew or should have known of the propensity to incur harm.

non-directive—An interview process in which the answer to a previous question will determine the tangent of discussion in an interview.

nonexempt—Not exempt from overtime payment.

norms—Standardized acceptable behavior.

nuisance—A legal settlement based on the opinion that the matter of dispute is not worth the time and expense to present a defense.

objective—A target for performance.

Occupational Safety and Health Act (OSHA)—The main federal statute providing for workplace safety requirements. Administered by the Occupational Safety and Health Administration, which has the powers of enforcement, investigation, and adjudication.

on call—Casual labor that works on an as-needed basis.

one-dimensional—Focus on a single side of the productivity model.

on-the-job training (OJT)—Training that takes place at the worksite during hours of operation.

open pay system—An open communication policy regarding pay and benefits in an organization.

open shops—Organizations with unions that do not require union membership as a term or condition of employment.

open-ended—A question that requires a response beyond a simple yes or no answer.

organization—A group of individuals brought together to accomplish a common objective.

organizational climate—The collective emotional temperament among members of an organization.

organizational culture—Shared values, attitudes, and beliefs among members of an organization.

organized—A collective group that is represented by a labor union.

outputs—Products or services produced by the company to earn revenue.

paradigm—A model that drives the thinking processes.

paradigm shift—A change in the thinking model.

part time—Those employees who regularly work fewer hours than full-time workers.

pending claims—Claims that are in the process of investigation for discovery.

performance appraisals—A comparison of actual performance to standards for performance.

perpetuation theory—A theory of discrimination that precludes employers from perpetuating past discriminatory practices that may have existed prior to the enactment of a statute.

perquisites—Rewards beyond benefits for organizational membership, usually for executive personnel.

piece rate—Pay per units produced.

plaintiff—The filing party in a legal dispute.

policies—Broad guidelines for performance.

policy manual—A document that explains company policies.

Polygraph Protection Act—The federal statute that prohibits the use of pre-employment polygraph testing for most employment scenarios, with certain exceptions.

position—An individual who performs a job.

positive reinforcement—Giving something pleasurable in response to a desired behavior.

PPO—Preferred provider option health insurance.

precedent—A matter of law as decided in a court dispute that has applications for cases with similar facts.

pre-employment—Activities that occur prior to an offer of employment.

preponderance of evidence—The balance of evidence in which a court decision is made on the slightest weight in one direction. This rule is applied in civil cases. Beyond a reasonable doubt is the rule of evidence for criminal cases.

pretext—A seemingly legal excuse to engage in discrimination.

prima facie—"First face" evidence, or the evidence at first glance. Those facts that are readily apparent.

privilege—Something that is given as a gift to a person or is earned by a person based on performance.

problem—A negative gap between actual performance and standards for performance in an organization.

procedures—Action steps required to achieve standards.

process theories—Theories describing how managers might motivate employees.

productivity—The relationship of resource expenses and revenue as connected by a transformation process and encircled by meaning and learning loops.

professional exemption—Exempt status for professional workers.

profits—Revenues less expenses that yield a positive balance.

progressive discipline—A process of disciplinary actions that include warnings concerning the consequences associated with future incidents.

promotions—Employees who are placed in positions that possess increased authority and responsibility within an organization.

protected class—Those who fall within the jurisdiction of legal protection.

public policy—Those factors that are in the interest of the general public within a society.

punitive damages—Additional awards designed to punish a defendant for willful harm to a plaintiff.

quid pro quo—Something of value that is exchanged for something else of value.

quid pro quo sexual harassment—Direct harassment by one person (usually a supervisor) which includes preferential treatment or avoidance of adverse treatment in return for a sexual favor.

racial bias—Instrument design that is not valid based on racial variables associated with subjects.

ranking method—An appraisal method in which all employees in a work unit are rated from first through last.

rater bias—Personal attributes influencing the rater.

rater error—Statistical error on the part of a rater causing an appraisal instrument to lose its validity and/or reliability.

ratification—Final approval of the majority of represented union members to an agreement.

realistic job preview (RJP)—The disclosure of both favorable and unfavorable characteristics associated with a specific position.

reasonable accommodation—The burden of responsibility placed on an employer that determines the legal level of accommodation, usually measured in dollar amounts relative to the resources of a given organization.

reasonable care—That which a person of sound mind would consider to be reasonable in a given situation.

receiver—The intended target of a message.

recency effect—Recalling a small portion of the appraisal time frame.

recruitment—The process of generating a pool of qualified applicants for a position.

reinforcement—Method to habituate new knowledge and skills to reach a state of unconscious competence.

reliability—Statistical measurement that demonstrates validity on a consistent basis.

responsibility—The duty to perform an action.

return on investment (ROI)—Money that is paid to investors.

revenues—Income earned through the sale of products and services.

right—Something that a person is entitled to from nature or law.

right-to-work state—A state that protects the rights of non-union workers to pursue gainful employment.

risk managers—Professional trained in reducing organizational liability through prevention and relations with insurance companies.

rules of conduct—A listing of the codes of conduct for employees in the workplace.

rules—Standards of conduct for individuals who are employed in the workplace.

safety committee—An organized decision-making body consisting of representatives from various departments and levels within the organization that takes primary responsibility for safety audits and prevention programs/campaigns.

safety programs—Systematic programs aimed at accident and illness prevention through audits and safety campaigns.

salary—Standard rate of pay from period to period.

scientific management—The first formal doctrine of management that is focused on the best way to do tasks and is efficiency based.

selection—The process of identifying individuals to occupy vacant positions within an organization; choosing the most qualified candidates for positions.

self-egoism—Acting in the interest of the self without regard for the harm caused to others.

self-managed teams (SMT)—Team that require little or no supervision.

sender—An individual with an idea to be communicated to a receiver.

seniority—Amount of continuous service in a position or an organization.

settlement—An agreement that is reached somewhere between initial demands and concessions in the collective bargaining process.

sex-plus discrimination—Gender-related factors resulting in discriminatory practices in the workplace.

shareholders—A stakeholder group consisting of the investors or owners of a company.

shop stewards—Employees of an organization that also act as liaison with business agents.

short-term gain—Financial returns over a period of one year or less.

situation—The environmental factors influencing a leadership style at a given moment.

slander—Verbal defamatory comments.

social audit—An external audit of organizational practices affecting customers and the community.

social responsibility—Duty to the community stakeholder group and society.

Social Security benefits—Federal government fund that provides supplemental benefits to retired, disabled, or family dependents of deceased workers.

sourcing—The process of locating potential qualified applicants to be added to the applicant pool for an organization.

staff employee—An employee who supports the line workers.

stakeholder group—Groups of constituents for an organization.

standard operating procedures (SOP)—A document that lists standards for performance and action steps to be followed to meet with the standards.

standards—Acceptable levels of performance in an organization.

statutory law—A federal or state law that is written by the legislature.

stewardship—Self-sacrificing service by a leader to the followership.

strategic planning process—A systematic process using the open systems model to construct plans that include objectives and strategies for future performance.

stress interview—An interview process intentionally designed to determine how an interviewee reacts under stressful conditions.

structured interview—An interview that uses a questionnaire that does not permit interviewer deviation from the standard questions.

succession-planning—Career development planning that combines forecasted promotional opportunities and development activities required to prepare a person to work at a more advanced level.

SWOT analysis—The analysis of strengths, weaknesses, opportunities, and threats to the organization.

synergy—An outcome that is greater than the sum of its parts.

synthesis—The ability to apply abstract concepts in a realistic setting.

systems model—A management model that all parts of an organization and its external environment exist as patterns of relationship to each sub-part.

theory of needs—Achievement, affiliation, and power needs.

tip credit—The difference between actual pay and minimum wage permitted for tipped personnel within a given state.

tort or common law—A law that is not written by the legislature that results from the interpretation of a judge, and is applied to other similar court cases.

trait—Characteristics or personality factors possessed by an individual.

transactional leadership—Leadership that focuses on the moment of leading only.

transformation process—The conversion of material resources into products and services.

transformational leadership—Leadership that focuses on the intrinsic desires of all involved parties that is applied to leading those parties.

turnover—The combination of voluntary and involuntary separation of employees within an organization.

two-dimensional—Balanced focus on inputs and outputs to enhance productivity.

unemployment compensation—A portion of wages or salaries paid from a state insurance funds to individuals who have lost their jobs due to layoffs or company closures.

unilaterally—An action taken by a single party to an agreement.

union contract—Collective bargaining agreements between labor and management within an organization.

union shops—Organizations that require union membership upon being hired.

universality—Unity in beliefs and behaviors beyond what is relative to a specific environment.

utilitarianism—A consequential approach to testing the ethics and morality of an action.

validity—Statistical measurement of intended outcomes associated with variables.

value-added manager—A manager who enhances productivity.

voluntary benefits—Those benefits that the organization chooses to provide for employees.

voluntary separation—Employees who resign from positions in organizations.

wage compression—Shrinking gap between newly increased start wage rates and pre-existing middle rates.

wages—Pay for time worked, usually by the hour.

Wagner Act—Another name used to apply to the National Labor Relations Act.

wellness programs—Programs offered to employees to assist with physical, mental, and emotional health.

whistle-blowing—Disclosing matters that violate public policy to third parties.

white-collar—Professional and administrative positions in organizations.

WIFM—What's in It For Me; the motivation for individuals to learn.

workers' compensation—Medical, disability, and death benefit insurance for work-related injuries or illnesses.

wrongful discharge—The discharge of an individual from employment for reasons that violate public policy, terms of an express or implied contract, or a covenant of good faith and fair dealing.

Index

Credits